Words, Wonders and Power

Words, Wonders and Power

UNDERSTANDING CONTEMPORARY CHRISTIAN
FUNDAMENTALISM AND REVIVALISM

Martyn Percy

First published in Great Britain 1996
Society for Promoting Christian Knowledge
Holy Trinity Church
Marylebone Road
London NW1 4DU

British Library Cataloguing-in-Publication Data
A catalogue record for this book is available from the British Library

ISBN 0-281-04855-X

Typeset by Latimer Trend & Company Ltd, Plymouth
Printed in Great Britain by
The Cromwell Press, Melksham, Wilts.

For Emma and Benjamin

Contents

Publisher's Acknowledgements

The author and publisher gratefully acknowledge the following for permission to reproduce copyright material.

Carcanet Press Limited, Manchester, for lines in Chapter 8 by Donald Davie, 'Ordinary God' in *To Scorch and to Freeze: Poems About the Sacred*, Carcanet Press, 1988.

CopyCare Ltd for the 'Family Song' by Steve Hampton in Chapter 4. Copyright © 1978 Scripture in Song. Administered by CopyCare, PO Box 77, Hailsham, Sussex BN27 3EF, UK. Used by permission.

Kingsway's Thankyou Music for kind permission to reproduce extracts from the following songs in Chapter 4, which can be found in *Songs of the Vineyard*, volume 1 (1987) and volume 2 (1989). All are copyright © Mercy Publishing/Kingsway's Thankyou Music, PO Box 75, Eastbourne, E. Sussex, BN23 6NT, UK. Europe (excl. Germany, Austria, Liechtenstein, Luxembourg and Switzerland). Used by permission.

'Lord, ask that You would come right now' by Bill Dobrenen, 1982 (*SOV* 1)
'I receive You, O Spirit of love' by John Lai, 1982 (*SOV* 1)
'As I close my eyes'/'Tender Mercy' by Peggy Wagner, 1985 (*SOV* 1)
'Hold me Lord, in Your arms' by Danny Daniels, 1982 (*SOV* 1)
'I give You all the honour'/'I Worship You' by Carl Tuttle, 1982 (*SOV* 1)
'Consider how he loves you'/'Sweet Perfume' by John Wimber, 1982 (*SOV* 1)
'You are the Vine' by Danny Daniels and Randy Rigby, 1985 (*SOV* 1)
'Lord, I love You' by Eddie Espinosa, 1982 (*SOV* 1)
'More love, more power' by Jude Del Hierro, 1987 (*SOV* 1)
'You are the Mighty King' by Eddie Espinosa, 1982 (*SOV* 1)
'Lord, I'll seek after You' by Eddie Espinosa, 1985 (*SOV* 1)

Author's Note:

Some of the terminology used in this book is quite technical. A glossary of terms is provided for the reader, and can be found at the back of the book. As a matter of convention, the male pronoun has been used for God, but as sparingly as possible.

Major works by John Wimber frequently referred to or cited in the text:

The Cross (manual with tapes), Mercy Publishing, 1986.
Power Evangelism: Signs, Wonders and Church Growth I (manual with tapes), Mercy Publishing, 1984.
Power Evangelism: Signs, Wonders and Church Growth II (manual with tapes), Mercy Publishing, 1986.
The Kingdom of God (booklet), Mercy Publishing, 1985.
Power Points (manual with tapes), Mercy Publishing, 1985.
Power Evangelism, Hodder & Stoughton, 1985.
Power Healing, Hodder & Stoughton, 1986.
The Dynamics of Spiritual Growth, Hodder & Stoughton, 1990.

Acknowledgements

I would especially like to express my thanks to the following for their help, support and encouragement: Professors Peter Clarke, Colin Gunton, Daniel Hardy, David Martin and Christoph Schwöbel. I owe much gratitude to the people and parish of St Andrew's, Bedford, who sustained me as I completed my doctoral thesis at King's College, London; it is that work which essentially forms the basis for this book. I would also like to extend my thanks to Philip Law and Catherine Mann of SPCK, and to Anne Borrowdale for her invaluable comments on the manuscript. Lastly to Emma, my wife, my constant partner in dialogue and unstinting supporter.

Introduction

Once upon a time, Christian fundamentalism was a religion for the few. Believers gathered together in tiny chapels, cut off from the storms of life and the reality of the world. They prayed, they preached and then they prayed again. Life was apparently very simple. Church was where you got saved. The world was where you got lost.

But fundamentalism is not the same any more. It is certainly not a religion for the few. In the USA, thirteen million viewers tune into 'fundamentalist' television stations every week. There are over a thousand religious radio stations, many of which are controlled by 'conservative' or fundamentalist groups. Fundamentalists are no longer confined to their chapels for fear of the world. Rather, they are engaging with it most forcefully, on a variety of levels. Fundamentalists contributed vocally and financially to Ronald Reagan's election victories of the 1980s. They picket abortion clinics, scrutinize school curricula, campaign against pornography, feminism and gay rights movements. Outside the USA, they march for Jesus, begin new denominations, and hold rallies and conferences that attract believers in their thousands. Beyond Christianity, they are active in politics in many societies, seeking to restore values and ideas they believe to be lost, and integral for social and moral survival. Fundamentalism is a worldwide force, touching governments, churches, education, social and ethical issues, and just about anything else you can think of.

However, since the late 1970s, the politicization of what some observers call the 'New Religious Right' has brought an end to the traditional theological neglect of fundamentalist movements. The maintenance of an ad hoc, critical stance over many years could no longer be sustained; a form of faith community once believed to be in its death throes was actually alive and well in a variety of guises, and attracting a large following. The theological response to the contemporary fundamentalist movement has often been either indifference or occasional critiques. It is true, of course, that theologians in general deal with fundamentalism more than they did previously, but overall, their responses to the movement have often lacked seriousness or empathy. For example, the majority of studies in the last two decades have either been historical analyses, focusing on the genesis and subsequent career of fundamentalism in the twentieth century, or, more popular studies conducted by persons on the margins of academic contexts.

Those theologians who have not taken this path have tended to respond to contemporary fundamentalism by focusing their interests on its politicized faction, or on 'evangelicalism', in which fundamentalism and 'new evangelicalism' are often carelessly lumped together as a monolithic reality. Although there is much talk about fundamentalism today, there are few theological critiques that see the movement as a tradition in its own right. An empathetic, critical and systematic analysis of the movement is important, if the power and attraction of contemporary fundamentalism in all its various forms is to be properly understood and critiqued. The approach to the fundamentalist movement in this book will therefore be significantly different from other works that cover the subject.

Fundamentalism as a movement (or individual fundamentalist exponents) may lay claim to be the 'Cinderella of theology'. There has been little in the way of serious theological engagement with fundamentalism in all its fullness. Certain types of criticism are particularly problematic. Some methodologies employed in analysis might lead one to believe that the critiques are just a developed list of complaints and personal dislikes. Although they contain much intuitive insight (which has some value), they tend to treat fundamentalism only as a matter of belief or, then again, simply as experiential and expressive. For example, authors like James Barr appear to read fundamentalism primarily in terms of its propositions, concluding that fundamentalists are at best simplistic and at worst anti-intellectual. This fails to take account of the fact that a fundamentalist orientation is a complex, systematic world-view in its own right. Fundamentalism *is* a way of relating, not just thinking. Most studies of fundamentalism fail to perceive that fundamentalism is a distinctive theological tradition and culture in its own right, with an accompanying, appropriate discourse and method. Such a complex system requires a systematic response, if it is to be respectfully engaged with and understood. Most critiques also fail to deliver a working definition of fundamentalism that is accurate, conceptually sound and properly descriptive. There is failure too, to hunt out the deeper impulses that drive the fundamentalist tradition. Too many works address the surface or expressive aspects of the tradition, critiquing the symptoms, but not attempting to locate the cause.

This book attempts to understand and interpret the theology and ecclesiology of contemporary fundamentalism. The approach that has been taken is what many would describe as 'phenomenological': careful searching, sorting and systematizing of texts and behaviour, read alongside theological, sociological and psychological insights. As such, it employs a methodology that is empathetic to the tradition, yet provides a coherent systematic account, which can lead to an assessment of the strengths and weaknesses of fundamentalism today, in terms of its contribution to modern life and the Kingdom of God.

I

Understanding Fundamentalism and Revivalism

A seven year old child from a family who belonged to a fundamentalist church once went to stay with some other members of the family who were not part of the church. For a treat, the relatives took the child on a day trip to an historic cathedral city, which included a tour of the cathedral itself. The guide was very informed, and throughout the tour the child was clearly enthralled. After an hour the tour ended, so they went for a cup of tea. 'Wasn't that an interesting tour?', asked the adult, 'I especially liked the stories about the architects – do you know who built your church?' 'Yes', replied the child, 'it was Jesus'.

The story is true, and gives an insight into the self-perception that most fundamentalists share, even a seven year old child. That is a belief that their church is as near a perfect incarnation of the body of Christ as is possible this side of heaven. Others may have their churches constructed from all sorts of physical, dogmatic and spiritual materials, but fundamentalists believe their church or body to be built by God. Some would say this is rank arrogance, but there is more to it than this. Fundamentalists are generally committed perfectionists, and part of the reason for the proliferation and diversity of fundamentalist churches lies in that relentless drive towards doctrinal and spiritual purity that in the end divides rather than unites.

This can be characterized by an old joke about fundamentalism, which tells of two fundamentalist pastors who go on a luxury cruise together around the remote Pacific islands. There is a storm, the ship sinks and all hands are lost apart from the two fundamentalist pastors who are washed up together on the same remote uninhabited island. Initially they get on well together, but within a week they have both started their own separate churches. It is an old joke, yet it does illustrate one of the basic difficulties that is encountered when one is trying to understand

fundamentalism. Quite simply, fundamentalism is an extremely
diverse phenomenon. Virtually all religions have within their ranks
people who would class themselves as fundamentalists, as do
political parties, reform movements, anti-reform movements,
football clubs and the like. In the post-modern age, in which we
live, diversity is usually something to be celebrated. It can be seen
as evidence of God's expressiveness and enjoyment of the universe.
Diversity does not always have to mean disunity. Indeed diversity
is not only desirable in the post-modern age, but necessary. It
points to the plurality of truth, experience, being and authority.
It is part of what makes up the human race. In terms of the
Church, diversity can also be a matter for celebration; grounded
in our common faith in the person of Christ, Christian theology
has traditionally delighted in the image of the body – a whole unit
made up of many different parts, each contributing in its own
way to the working out of God's own purposes in the world.

Like it or lump it, fundamentalism is part of that body. Most
denominations and churches contain within them people who
regard themselves as fundamentalist. Many a good doctrine that
forms the Church contains within it the seeds of fundamentalism.
And fundamentalism itself is alive and kicking in the post-modern
world. In the early part of this century fundamentalists reacted to
modernism, namely the suggestion that there might be one unifying
idea, or a collection of unifying ideas that might bind society
together and give it a better future. Fundamentalists argued for
an alternative view. They rejected the optimistic liberalism that
had turned to ashes after the First World War. Instead, they pressed
for a return to biblical values and ideals, which would be protected
by a view of scriptural inerrancy that would safeguard the
foundations for such a society. In our present post-modern era,
fundamentalists have proved to be more than adaptable to the
current climate. They accept the plurality of belief and authority
that operates in most societies and keenly compete in the 'free
market' of spiritual and social values as and when they wish.

The fact that fundamentalists have adapted themselves
successfully to the conditions of post-modernity is beyond question.
Any glance at the 'family tree' of contemporary Christian
fundamentalism reveals a wide scope for diversity, originating with
American conservative Protestantism and the rigorous
individualism and sectarianism so indigenous to American society.
The family extends to Pentecostals, neo-Pentecostals, mainline
evangelicals, non-mainline evangelicals, Southern Baptists, new

fundamentalists, old fundamentalists and charismatics of various shapes, sizes and colours. It is a very big family. And as in all families, not all of the members speak to one another. Some habitually squabble, others get on well, whilst some are not very sure that they actually 'belong'.

What is it, then, that binds the fundamentalist family together? Opinions vary enormously, usually according to the critical discipline that is applied to the fundamentalist group being studied. Certainly a popular picture is based on the caricature of old-fashioned fundamentalists. Preachers who denounced evil in 'the world' in order to 'shepherd' their flocks away, into strict isolation from it, images of tiny rural chapels where true believers seated on rickety folding chairs professed born-again faith quickly come to mind. But we must add to this handsome stately churches with memberships the size of small towns. Fundamentalism is a powerful, confident and important force in worldwide Christianity. Popularly associated with stern opposition to such personal 'sins' as drinking, smoking and gambling, fundamentalism draws on the entire heritage of American revivalism, with its code of personal piety and its insistence upon conscious commitment to Jesus Christ as one's 'personal Saviour'. But many people share that style of religion without being fundamentalist. Characteristically, many regard the heart of the movement as being cemented by two things: an unbudgeable belief in the word for word accuracy of the entire Bible, and a spirit of hostility towards anything in the Church or society that is thought to conflict with scriptural commands. The Bible is considered 'inerrant' – free from error as it was originally written, not only in spiritual and moral teaching but also in historical details. However, there is a great deal more to fundamentalism than this. As we have already noted, fundamentalism is not simply confined to Christianity or other religions, but is an attitude that can be located in politics, pressure groups and movements and a variety of other arenas. This book considers fundamentalism in contemporary Christianity, and begins with an investigation of what the term 'fundamentalism' means.

Fundamentalism: Clarifying Definitions

A number of scholars have argued that the term 'fundamentalism' is now so broad as to be useless.[1] So many groups are now labelled as 'fundamentalist' that the concept has indeed become somewhat 'spongy', and is in need of redefinition. Conventionally, the word has usually been applied to individuals or organizations that operate by 'strict adherence to traditional orthodox tenets (e.g., the literal inerrancy of Scripture) held to be fundamental to the Christian faith', as well as 'being opposed to liberalism and modernism'.[2] Whilst this definition tells us something about the nature of fundamentalism, it does not go far enough. Fundamentalism is not just a set of constructive propositions designed to oppose modernist thinking, and advance what is held to be original orthodoxy. It is a relational phenomenon too, a way of being in the world, offering a social and mythic construction of reality for participants that offers a secure identity along with personal and corporate value.

Following this, church historian Martin Marty has characterized fundamentalism as 'a worldwide reaction against many of the mixed offerings of modernity', appealing to those who look for 'authoritarian solutions' in relational problems.[3] He notes that differing fundamentalist groups are often deeply hostile to each other, even if there is a measure of broad agreement on the nature and location of fundamental articles of faith. Marty's explanation for this is that fundamentalism appeals to a particular class and personality type. Indeed, he sees the actual fundamentals themselves as a smoke-screen, and goes so far as to state that fundamentalists are not so much motivated by religious belief as by psychological disposition, social forces and historical circumstance. Noting that Catholic, Jewish, Christian and Islamic fundamentalists all share the same mindset, he states: 'It is not productive to dwell on fundamentalist theology and point out its contradictions and errors. The [fundamentals] . . . are merely tools, excuses or alibis for the fundamentalist mindset. Without the mindset, the doctrines wither.'[4]

Marty's observations are useful, yet he himself still tends to treat fundamentalism as though it were a unified phenomenon, its many adherents believing roughly the same thing, behaving essentially in the same way. This is extremely problematic, since if we analyse how fundamentalists define and describe themselves, a wide polarity of views quickly begins to surface. These defensive clarifications of fundamentalism in fact only serve to underline the scale of our systematic problem.

For example, many self-defined fundamentalists believe the charismatic (or Pentecostal) movement is, at best, contrary to the will of God: 'On the basis of Scriptural evidence we have concluded that . . . the modern tongues movement is not of God'. Meanwhile, Pat Robertson, another self-confessed fundamentalist, points out in his *The Fundamentalist Phenomenon* that the 'Pente-costal-charismatic movement . . . is based upon the funda-mentalist doctrinal foundation'.[5] Other fundamentalists deny the right of people like Billy Graham to own the title 'fundamentalist' – he is too liberal, they claim, and co-operates with Roman Catholics.[6] J. I. Packer, author of *Fundamentalism and the Word of God* (1958) would disagree however. Although uneasy about the term 'fundamentalist', he nevertheless, as an evangelical, concludes that evangelical doctrine is fundamentalist, and the term 'fundamental' pervades most apologetic work done by self-confessed evangelicals, anxious to distinguish themselves from some fundamentalists, whilst wanting to own some fundamentalist doctrine. It is difficult to see, for example, what upsets them most about James Barr's *Fundamentalism* (1978) – his critique, or his terminology? Carl F. H. Henry conducts a sustained attack on Barr in volume 4 of his *God, Revelation and Authority* (1979). He questions Barr's 'broad and tireless use of the term *fundamentalism*', but then warns his readers not to reject evangelicalism, which affirms 'the literal truth of an inerrant Bible'.[7]

I have pursued this question of terminology here because it is an acute difficulty for many of its subjects, and with good reason. Fundamentalist attitudes can be found in a wide variety of individuals and communities, and few wish to own a title with such pejorative connotations. Yet from our brief survey so far, the term 'fundamentalism' can at least be used to describe a set of common outlooks on society, theology and the Church, shared between traditional fundamentalists (i.e., anti-Pentecostal), some evangelicals, and those from the charismatic movement or Pentecostalism. There are five marks which characterize funda-mentalism, which will give it a sharper definition.

1. Contemporary fundamentalism is a 'backward-looking legitimation' for present forms of ministry and belief.[8] Present patterns of operation are justified in legalist and historicist fashions via a claim on an exclusive validity for one line (or a very small core) of development from Scripture, that refuses to recognize the diversity and development of others. In other words, an absolute authority must be established. This in turn affords participants a viable perception of reality in the modern world, a template through which experience can be processed. Some of these experiences

themselves – as in the case of charismatics or Pentecostals – can then become actual fundaments or basic beliefs, although the validating line of interpretation – usually an interpretation of a text or texts, or possibly a written creed or articles of faith – often remains the supreme authority. This backward-looking legitimation is subsequently represented by a myth or constellation of myths that are 'at home' in the modern age. The metaphor 'home' is not meant to suggest an impression of happiness or comfort. Instead, it suggests that these mythic constructs provide a perception of reality that is more usually opposed to many aspects of western culture. It is 'at home' however, because it eclectically 'maps' traditional Christian mythologies and symbols on to the modern situation, thus forming a basic comprehensive cognitive picture of how the world is, how it should be, and how it will be. This cognitive picture is comprehensive enough to influence, amongst other things, attitudes to family life, the role of women, politics, other faiths, ethics and questions about life after death.

2. Fundamentalism exists in relation to and opposition to trends in society that it perceives as modernist (i.e., where the authority of the existing tradition is challenged), pluralist (i.e., where beliefs and moral, religious values have to compete for attention), or compromised. Thus it aims at reversing certain traits and establishing a new type of order or perception of reality. This is most commonly expressed in the symbol of 'Holy War'. Fundamentalists see their enterprise as a struggle, in which the order they seek to advance must overcome the present (ungodly) order. The trends of modernity that fundamentalists oppose are to be resisted precisely because they represent a threat to the authority that they place themselves under. Therefore, fundamentalism refuses to engage in dialogue. It has nothing to receive from the world, since the world must receive it first, wholesale. Some sociologists of religion (such as Bryan Wilson) identify this phenomenon as sectarianism, which is usually quite correct. However, caution needs to be exercised in using that word, since it might indicate that fundamentalists are somehow retreating from the world. In fact the opposite is true; they are engaging with it most forcefully, yet with a faith that arises out of their authoritarian dogma and is expressed by monologue rather than dialogue.

3. Although fundamentalism now enjoys considerable breadth of expression, including competing sectarian factions that deny

each other the right to own the title, there is nevertheless a traceable phenomenon that we can call 'fundamentalism'. By viewing it as a *tendency*, a habit of mind, rather than a single movement, it is possible to discern a phenomenon that is widespread, yet with common features. It is an attitude, sometimes selective on subjects (e.g., sexuality) and found within traditions that are otherwise quite catholic or plural. These features generally include a hostile reaction to the mixed offerings of modernity, and to combat it, a set of 'fundamentals', such as a 'core doctrine', an absolute source of authority, a specific programme that is to be imposed rather than shared, clear patterns for mediating authority and power, and authenticating procedures (e.g., 'Have you been born again?') that validate and recognize existing members and potential recruits.

4. Fundamentalism, like liberalism, is not just a theological perspective localized to a particular denomination (or even religion). It is a phenomenon that crosses denominations denoting standpoints, attitudes, patterns of behaviour and theological methods. Although it has its origins in the emerging evangelicalism of the eighteenth century and in the 'historic fundamentalism' of the early twentieth century, it is a diverse socio-theological movement. It understands itself to be concerned with upholding certain doctrines of the Christian faith that are regarded as essential to authentic Christianity. Contemporary fundamentalism's chief enemy is theological and ethical liberalism, which it opposes in varying degrees. In fact, what distinguishes fundamentalism from other similar faith perspectives is its opposition to liberalism: where opposition to liberalism is lacking, I hold that one cannot speak of true fundamentalism, but only of a close relative. At first sight, this might appear to rule out many charismatic or Pentecostal groups, but not so. These groups are just as anti-liberal; they simply construct their remedial programme differently. A good example of this is the British Evangelical Alliance, an umbrella organization incorporating many different fundamentalist groups from different denominations, in order to bring a greater degree of pressure to bear on certain issues.[9]

5. Fundamentalism is a cultural-linguistic phenomenon.[10] Too many of the studies discussed regard fundamentalism as a primarily noetic phenomenon, concerned with certain beliefs and doctrines, and propagating informational propositions. We have already noted this problematic aspect in Barr's treatment of fundamentalism, namely his habit of treating fundamentalism as

a (primarily) credal phenomenon. For example, the doctrine of inerrancy does not just exist to counter the excesses of form criticism and Darwinist ideas about the origin of man. It is more subtle than that. The cognitive approach does not do justice to the rich intricacy of the fundamentalist universe; it fails to attend to how a doctrine like inerrancy helps constitute a habit of mind, viable perceptions of reality, in short, a whole world. Stories also help constitute communities, not just propositions; it is often the group's own narrative that shapes its theology, as, for example, in the case of fundamentalist Afrikaaners.

Equally, fundamentalism cannot be regarded as just a matter of expressing experience. There is more to fundamentalism than a primordial religious experience, which when articulated becomes thematized into a type of determinate 'mystical' language. For example, Methodists do not all seek to have their hearts 'strangely warmed' as Wesley did. It is the telling of the story, with its message of immanent change, the hope of transformation, and the renewal of inner being that helps place that story centrally in the Methodist tradition. The point of expressing experience belongs in a wider context. Thus, fundamentalism must be read as a comprehensive interpretative schema, employing myths or narratives that structure human experience and understanding of the self and the world.[11] This view recognizes the power of language to shape, mould and delimit human experience, to the extent that it may be said that the way language itself is used can give rise to certain experiences. If fundamentalism can be seen as a cultural-linguistic system, the operating scaffold of symbolism within can be shown to be part of the idiom that describes realities, formulates beliefs and the experiencing of inner attitudes, feelings and sentiments: in short, a complete interpretative framework. Like a culture or language, fundamentalism as a tendency is a communal phenomenon that shapes the subjectives of individuals and the objectives of communities, rather than being a manifestation of them. It comprises a vocabulary of discursive and non-discursive symbols, together with a distinctive logic or grammar in terms of which this vocabulary can be deployed. It is a form of life, with cognitive and behavioural dimensions; its doctrines, cosmic understandings, myths and ethics relating to the rituals practised, the sentiments and experiences evoked, the actions recommended, and the subsequent institutional form that develops. All this is suggested in comparing fundamentalism to a 'cultural-linguistic system'.

These five hallmarks suggest a very wide definition of fundamentalism. Indeed, much of what could be described as Christianity fits this description: but this does not invalidate the definition. Much of Christianity *is* organized around fundamental articles or excluding creeds, and many scholars have affirmed that Christianity has been a form of fundamentalism for much of its history. So, is there anything that separates fundamentalism from 'ordinary' Christianity, that simply organizes itself around a set of fundamentals? I would suggest there is, with the difference locating itself in a variety of arenas, of which two are singled out here (more will be said about these in the conclusion). First, the fundamentals are held differently: doctrines tend to be 'tight', rigorously defined, and used as a controlling mechanism for the establishment of order in the Church. The doctrine of an inerrant Bible is a clear example, being a symbolic reminder that revelation is closed and complete. In contrast, non-fundamentalists generally recognize that their faith and knowledge is incomplete (cf. I Cor. 13.9), resulting in a commitment to dialogue and openness rather than monologue. Second, and linked to this, is the question of the nature of truth. Fundamentalists deny the ambiguity of truth, seeking to press for a uniformity that will effectively govern life. Truth emerges as an exclusive concept, with no space for error, alternative interpretation or appropriate ambiguity.[12] Non-fundamentalist Christians acknowledge the necessity of contradiction in truth, which generally gives rise to a higher degree of tolerance for plurality.[13] So, there is a clear difference between fundamentalism and other forms of Christianity that might be organizing their theology and doctrine of the Church around a group of fundamentals.

Case-study, Texts and Methodology

This book concentrates its critique on the extensive work and writings of John Wimber, a pre-eminent contemporary fundamentalist in the 'revivalist tradition', still practising his ministry. This focus on one individual helps to avoid Barr's rather selective analysis of fundamentalism, that at times seems to focus on extremes and aberrations within the movement. However, in choosing one case-study there are significant implications for the study of other fundamentalists.

John Wimber has been chosen as a case-study for a variety of reasons. First, although an American converted via a

fundamentalist-evangelical tradition, his appeal is international
and crosses denominations. In the United Kingdom, he has strongly
influenced significant portions of the Anglican Church since 1980,
largely through his association with Canon David Watson (now
deceased),[14] and latterly, The Right Reverend David Pytches,
formerly Bishop of Chile and now vicar of St Andrew's,
Chorleywood. Since the mid-1980s, his involvement with British
Christians has steadily extended, and now includes a 'network' of
many denominations, including what are commonly known as
'house churches'.[15] Since 1988, Wimber has been establishing his
own churches in the UK (called 'Vineyards'), and has also associated
himself in leadership with churches and Christian leaders who
aspire to the particular form of Christianity he espouses.
Worldwide, Wimber supervises over five hundred churches.

Second, Wimber fits well with the fundamentalist criteria
discussed earlier. He looks to the past to legitimize his present
practice, affirming the doctrine of scriptural inerrancy.[16] Wimber
is constantly looking to Scripture for endorsement of his ministry,
seeing this as the unalterable yardstick by which he and his
followers must be measured. Yet he is actually much broader in
his choice of fundamentals, being a fundamentalist in the 'revivalist'
tradition. Part of what makes Wimber such a fascinating case-study
is that his fundamentalism does not just depend on a few articles
of faith, but on his followers actually experiencing and promoting
'signs' of God's presence. In fact, Wimber is a good example of a
sophisticated fundamentalist. He is seldom crude, though often
very simplistic, and illustrates my belief that fundamentalism
cannot be reduced to a few basic issues.

Third, Wimber's fundamentalism is a *tendency*, functioning
programmatically. Wimber has a greater range of fundamentals
than some other fundamentalists, but he owns them and uses them
in the same sort of way. He seeks the spiritual renewal of the
Church, by propagating a whole host of phenomena that have
come to be associated with contemporary charismatic renewal:
'spiritual gifts', 'signs and wonders', healing, prophecy, deliverance,
speaking in tongues, and so forth.[17] Wimber is thus engaged in his
own particular 'Holy War' against weak, powerless or 'dead'
churches although using the highly mythical language of demons,
powers and principalities that must be engaged with and opposed.
He rejects dialogue, regarding engagement with critics as a waste
of energy and resources: 'The Bible is full of examples of Christians
who defend themselves against false accusations and criticism. In

my case, however, God has told me not to'.[18] Lastly, Wimber's particular theological methods, with their tactile emphasis, form the basis of his social organization in all its distinctiveness, as well as characterizing his opposition to other belief-systems. Analysing his work will highlight how this form of fundamentalism offers a complete interpretative framework for participants in which their understanding of God, the self and the world is formed through the words that are used and the experiences and behaviour that are valued.

The analysis in this book is based on a study of Wimber's published works. A prodigious writer and speaker, he has produced a large number of 'courses' for his followers, which generally consist of a written manual, with recorded audio cassette tapes of him speaking. The subjects covered include healing, prophecy, deliverance, 'spiritual warfare', the 'End Times', evangelism and church growth. He has contributed to a number of books that touch on issues central to his concerns, and has written himself: *Power Evangelism* (1985), *Power Healing* (1986), *Power Points* (1985) and *The Dynamics of Spiritual Growth* (1990).[19] He is also editor-in-chief of his own magazine, which runs under the title *Equipping the Saints*, and is internationally available. Around this material lies an even larger belt of commentary and occasional critique. Many of Wimber's more notable followers (e.g., Bishop David Pytches, Professor Peter Wagner, Fuller Theological Seminary, etc.) write in favour of the principles that he advocates, and actively support him. Some books bear testimony to the success-claims of Wimber's ideas and ministry, such as *Riders of the Third Wave* (1987) and *Some Said it Thundered* (1990). Perhaps inevitably, there are some fundamentalists who dislike Wimber's particular style and emphasis, and a small number have written critiques.[20] But there are no serious theological or sociological critiques as yet.

In addition I have been to Wimber's conferences in England and Scotland, as an observer. Because fundamentalism is also a matter of conduct, it seemed important to experience first-hand how Wimber and his followers operated in their preferred context, and my observations of them inform my critique. Fundamentalism is not a static thing: it moves forward as its people grow, develop and encounter what is new. Yet it also appeals to core, unchanging boundaries. What is required is a methodology that will encounter fundamentalism in all its dynamism, comprehend it, and then critique it. This book approaches the problem of interpreting

Wimber's constructive theology by treating seriously the language, concepts and manifestations of power which permeate all his work and works. Though Wimber's work, like that of so many other fundamentalists, is complex and multi-layered, interpreting him via the theme of 'power' will offer significant vantage points, from which other forms of fundamentalism might be assessed in the future.

Power as a Principle of Coherence for the Interpretation of Wimber

Most forms of fundamentalism are attempts to organize a culture around a given community's sense of where God's fundamental or primary power might lie. For example, for some fundamentalists the power of God is perceived to lie mainly in the text of Scripture, through which God is deemed pre-eminently to express his self-communication. So, God is perceived to have invested his power in the capacity of words to transform, and consequently, the community receive God via his words. Symbol, sacrament or mystical experience are rejected, since they threaten the autonomous power of words alone. The fundamentalist community therefore puts most of its energy into understanding 'the word', living under its authority, and spreading it abroad, as a means of demonstrating and sharing God's power. Consequently, its churches often revolve around preaching, Bible expositions, biblical studies and commentaries. Because the power of God lies in 'the word' and its capacity to transform, save and convict, members of such communities constantly measure themselves against texts, in order to gauge how much of (the power of) God they have understood and received.

For Wimber, however, the location of power is different. He does contend that God has powerfully revealed himself in an inerrant canon, but he parts company with his Quaker-evangelical roots in his insistence that the power of God is by nature a visible, tangible phenomenon. God reveals himself in signs, wonders, healings, miracles and church growth. Just as some fundamentalists limit the primary power of God to texts, thereby excluding other options, so Wimber locates God's power in activity, thus also excluding other avenues in which God's power might be manifest. For example, Wimber's view of God's power does not usually permit him to see God revealing himself (equally) in failure, sickness or powerlessness.

Even the most cursory glance at Wimber's books and courses will impress the reader or listener with the frequency of the use of the word 'power', or words that might be associated with it, such as 'force' or 'energy'. At times the words are employed as literary devices, as when he describes the path to spiritual growth: 'experiences of God's truth ... *boost* us along ... *catapult* us towards maturity' (*The Dynamics of Spiritual Growth*, p. 5). Also typical of Wimber are his own 'power stories' which appear scattered throughout his works, and are used to illustrate doctrine or practice, most notably in the ministries of healing and evangelism. 'Power metaphors' and symbols punctuate Wimber's worship materials, 'power concepts' govern his understanding of church history and God's current activity in the Church.[21] Most importantly Wimber pursues a notion of God as an empowering transformer who creates, redeems and renews via the unequivocal disposal of various forms of power.

Power language occurs with such unusual frequency, and at such significant points that categories of power are clearly central both to Wimber's analysis of God in church history, and to his articulation of the Christian message. Proof that sensitivity to power factors habitually conditions Wimber's thinking may be found even when no explicit 'power' words are used. The following passage – Wimber's summary of the place of 'signs and wonders' in the Church from *Church Growth: State of the Art* (1989) – illustrates the point:

In Athens, he [Paul] had used persuasive words with meagre results. At his next apostolic stop, Corinth, many believed. It appears that in Corinth Paul combined proclamation with demonstration, as Christ had done throughout his ministry. What we are dealing with here is both content (proclamation) as well as context (the situation impregnated with God's mighty presence). The word and works of God, coupled in an expression of divine will and mercy, culminate in the conversion of individuals and groups.

I call this type of ministry that Paul had in Corinth power evangelism: a presentation of the gospel that is rational but also transcends the rational. The explanation of the gospel comes with a demonstration of God's power through signs and wonders. It is a spontaneous, Spirit-inspired, empowered presentation of the gospel. It is usually preceded and undergirded by supernatural demonstrations of God's presence.

... One of the indicators of the Messiahship of Jesus was the demonstration of God's power in his ministry ... He viewed His ministry from a different perspective. He saw it from a power demonstration point of view ... The early church was effective because it understood evangelism from this same perspective – power demonstrations! (pp. 223–4)

This description of the signs and wonders ministry highlights the important stress Wimber gives to the relationship between words and works. He sees words as potential vehicles of power to persuade and transform, although it is the work (or demonstration) of power that holds his interest. As he says in *The Kingdom of God* (1985):

There is no difference between the *words* and *works* of Jesus. The *works* have exactly the same message as the *words*. The message and words concentrate on the announcement of the Kingdom of God. The miracles and works show us what the Kingdom is like. The preaching and parables were verbal announcements of the impending arrival of the rule of God and destruction of Satan's rule ... The miracles were concrete parables. With his *works*, Jesus came and destroyed Satan's grip and ushered in the rule of God, restoring God's control over what Satan had seized. (p. 41)

So for Wimber, the Kingdom of God is a kingdom of power – announced, then practised – which overthrows the controlling power of Satan. One of Wimber's central themes is that there has been a 'shift of powers in the Church',[22] which has displaced the life of God in it. The spiritual and the immediate have been subverted by the human and the institutional; words have often been unaccompanied by deeds; programmes have replaced a reliance upon the Holy Spirit.[23]

I want to argue that concepts of power form the basis of Wimber's thought. The recurring themes of God dynamically intervening in history, of movements fostering the charismata, of signs and wonders being transformative, of conflicts between the forces of darkness and of light, are all power themes. Wimber views the record of the ministry of Jesus as a clash and interplay between various powers, in which, ultimately, the power of God is revealed. 'Signs and wonders' is a phrase that most students of fundamentalism would associate with Wimber, but it is used interchangeably with another phrase: 'power encounter'. For Wimber,

> Signs and wonders being manifested is a *power encounter* ... a visible, practical demonstration that Jesus Christ is more powerful than the false god(s) or spirit(s) worshipped or feared by members of a people group. When these divinely appointed encounters occur, the church grows – although not on every occasion. Sometimes there are other mitigating factors which keep the church from growing, such as ... the negative backlash of power entities in the community who are threatened by God's display of power.[24]

One is justified in speaking of these motifs in Wimber in terms of power rather than simply dynamism for several reasons. The first is that they are the terms in which Wimber himself chooses to speak. The second is that the dynamism Wimber advocates is traceable to the importance he places on the person and work of the Holy Spirit, who animates, renews, restores, convicts and *acts* (powerfully) for God. Wimber's doctrine of the Spirit, as we shall see later, can only be understood properly if it is seen in power terms. The third reason why it is appropriate to describe Wimber's thought in terms of power is that the themes of conflict and resistance are prominent in it. Max Weber's classic definition of power, to which the notion of resistance is central, illuminates much of Wimber's thought: wherever issues of conflict and resistance are a focus, it is appropriate to speak of a language of power.[25]

Of course, Wimber's primary interest is the power of God and the powerfulness or effectiveness of the gospel's capacity to confront and transform the present powers at work in individuals and societies. His work asserts the superiority of God over what is 'natural' (Wimber's term denoting 'worldly'), and represents an affirmation of the ultimate power of God in the human situation. When Wimber emphasizes power as central to the Christian religion he is not doing anything new, but rather affirming a simple and most basic Christian tradition, of an *almighty* God, of Jesus as *Lord*, of the Holy Spirit in work and deed as active and transforming. What is most intriguing about Wimber's work is that it presses for a particular vision of the *kind* of power God exercises, *how* Christians receive it, and *what* its effects are likely to be.

2

Fundamentalism and Revivalism: Religions of Power

In order to comprehend why individuals become and remain fundamentalists, it is important to understand how God, the Church and the world appear to the individual *inside* the movement. I therefore want to analyse the role, both perceived and actual, that the power of God, Church and world play in making up the fundamentalist universe.

The definition of power I am working with holds that power is a multi-faceted reality, like fundamentalism itself. It is the 'force' that can apply itself through and reify itself via agents (tools). It is dispositional, in the form of ideas, manners, bonding and unity. It is also episodic, in the form of specific instances, interventions and moments. It is a phenomenon present within all epistemological and social frameworks, usually encountered via its agents rather than the source itself. Power is a *function* of systems of social interaction.

Understanding fundamentalist belief and organization requires the careful use of sociological tools that can bridge the gap between the language and models of fundamentalist theology and the language and models of its modern organization. The omnipotence of God, the Lordship of Jesus and the power of the Holy Spirit, place the concept of power at the centre of theology; in organizational theory, a grasp of relationships and hierarchy (power) are essential to understanding any institution. Using the concept of power to interpret fundamentalism enables an understanding of how individual fundamentalists regard God, as well as the communities in which they seek to serve him.

A Religion of Power: Exploring the Key Issues

A religion has a set of beliefs, either dogmatically set forth or instinctively recognized and accepted by those who hold them.

This set of beliefs includes an element of faith or trust, and, perhaps, a primitive view of cause and effect. Following certain religious conventions ensures for the believer a better, more interesting and ultimately rewarding future: these promises are implicit in almost all religions. Power is clearly a fundamental issue in any such religion, and especially so in fundamentalist expressions. Even writers sympathetic to American Protestant fundamentalism recognize that 'there is a striking difference in the desire of [contemporary] fundamentalism for power', that holds the system together, and magnifies it.[1] Of course, that desire in fundamentalism is manifest in many different forms, and becomes concretized in various social and sacred activities. Political power, if achieved, can promote 'spiritual values' on a wider social scale. Liturgical power can organize and routinize a community. Access to charismatic power can enhance the position of a leader as the best mediator between God and humanity.

Cheryl Forbes, in her influential critique of power in the contemporary American evangelical scene, notes that 'the point of power is to be visible, and it promises visibility to the worshipper'.[2] She chides modern evangelical leaders for their pursuit of *success* (Forbes equates this with power) – in all its spheres – and suggests that most churches fail to own up to their preoccupation with power, and choose instead to mask it under a new vocabulary, with words such as 'leadership', 'authority' or 'simplicity'. Although her aim is to exorcize the influence of 'possibility thinkers' from evangelicalism,[3] she makes a number of useful observations. First, she notes the tendency of evangelicals and fundamentalists to use well-known personalities who have become Christians in their evangelism. The appeal to a powerful personality who is a convert, she suggests, is a 'power-game'. On one level, it assures 'more average' believers (or interested non-believers) that they are correct in subscribing to this particular form of Christianity. Yet at a deeper level, she suggests that the use of a powerful personality from a profession (acting, politics, sport, etc.) is a way of *not* talking about *powerless* people who might also believe. She maintains that this is because the powerless, those who are sick, poor or handicapped, are not usually used in the service of the Church's evangelism because their lives do not immediately speak of God's power. Thus she concludes, fundamentalists use power in the service of greater power. She carries this argument over into the realm of miracles, signs and wonders, and questions evangelicals and fundamentalists as to

whether or not they have 'moulded' God in their own image,
and then turned themselves into 'power-brokers', with potentially
damaging results.[4] This reaches a peak for Forbes in her engagement
with the Charismatic movement (emphases added):

> I attended the 'First International Conference on the Holy Spirit'
> as a reporter. Most of the attendees spoke in tongues and were
> convinced someone wasn't 'completely' a Christian if he didn't.
> Since I was not a charismatic, I became the object of much
> witnessing. People badgered me about speaking in tongues (there
> is no other way to describe it). One otherwise charming elderly
> woman told me that *God had sent me to the conference just so I
> would begin to speak in tongues.* And there were others, not quite
> as charming, who *upbraided me for not submitting to the Holy
> Spirit,* for being proud and defensive. *These people wanted power
> over my relationship with God.* They used every spiritual tactic
> they could think of to shame, harass, embarrass, and propel me
> into an experience that was for them the mark of a Christian.[5]

The experience of Forbes demonstrates the multi-layered way
in which power is functioning in a charismatic community like the
one she describes. She is perceived by the conference participants to
be lacking in some fundamental aspect of God's power.
Consequently, power in the form of pressure is applied to her,
with those applying such pressure presumably (and sincerely)
seeing themselves as agents of God's power, through whom Forbes
might ultimately be blessed.

All this seems a long way away from the assessment of
charismatic phenomena and their influence on church doctrine
made by David Ford and Daniel Hardy, in *Jubilate: Theology in
Praise* (1984). Although they recognize that in charismatic renewal
'the power of the real thing is paralleled by awful examples of
what its imitations and perversions can do' (p. 20), they portray
a much more positive picture of the place of power in religion.
The focus of their concern is to 'participate in the free and
unconstrained activity of God' by constructing a theology of praise.
They equate Pentecostalism and charismatic renewal with what
they call 'the jazz factor'; the worshippers literally become
instruments of praise in this analogy, with spontaneity, freedom,
innovation and harmony implied, though without the constrictions
of order that can sometimes stifle free response.[6]

This affirmative portrayal of Pentecostalism or charismatic

renewal partly sets the agenda for the authors' understanding of power in religion, and it deserves careful attention. Beginning with the observation that 'the question of God's power and action in the world is one of the most important in theology', they continue:

A great deal of theology and daily existence is bedevilled by inappropriate ways of understanding God's power. One of the commonest pictures is of God's power in competition with his creation's freedom, and people needing protection against his overwhelming omnipotence. The model of power in this picture is a crude one of the coercive use of force.[7]

They suggest that the central question is to ask how God's power is a primary cause in the world. They locate the answer in the sphere of speaking, noting that 'at its best it works by invitation and information rather than by manipulation'. On this model, even the crucifixion is 'God's speech expressed in suffering. He lets people be themselves, lets them have their freedom even to be wrong, to ignore him and to show disrespect to the point of killing'. So, in the view of Hardy and Ford, the power of God if rejected or opposed is not met with counter-force by God, but with a willingness to respect the power that has been given to the world. Even the resurrection is not a reversal of this: rather, it is an overcoming of evil and death that respects the world, yet also judges it and probes its limits.

In spite of Ford and Hardy's positive view of Pentecostalism and charismatic renewal, their liberating and rich view of the power of God is not reflected in the Christian community under investigation here. This is not meant to sound harsh or dismissive. Certainly, Wimber is attempting to recover an apparently lost sense of the immediate power of God to the Church and to the individual. But the recurring question is, what kind of *powers* is Wimber attributing to God and then, in turn, to the Church?

For instance, in Wimber's churches 'words of knowledge', reputedly supernatural in origin, are used to persuade, convict and transform individuals, in order that they might respond to God (*Power Evangelism*, p. 47). Although there is some biblical precedent for such approaches (e.g., Jesus and the woman at the well, John 4), the problem with Wimber and his followers' *use* of words of knowledge is that they frequently do not permit a free response, or constitute an invitation. They can be tools for persuasion, alteration and coercion; thus, Wimber writes: 'In power evangelism, resistance to the gospel is supernaturally overcome' (*Power Evangelism*, p. 47). So the speech of God for Wimber, here in the form of words of knowledge, is a notion of the power of God that competes with the freedom God has given in creation, ultimately quashing it. In Wimber's view, God will use any form of power – including coercive words – to gain the response of an individual.

This view of power has an implication in church communities, though it is masked in authority structures. Some of Wimber's followers, and perhaps Wimber himself, believe in what they call the recovery of 'the Ananias and Sapphira scenario' amongst their churches (Acts 5.1–11). Followers who resist or lie to leaders are deemed to be resisting or lying to God, and are therefore immediately liable to the power of God in the form of judgement.[8] This invests the leaders of Wimber's churches with a high degree of authority, since they can already receive words of knowledge concerning an individual's secret or sinful state. Thus, the room to respond to a word of knowledge is severely restricted, with the result that the power of God is often perceived as being the irresistable force meeting the movable object. Similar attitudes to power in Wimber's thinking and churches can be traced in the phenomenon of 'being slain in the Spirit'.[9]

These observations are necessarily critical, yet Wimber is trying to do no more than conform the way in which power works in the Church with the way in which he believes God exercises power. What appears to have gone wrong is that God's superabundance has been fundamentally misunderstood. For example, phenomena like 'speaking in tongues' should mirror the 'overspilling of the internal trinitarian process of communication',[10] resulting in a 'cathedral of sound' being created, that reflects the glory of God. This form of communication ought to be invitational and inclusive in orientation (1 Cor. 14.22–5), prompting even those who do not understand it to recognize the authentic presence of God. Yet frequently, this is not the case, with 'speaking in tongues' being used as a tool that demonstrates the power of God, and therefore of the church concerned in their *capacity* to receive and handle it. This was the problem Cheryl Forbes experienced with the people she met at the 'Conference of the Holy Spirit', who wanted her to know the power of God. But their perception of that power as a *necessary* hallmark for the spiritual completeness of the individual Christian places a limit on the freedom of people to respond as they wish, as well as reducing the power of God to that of a coercive agent. The form and content of God's power is not that of a totalitarian ruler: it is, like the inner life of the Trinity itself, an inclusive sharing that necessarily expands to include all of creation, whilst respecting its freedom to respond appropriately or inappropriately.

(i) THE NATURE OF THE PROBLEM
There are two socio-theological reasons why it is important to understand what is meant by power. First, power is one of the primary religious ideas; humanity's awareness of God is an awareness of him as powerful. It is seen as a fundamental attribute of God. The possibility and existence of God reside in his omnipotence. In the Judeo-Christian tradition the election and guidance of Israel are viewed as being marked by specific manifestations of power; Jesus' good news concerns the reign and Kingdom of God, that is, the perfect expression of his power; as Christ and Lord, Jesus shares in that power, revealing a new knowledge of the love of God which is now disclosed as being the central feature of God's power. Second, a right attitude to power is fundamental in human social relations. The source, practice and goals of power are important here. To Christ, all power in heaven and on earth is given, and the Christian's citizenship of heaven implies that a personal appeal may be made to a transcendent form of power. Yet the earthly authorities are also to exercise power and are to be obeyed by citizens, as they carry out their work of administering justice as God's agents. Both observations are crucial. In the type of charismatic fundamentalism under investigation, the distinction between works of God and human activities is blurred to the extent that is difficult to perceive their precise nature and (subsequent) proper relationship. The use of the word 'distinction' is not meant to imply a separation: it is recognized that all human action is dependent on God as its creative ground, and equally, that God's power must be made known through some form of created – often human – agency.

(ii) THE NATURE OF POWER
Power is most often in question in the sphere of social relations, since social power can be the will of individuals or groups exercising a determining influence on the communal life of a number of people within an organized structure. Such a will is powerful when it can impose what it wishes. If it does this by the free consent of

others, power assumes the form of authority. If it acts directly on other external realities, it can assume the form of force. But power and authority are at their strongest when they are consented to, since power can then be drawn from within, and not merely from outside.

These observations have rich implications for our study of Wimber. The powerful will must be at one with the consenting will of others, and yet it must also be at one with itself. This demands that what it wills ought to exist and its act ought to be posited (in this case, the nature and activity of God understood through a working 'power theology' that will shape church behaviour and destiny); that is, this form of power must be good and rightful. Thus, the real purpose of power can be partly expressed here as (visible?) goal-attainment, namely increasing the power and influence of what is said to be good and right, in the interests of a common good. So, power has both a horizontal and vertical dimension to it: horizontally, it harmonizes community will, and vertically, it attempts to be in harmony with the higher goals of what it believes to be 'normally' right and good. In short, as far as Wimber and his theology are concerned, power is the effective ordering of his communities in relation to God and in relation to the world. For such purposes, both authority and force are legitimized in social relations and theological dynamics.[11]

The exercise of power in Wimber's theory and practice is intrinsically linked to the blur that results from the confusion over what is God's work and what is humanity's. The fact that this confusion has arisen at all is traceable to the very foundations of Wimber's movement. Wimber is seldom clear in distinguishing his own powers from that of God's power working in him: rather than trying to clarify this tension, he seems to have gained from it. The results – often traceable in other forms of (charismatic) fundamentalism – have been threefold. First, clear patterns for mediating social and theological authority have emerged: one primary leader (Wimber), supported by a group of 'anointed' underlings. Second, the authority or force of God has become merged – for the whole community – in the office of the leaders, making the distinction between human and divine power difficult to actualize. Third, the leaders have become the chief mediators of God's power, via the agency of, say, healing, prophecy, or renewal. Therefore, the *nature* of power for the community concerned becomes identified with *how* that power is actually exercised.

(iii) THE CONSEQUENCES OF POWER

Power is one of the important means of social organization. Agents are 'things' capable of moving or impelling power. Agents can be people, instances, doctrines, situations, and so on. Within a given world-view, agents are the fixed points that allow access to power, provide markers or boundaries for a circuit (group, identity, etc.), and ensure the connectedness of the power relations. Charisma can be an agent as much as an individual doctrine, and each agent will have its own structure made up of other nodal points. The likely effects of a 'power theology' and 'power community' on itself and on others can be summarized in the following suggestions:

1. Finite power is always tempted to establish itself in self-assertion, to shut itself off and try to be independent in the face of competition from other finite wills. This leads to the community and its main sponsors rejecting dialogue, and ultimately becoming sectarian. In Wimber's case, this has already happened: he has a 'policy' of not answering criticism, or of engaging with critics, on the basis that it drains his energy and diverts the attention of the community.

2. If divine power is conflated with human power in the face of this stance, the leaders themselves will become 'fundamental' instruments of God. Charisma bears witness to the leader as God's elect, and this often makes the community unmanageable after his or her demise, even if the ideology remains intact.

3. The failure to distinguish between divine and human activity leads to a distorted view of the Church. The preservation of the community's identity becomes too vital a task, since it identifies itself and its goals too closely with God and his purposes. Thus, what the community and its leaders want is what God wants. So, the task of the community moves from being an open engagement in social interrelationships quickened by the Spirit (mission), to being a closed agenda, in which God and the community only confront the world in a defensive fashion, yet with clear targets in mind.

4. The 'power theology' of Wimber is too stipulative and programmatic. Although individuals may find it progressive initially, as a form of truth it ultimately fails in its obligation to set people free. The church structure – funded by charisma and ideology – is partly to blame. But at the root of this, lies a theology that has not dared articulate the limits of power and its implications, and has attempted to possess and own

God's power (albeit for apparently worthy causes), rather than
be owned by it.

5. Wimber's view is too mechanistic. Against the threat of
randomness that modern plurality seems to suggest, Wimber,
like many other fundamentalists, offers a God who is in tight
control of the world, even when the nature of his creation
seems to rule out such totalitarianism. Logically, it is almost
impossible for Wimber and his followers to avoid determinism
and its theological offshoots such as predestination. The
evidence of such notions can be traced in Wimber's churches,
as we shall see later.

These are serious charges, but the rest of this book will bear
them out. As Sykes says: 'the language of sociology and the
language of theology may be separate, but the reality of divine
and human power is not. It is not parallel or merely co-ordinated,
it is inevitably, and dangerously, mixed'.[12]

Ultimately, the 'Religion of Power', like all forms of
fundamentalism, will be shown to be an insecure response to the
modern situation. Instead of grounding ecclesial, individual and
theological identity in an open movement towards God and others,
the search for the power of God has been laid to rest prematurely.
The desire to channel the energy of God leads communities to
refer what is finite and fallible only to itself and idolize it as
infinite or infallible.

The Historical and Theological Context of Wimber's Concern with Power

Two questions arise from Wimber's historical and theological
concern with power. First, how does Wimber himself see history,
and does this authenticate the procedure and method chosen?
Second, but related to the first question, what historical roots
might Wimber possess that lead him to construct his theology and
doctrine of the Church in the way that he does?

Wimber's treatment of signs and wonders in church history
illustrates his use of 'power'. In two important appendices, Wimber
divides instances of signs and wonders into four periods: patristic,
medieval, reformation-modern and twentieth century. Wimber's
strategy is to show that signs and wonders have always been part
of the witness of the Church and, therefore, his present enterprise

stands within a credible tradition. The execution of this strategy, however, is somewhat simplistic, and its use as 'proof' owes much to Wimber habitually not treating his sources critically. For example, citing instances from the *Journal* of John Wesley, he notes:

> What I discovered was that our experience at the Vineyard Christian Fellowship was not unique; people like John and Charles Wesley, George Whitefield, Charles Finney and Jonathan Edwards all had similar phenomena in their ministries ... For example, on May 24th 1739, John Wesley wrote in his journal ... 'About three in the morning as we were continuing instant in prayer the power of God came mightily upon, insomuch that many cried out for exulting joy and fell to the ground ...'.[13]

Wimber handles an historical phenomenon with a view to exposing its power dynamics. His works are littered with similar examples of historical phenomena 'processed' for their relation to power, although I would contend that his hermeneutical skills are weak.[14] He is not choosy either, about where he draws examples of power-related phenomena from. Sources range from Prophet Harris (founder of a Nigerian charismatic cult) to the recorded healings at the shrine at Lourdes, from the more familiar Azusa Street Revival (1906) to the modern missionary campaigns of Reinhard Bonnke. Even so, it is clear that Wimber's primary power interest is the power of God and the empowered community as it celebrates the effectiveness or powerfulness of God's action in its life, drawing individuals into a deeper bond with God. Furthermore, Wimber contrasts this power – a liberating, transforming force that is made known through the Holy Spirit – with what he sees as the more traditional powers of the Church, namely that of constraint, and the deadening effects of tradition, rationality and orthodoxy.

Consequently, Wimber is constantly pressing the superiority of the power of Christ over every aspect of nature. The power of God can be ultimately affirmed in Scripture, in history, and also in the present. 'The power of God' for Wimber means that human, economic, geological, social and organizational powers – in fact power of any kind – can be subject at any moment to the superior power of God. Thus, the mission of Christ in Wimber's view becomes an historical event in which power is lost and won: on the cross, the power of sin is defeated, the power of Satan destroyed,

and the superior power of Christ revealed over all other powers.
The question naturally arises as to how Wimber accounts for
defeat and failure? One answer is given through the analogy of
the D-Day landings, June 1944. From that point, Hitler's downfall
is assured, but he is not yet defeated, so suffering, occasional
defeat and setbacks continue until the war is finally won.[15] The
Church, claims Wimber, is embroiled in a similar struggle. The
present and future can therefore be characterized in the following
way:

> A war is going on! Cosmic War! Jesus is the divine invader sent
> by God to shatter the strengths of Satan. In that light the whole
> ministry of Jesus unrolls. Jesus has one purpose – to defeat Satan.
> Jesus was aware of this war. Paul wrote about and waged the war
> (Ephesians 6.10ff). Peter was cognizant of it (1 Peter 5.8). Nothing
> has changed. The war goes on and will continue until Jesus returns.[16]

The second question is why a concern with power understood
in this particular way should constitute a focus for Wimber's
thought and work. Several factors no doubt play their part. The
first would be its accordance with Wimber's personal religious
experiences shaped, as they often are, by a form of dramatic
intervention. These experiences in turn could well have been
confirmed and built upon by his initial evangelical upbringing,
with its stress on personal conversion, an immanent experience of
being born again, and a commitment to seeing the gospel as
something active and effective in others. This framework was
developed by his encounter with 'Jesus People'. Another factor
would be Wimber's theological education, at Azusa Pacific
University, where he could have been exposed to teaching from
Pentecostal and evangelical lecturers, although curiously, Wimber
denies any familiarity with a Pentecostal education (indeed it
would probably have been initially unacceptable to his original
Quaker–evangelical church at Yorba Linda). After graduation, he
was exposed to evangelicals who were familiar with the power of
the Holy Spirit via their own experience of charismatic renewal:
the influence of Peter Wagner has already been mentioned, but
figures such as George Eldon Ladd and James Kallas have also
played their part.[17]

A third factor lies in the apologetic resonance of interpreting
Christianity in terms of power. Power is a concept which current
intellectual, political and economic developments constantly place

in the foreground of people's thought, and so an account that speaks in terms of power stands a good chance of gaining attention and of being understood. Indeed, as we have hinted before, one of the things which drives fundamentalists so hard is the conviction that the power they serve is greater than the combined forces of plurality and modernity. The fundamentalist endeavour is therefore frequently concerned with channelling and directing that power against the prevailing powers of the age. A form of fundamentalism that articulates this explicitly is bound to be appealing. Developments in theology and the Church in the twentieth century may also have contributed to Wimber focusing on the power of God. Troeltsch points out that prior to the Enlightenment the Church established its proofs of the divine power in terms of miracles and the fulfilment of prophecy, but that when it departed from a strong emphasis on external proofs, the internal, psychological miracle of divine power working within the soul became more important.[18] Although Wimber has a high place for the internal activity of divine power in his work, he nevertheless seems to be striving to recover what has apparently been lost since the Enlightenment. This partly accounts for his repeated attacks on post-Enlightenment 'western world-views'. Another factor which seems to promote Wimber's interest in the subject of power is his distress about the present state of the Church (so often referred to as 'dead', 'asleep', etc.), which in his view allows Satan and his advocates too much opportunity to extend their power:

> The struggle we are in is not a civil war within a kingdom. It is the Kingdom of God against the Kingdom of Satan. The strong man's house (i.e. Satan's Kingdom) is bound ... Satan's power is curbed but obviously he is not powerless ... God desires to raise an army, not an audience. He wants us to be aware of the enemy's plans and weapons. He longs to equip us with His weapons. His wish is that we may fight the good fight of faith. (*Power Points*, manual, p. 43, and tape 5a)

Another factor that cannot be overlooked is the social and cultural conditions from which Wimber's power theology has emerged. We might 'dub' this the 'Californian factor', and it operates at a variety of levels. California itself has a number of Pentecostal seminaries, universities, graduate schools and Bible colleges and a strong tradition of charismatic renewal beginning with the Azusa Street Revival of 1906 in Los Angeles, continuing

right through to the 'Jesus People' of the early 1970s. Californian
people, especially those with Christian backgrounds, are perhaps
peculiarly sensitized to the issues of power. This is partly because
of the rapid pace of change that seems endemic to California (in
social trends, ideals and the Church), and partly due to the idealism
and romanticism that seem to characterize the pervading mood of
society. Wimber appears to be both a master and a victim of the
culture in this respect. Although his churches enjoy considerable
support abroad, his own power-base at Anaheim (in the form of
numerical support: rising to 4,000, then 10,000, then falling to
5,000) is constantly prey to the contemporary 'Christian fashion
scene' that is part of Californian Christianity. For example, within
a few miles of the Vineyard at Anaheim is a considerable variety of
styles of Christian worship: Robert Schuller's 'Crystal Cathedral',
Chuck Smith's Calvary Chapel, Jimmy and Tammy Bakker's
Trinity Broadcast Network (tele-evangelism), to name but a few.
The Californian Christian culture appears to be able to support
and accommodate all these diverse bodies quite comfortably, as
they compete for interest and income.

In the wider context of American culture in general, the interest
in power and success that permeates many areas of society must
also be noted. It is a country that was founded by competing
sectarian groups that initially migrated from Europe, although this
net has now widened in the twentieth century to include all other
continents of the world. At the heart of the invitation to be an
American lies a popularized or idealized concept: power in the
form of equal rights, and the opportunity of extending one's power
via wealth or success. It is probable that no other culture in the
world could spawn and nurture the kind of theology and doctrine
of the Church that Wimber espouses. Of course, it is exportable
to other cultures like any other commodity passing from its own
distinct context to another. Nevertheless, Wimber's power theology
and ecclesiology is recognizably American in origin, with notable
West Coast/Californian distinctives. This climate of power and
success in American social, individual and church life is no doubt
sufficient to explain at a basic level why Wimber's theology and
ecclesiology interest his hearers so much, but it is more complicated
than that.

First there is a sharp distinction in Wimber's thought between
political and religious power, which is no doubt traceable to his
evangelical upbringing. Wimber does have an interest in politics,
but only in so far as he sees politics being subject to demonic

influence rather than Christian influence. Essentially, Wimber's dualism only permits political power the choice between God's way and that which might be pervaded by the 'personality of Satan' (*Power Points*, manual, p. 46, tape 5a). Then there is also the influence of several 'isms' to contend with, of which 'rationalism' is perhaps the most important. Wimber and his followers are deeply convinced that the powerlessness of the contemporary Church lies in its over-commitment to reason. One of the principal reasons Wimber advocates the 'power encounter model' of evangelism as the goal of Christian mission is that it, to quote Wimber, 'blows your mind open', breaking up westernized patterns of thinking that have left little or no room for the miraculous. In addition to the influence of opposition to rationalism in Wimber's thought, his positive evangelicalism cannot be ignored. This also helps to frame a power idiom for Wimber's description of the Christian's inner life. Its emphasis on new life, transformation, sanctification and various moral imperatives based on Scripture and traditional behavioural conventions constantly recurs in Wimber's writings.

We might expect Wimber to trace dogmatic beliefs back to the actual experiences of divine or spiritual power that prompted them, especially in the light of his reading of history. Yet he is hesitant about such an undertaking, and appears to be willing to explore the subject in only a limited way. Like many other classical Pentecostal or 'Holiness' movements, he does not probe *how* divine power actually operates on the individual. Two consequences result from this, which are familiar themes in early charismatic Quakerism. First, the feelings of the individual's heart are used as the only reliable register of God's activity and power. Second, individual and corporate holiness are seen as the only appropriate response to the mystery of God's power. Both drives are demonstrated in Wimber's treatment of spiritual power, and significantly both are forms of institutional responses to unanswered questions.

It certainly seems odd that for all Wimber's talk about the power of God, and its immediate availability for transformation and redemption, there is little attempt to explain its capacity, particularity, and identity. This is still true even if one takes into account his occasional crude mechanistic tendencies. There is certainly no doubt that in asking questions about spiritual power one is searching the very heart of religion, and that the consequences of the questions could be far-reaching. Reverence and awe on the part of believers do account for some hesitation: how do mere humans discern the depths of the divine, asking not only what God has done, but how it is done? Widespread discomfort with the subject of power in general also plays a part: fear is a factor that inhibits deeper investigation in many disciplines at many levels. Perhaps in Wimber's case there is a fear that a deep probe into his major fundamental – the power of God – may have the effect of starting a reductive (or deconstructive) process in himself and his followers, leading to foreseeable consequences: the power of God becoming a psychological trait, words of knowledge becoming simply auto-suggestion, the immediacy of God in his community emerging as just a method of relationality. To question the power of God implies that there might be some uncomfortable conclusions: which fundamentalist in the revival tradition would want to face those?

Something else which restrains Wimber and others from pressing the question of God's power is that it might imply partial unbelief. Again, it was Troeltsch who observed that miracles and psychological or inward manifestations of power are something of a last bastion for transcendence. Only those who are unsure of God's power are likely to probe its limits in an effort to gain reassurance. If the world exhibited abundant evidence of God's almighty power in redemption and creation, such questions might not be necessary, or be of only mild academic interest. But the question has a profound existential relevance, for humanity inhabits a world in which divine power seems weak, erratic or absent, with other powers holding sway. The would-be fundamentalist therefore confronts the proclaimed tradition of God's supreme sovereign power with a belief and hope, yet is surrounded by contrary evidence. Inevitably, the problem must be solved as it usually is for most fundamentalists, either by reference to eschatological dynamics (which must remain mythic-speculative), or by resorting to a complex, systematic dualism: both can be located in Wimber. Ultimately, Wimber's work offers a satisfying and plausible way of being for his followers. His own optimistic cheerfulness and immense productivity, coupled with his deep sensitivity, may also help to assuage any doubters in his ranks.

Categories of Power in Wimber's Works

Wimber has not developed any particularly specialized vocabulary for discussing power, and neither has he laid out any formal

typology for the different kinds of power he speaks of. Therefore
in the interests of clarity, some attention needs to be paid to the
terminology he uses, which falls into three categories.

(i) THE POWER OF GOD AND THE EMPOWERMENT OF THE CHRISTIAN

When Wimber writes or speaks of 'the power of God', of
'spiritual power' or 'the power of the Holy Spirit', the 'of' is
crucial: Wimber sees a certain type of power as belonging
entirely to God, to be dispensed as he wills. As such, it is
something beyond social or political enquiry, although social
and political consequences naturally arise from its use. Thus
for Wimber, there is a real dichotomy between sacred and
secular power. The two only really engage in conflict ('power
encounter') for Wimber, when secular power – in the form of
institutions, tradition, etc. – actively prevents the operation of
divine power. Though even here, as has already been hinted,
Wimber invests such encounters with a sacred–satanic
interpretation rather than sacred–secular.

Thus, the double-dualism (sacred–satanic, sacred–secular)
provides Wimber with a framework for speaking of a type of
power that belongs to God alone, although it can be passed to
or through Christians, who then become agents for that power,
provided they co-operate with its intentions. In turn, Wimber
locates the operation of divine power, though not the subject
of divine power, firmly within the category of outwardness. For
Wimber, God is the one who wishes to achieve certain things
via his agents, in order to demonstrate his love and his power.
In an interesting passage in *The Dynamics of Spiritual Growth*,
Wimber illustrates this in his attempt to describe the person of
the Holy Spirit, not just his works. Yet the attempt fails
altogether: what describes the personality of the Spirit for
Wimber is just a long list of what the Spirit does, and each of
these activities has its orientation in outwardness. For example:
'He provides resurrection power...He empowers and guides us
in our witness and service...He produces spiritual growth...'
(*DSG*, p. 133).

Thus, the power of God is something placed in the Christian
as a means of expanding God's economy of productive activity.
This economy is ultimately a conformist one (some would say
coercive), in which everything is responsive to manifestations
of power in accordance with how that power would wish it

to be. Christians do not, therefore, have much choice about
how the power of God is to operate: they must simply remove
any personal obstacles to that power, and prepare to be filled
by it. This activity will always result in an outward movement
either into the secular or against the satanic, resulting in a
'power encounter' which will confront further blockages to the
power of God.

This rather vacuous notion of what Christians are for is
persistent throughout Wimber's works. Instead of humanity being
creatively and directly involved, with their individuality and
corporality by the Spirit, they instead become 'tools'. (This
mechanistic image of Wimber's, used to refer to the gifts of
the Spirit, also, ultimately, refers to the wielder of the tools.)
Consequently, the role of the Spirit is reduced to that of a
transformative force or tool in the hands of God, devoid of
personality, individuality or real nature. The only place for an
'inward' role for the Spirit is in 'witnessing' or 'convicting'; yet
these things themselves will only be shown to be genuine if they
result in outward, visible signs of the inward event. Christians are
thus agents of God's power, which is a force or energy that 'attracts
us to Jesus'. Indeed, such is Wimber's view of the power of God
in its relation to the Christian, that he writes: 'God's intent is to
transform us into *replicas* of his Son.'[19]

(ii) 'POWER POINTS': AGENTS FOR ENERGIZING
Given that Wimber sees the Christian development as being the
progressive objectification of the Spirit and the progressive
domination of all that might hinder this, how might this be
achieved? The short answer is, via agents that effectively
communicate the power of God *to* their intended goal. To explain
this, Wimber employs some of his most specific power language,
by referring to what he calls 'power points': 'Power points are
based on our interaction with objective markers of core Christian
truths that direct us towards maturity; if we follow them well,
they change the direction of our lives'.[20]

Wimber's 'power points' are moments in which radical
transformation takes place, resulting in a new knowledge of God
or experience of his power. Thus, the acquisition of 'power points'
gives the believer power to do more, or greater energy. So, the
outwardness of the Christian's power, given by God, is stimulated
by other agents (such as a fundamental principle), also given by
God. Hence, Wimber continues (note my emphases): 'they [power

points] are experiences of God's truth that *boost* us along, that *catapult* us towards *maturity* . . . [they] *raise* our *vision* and sense of calling. *Elevated vision* in turn creates an *expectant, highly motivated* environment'.[21]

The somewhat vacuous notion of power, humanity and the person of the Holy Spirit previously discussed is here alleviated by providing nodal points that the Christian can grasp, which provide a series of steps or levels, which might indicate the level of power that is potentially operative in the individual. The believer does not simply have to be open to the power of God, with no thought to the consequences. This could easily lead to disagreement over what is the objective sign of power in the community and the individual and what is not. Instead, what the believer has is a power or energy network, a series of interconnected 'points' that convey power, each with its own heart of biblical truth. The task of the believer, in their desire to progressively make real the power of the Spirit in their lives, is connected to the power points in such a way that the energy from within them might dispose of its transformative power. For example, a commitment to a form of biblical inerrancy is said to be a 'power point', since not believing in inerrancy would 'undermine our *confidence*' (*DSG*, p. 40) in Scripture as an agent of God's power.

Thus, we can see that Wimber's terminology for fundamental articles of faith can actually be expressed in terms of 'power points'. For Wimber, it is via these points that God offers either steps or a path into his power. When they have been grasped or 'mastered', the believer ascends into a greater experience, expression and understanding of God's power. As such, the fundamentals require a response: they are the points through which God offers his empowerment, and as agents of power, must be engaged with if progress is to occur. However, the 'power points' appear to have no power of their own: Wimber does not advocate the independent power of inerrancy, doctrine or the like. These things are only power points in so far as the grasping of them leads to a greater experience of God's power. So, as with the individual believer in the previous section, these objective markers are also somewhat vacuous: objects waiting to be used for empowerment as a means to progressive activity.

(iii) POWER AS AUTHORITY: OVER NATURE, SUPER-NATURE AND THE CHURCH

Intrinsic to Wimber's idea of power is a notion of conflict. The power of God is operating in the life of believers, but its full potential is not realized because of natural resistance, supernatural resistance, or confusion over structures and priorities (authority). Each one of these will be dealt with in turn.

It is important to begin by noting that Wimber does not articulate any theory as to the limits of God's power. Therefore any resistance to its goals can be overcome if the individual or community 'takes authority' over the particular problem. Most commonly for Wimber, this is focused in the area of healing. Wimber does not believe that all illness is satanic in origin: he regards it as a condition of human nature which entered creation via 'the Fall'. However, the victory of Christ on the cross for Wimber necessarily indicates that what is apparently natural may no longer be pre-eminent over the supernatural. The power of Christ can heal everybody, provided the right methodology is employed. Those who are not healed have simply not been correctly or adequately exposed to the power of God.[22] The power of God is therefore a seal of authority over what is natural and normal, and the task of the believer is to claim, realize and practise that authority in everyday situations, as, it is claimed, Jesus did himself.

Power as authority is also manifest in the supernatural realm, where again, Wimber calls for believers to exercise their God-given authority in the form of power, by resisting the devil. Although Wimber ascribes tremendous powers to both Satan and to demons, he sees the power of God as being consistently triumphant, since the power has an authority that other powers do not possess. The nature of this authority is essentially that of controlling. If the right techniques are employed for, say, a deliverance, the demon must ultimately comply with the wishes of those praying, since they may 'bind and loose' in the name of Christ. This is important, since it suggests that the power of God, in the form of authority, can be realized in any conflict, with a positive, progressive result.

Similarly, in the Church, authority is a form of realized power. Only when individuals have 'submitted' to principles, and placed themselves under the authority of leaders or certain principles, will empowerment follow. The power of God therefore lies in the *authority* of its agents. To question their authority is tantamount to questioning the power of God. Consequently, non-acceptance of authority results in not receiving empowerment, and therefore being exposed to the elemental (natural and supernatural) powers of the universe, with appropriate consequences.

These three overall categories of power will be analysed in more detail later on. It is clear, however, that the power of God in Wimber's thinking is extremely conflated with that of the agents he suggests it arrives by. Further questions are raised by his view of God's power as outward, progressive and authoritarian, and to these we must now turn.

3

Power, Agency and Charisma*

Introduction: Some Perspectives on Power from Social Sciences

In ecclesiology, and perhaps to a lesser extent theology, power has been a neglected, even despised, concept. The common error of over-simply equating power with coercion has meant that theology has been reluctant to find a legitimate place for it in its doctrine. Embarrassment over the reality of power often leads to the concept being cloaked or misrepresented through the use of terms like 'authority', 'Lordship' or 'headship'. Evidently, before we can work with concepts like power and power structure in fundamentalist communities, we need a broader understanding of power, and for this we must turn to social theorists and philosophers. Once we have a grasp of how the concept functions in organizational theory, we can bring it back into theology, and fundamentalist thinking, in order to see if we can make use of it.

However, before beginning our discussion of power, we ought to clarify our terms of reference with regards to the concept of agency. A preliminary definition was advanced in Chapter Two, but it is now necessary to be more precise about the usage of the term. Working on the assumption that it is not possible ever to encounter the pure power of God, which would, presumably, constitute meeting God (himself) face to face, theologians have to accept that God is encountered through agents of that power. These agents can either be of divine origin, as in, say, the case of creation, or they can be of human origin, as in, say, the case of a work of art. Of course it is sometimes difficult to decide what is

---

* Some of the material in this chapter may be quite difficult for the general reader. Although it will repay careful study, some readers may prefer to move on to Chapter Four and return to this chapter later.

a human agent, and what is a divine one, particularly in fundamentalist communities, where the power of God is often conflated with other powers at work in the community. For example, charisma has an ambiguous identity as an agent in Wimber's Vineyards. The distinction between divine and human agents is sometimes quite clear in Wimber's work. For Wimber, designed 'programme evangelism' is a human agent, through which the power of God can work. He clearly sees this as inferior to 'signs and wonders', which he regards as an originally divine agent, which is given to the elect for using to draw humanity into the power of God.

We should not be surprised at this sharp distinction. Actually, fundamentalists tend to treat their primary agents for delivering divine power virtually as divine agents. Thus, an inerrant Bible is seen as a 'God-given' agent in the same way that 'signs and wonders' might be. However, the *methods* for using these agents or interpreting them are widely regarded as examples of human agency. In all cases, the primary function of an agent is twofold: (i) to *reify* power, and (ii) in so doing, to *control* people, doctrines, standards, etc., by the exercise of that power: that is to say, produce a product or benefit from its use. When the term 'agent' or 'agency' is used here, the following assumptions can be made: when the term is linked to fundaments, divine agency is implied; with methods or programmes, human agency is implied; and with concepts such as charisma, there is conflation between the divine and human. How though, does this discussion connect with ideas about power?

Addressing Some Aspects of the Nature of Divine Power

There is little agreement among social scientists about how power language is to be read. With no definitive experts to consult, theologians must find their own way amongst the many treatments of power available. As a working definition of power with which to begin, Max Weber's is still adequate, i.e., that power is 'the probability that one actor within a social relationship will be in a position to carry out his own will despite resistance, regardless of the basis upon which this probability rests'.[1]

With this definition, a number of qualifying terms begin to develop around the bare word 'power': social relationship, will, resistance. More is to follow. Clearly power occurs in many and varied forms, and the work of social scientists reflects this variation to a large degree.[2]

The work of sociologist and theologian Peter Berger stands out sharply in contrast to that of other contemporary thinkers. When theologians write about divine or spiritual power they often do so with hesitancy and imprecision: discussions often concern themselves with institutions, authority or the appropriate place of service. Even those who have become critical about social and political power continue to handle spiritual power in a simple manner.[3] By radicals it can be 'debunked' and declared only to be a 'mythic legitimation' of the altogether human power of religious institutions. By fundamentalists and revivalists, it is often celebrated as a kind of magical electricity, offering immediate and direct solutions, and though phrases like 'the power of the Holy Spirit' may be scattered liberally around, actual discussion of the nature and method of operation of divine power tends to be sparse and stereotyped. Theologians who do not fall foul of either of these extremes are usually preoccupied with what divine power can and cannot do, and how it is demonstrated.[4] Yet the subject is of vital importance in apologetics: theologians and fundamentalists alike must all address the issue at some point.

Berger maintains that whenever fundamentalists or theologians attempt to deal with the phenomenon of the power of God and of the spiritual power active in and available to believers, varying strategies are adopted. His book, *The Heretical Imperative* (1980) makes a valuable attempt to systematize the chaos. Though having a slightly wider frame of reference than that of divine or spiritual power, his work is nevertheless fully applicable to this area. With reference to fundamentalism, Berger begins by noting that the strategies originated in the desire to combat the apparent problems posed by pluralism, and the general secularity attributed to modernity. Berger suggests that there are three main approaches to the problem, and these enable a better appreciation of the context and method both of Wimber's attempt in this field, and those of other fundamentalists.

For Berger, experiences of the supernatural and sacred create ruptures in mundane reality and give rise to new perceptions of the self and others. Echoing Weber's 'routinization of charisma' (see Glossary) theory, he notes that religious experience, which is initially self-authenticating, inevitably over time becomes embodied in religious tradition which becomes an authority, supported by social institutions, consensus and control. But, he notes, our situation, the religious situation of modernity, is one of pluralism, of a choice to be made from among competing traditions. This poses a threat to the reality, security and objectivity of each and all traditions.

Berger's emphasis on the challenges of pluralism and modernity fits the fundamentalist situation well. As was noted in Chapter One, fundamentalism is a counter-cultural phenomenon, a reaction against aspects of the modern situation that are deemed to threaten or undermine religious faith. In the face of the threat of pluralism, Berger outlines three possible strategies which will enable faith to be defended. The first he calls the 'deductive possibility', in which 'the tradition is affirmed anew, after an interval when it was not affirmed. The problem is, quite simply, that it is very difficult to forget the interval ... This is why neotraditional and neo-orthodox movements come with particular vehemence ...' (p. 68).

Berger cites Karl Barth's Protestant neo-orthodoxy as an example of this first possibility, in which faith in the Word of God is the starting-point: there is no method of knowing God, no natural human capacity to know God. Only the Word gives one the capacity to affirm it. Christianity's uniqueness and validity are simply given, *a priori*. Because it has been questioned in liberal Protestantism, the authority of the tradition must now be reasserted with greater force. If one can accomplish this, the gain is one of certainty, and one can once again deduce propositions from the old tradition. At first sight, this strategy might appear to be a good description of fundamentalist methodology, but as I shall show shortly, this is not quite the case. Undoubtedly, aspects of fundamentalist strategy look like this, but as an exhaustive account of fundamentalist methodology, it is inadequate.

The second response suggested by Berger is the 'reductive possibility'. This starts from the assumption that modern consciousness cannot accept the supernatural, and that this constitutes an advance. But desiring at least to salvage the core of the tradition, this strategy translates the supernatural elements of the mystical tradition into a variety of guises. Sometimes it can be ethics or mystical experience, a common feature of some classic liberal exponents, such as Tillich. Alternatively, the translation may be into existentialism (e.g., Bultmann), popular psychology (e.g., Norman Vincent Peale and other Americans of the 1950s), or politics (e.g., liberation theology). As with the first strategy, there are aspects of fundamentalist methodology that 'fit' with this. Some of the mechanistic tactics and theology of the church growth movement appear to have originated from a thorough reductiveness that places a great emphasis on productivity. The work of Donald McGavran, for example, certainly reduces the task of the Church to being that of the community that fulfils what he calls 'the Great Commission' (Matt. 28.16–20). The effectiveness of the Church can be measured by its ability to achieve certain goals, which, it is claimed, God is attempting to reach (e.g., 'making disciples of all nations').[5] However, although reductiveness is sometimes a feature of fundamentalism, fundamentalism itself is not necessarily primarily 'a modernizing of the tradition' as Berger describes. In addition to this, fundamentalists would not share the notion that their God was simply the symbolic goal of human reality, as some reductive thinkers and strategies might be prepared to acknowledge.

The third response is the 'inductive possibility' – a moving from tradition to experience. When the tradition comes to be questioned, this strategy seeks to trace back to the religious experiences which began it. Thus, historical development and the analysis of religious phenomena become important. Taking human experience as a starting point for religious reflection, the inductive strategy generally uses the methods of historians to uncover those human experiences which have become embodied in the various religious traditions. Schleiermacher's liberal Protestantism is a good example, and Berger also cites Adolf von Harnack's search for the core experiences that gave birth to Christianity.

However, when the inductive strategy is brought together with the issues of spiritual power, there appear to be two different ways of practising it. The first is intellectual and analytical – like that of Harnack – and fits easily into Berger's description: through history and reflection on the historical religious experiences of humanity, one can seek to describe the core experiences of divine power. But there is a second variant which is more active, and emphasizes the necessity of confirming and supplementing historical analysis by seeking direct religious experience at first hand. Such an approach is typical of many mystical sects. But crucially, it is also characteristic of fundamentalist and charismatic writers, who attempt to authenticate traditional truth-claims about the power of God by demonstrating that power in the present. In Wimber's case, truth-claims are validated by 'signs and wonders', yet the strategy fits non-charismatic fundamentalists as well. For example, those committed to rigorous biblical inerrancy also seek to confirm the power of God in the present by pointing to the effectiveness of Scripture in its capacity to change lives. Thus the power of God is here validated in words, unlike Wimber, who authenticates by manifestations.

Berger repeatedly reminds his readers that religious experience is self-authenticating at the time, but that the authentification has a tendency to fade over time, especially when the experience is only known second-hand. Thus there is a perennial problem of certainty, and a continuous need for authentication.[6] This can be traced quite clearly in Wimber's career: the constant pursuit of 'signs and wonders' that suggests that God's activity is coincidental with the growth of his Vineyards. Consequently, there tends to be less emphasis on argument and interpretation in these types of fundamentalist communities, and more on biography. This in turn can lead to aberrations in the quest for direct experience, as serious theological reflection can often suffer in the journey.[7] Yet as was noted before, the existence and widespread influence of the inductive strategy in approaching the subject of divine power, particularly in fundamentalist groups, renders it worthy of serious study.

Power in the Community

In any community, the forms of power are clearly many and varied. How divine power is addressed will usually dictate how the community is formed to some degree, so in this section we shall be searching for a sociological framework that makes sense of the existing inductive strategy we have already identified. In assessing various forms of power, we can see that questions of intentionality, effectiveness, balance, and latency can never be fully solved. Power – be it allegedly divine or human – is sometimes consciously mediated through coercion by authority, or some other form such as persuasion. Equally though, power lies dispositionally at the heart of any religious polity, although it can be traced via agents or facilitative processes. And yet, the mediation of a form is not always necessarily a conscious act on the part of leader or subject. What we can say about power is that the combinations and interrelations of forms demand a multi-dimensional appreciation, if we are to understand the anatomy, operation and possible identity of power within a given fundamentalist community like Wimber's. So it is to a concept of circuits of power I have turned,[8] following the work of Stewart Clegg (*The Theory of Power and Organization*, London, Routledge & Kegan Paul, 1979, and *Frameworks of Power*, London, Sage, 1989), in an attempt to examine the character and framework of power in Wimber's community structure.

It should be clear by now that any generally applicable theory of power will also be a theory of organization. Much of the theory of organizations has been orientated towards explaining how organizational obedience is arrived at.[9] This could lead us into a great deal of organizational analysis, but that is not entirely necessary for our discussion here. We will later note the features of Wimber's organization in Chapter Six, and the apparent absence of a 'still point' in his theology (unless it is connected to power or control), which means the terrain of his ecclesiology and missiology is constantly shifting, unstable and usually always in motion. And yet behind this, a field of force in which power operates has somehow been fixed – possibly via the inductive strategy referred to by Berger – which contains Wimber's principles and agents of adherence. So, in spite of the apparent lack of a still point or centre on the surface, there are certain 'nodal points' or fundaments of belief and practice which conduct and direct the forces or forms of power within Wimber's theology and ecclesiology (we will show in the conclusion that these revolve around power and control). These nodal points can be ones of either rationality (e.g., inerrant text or person) or of efficiency (e.g., signs, charismatic leadership), or a combination of the two, culminating in the nodal point being one of ultimate legitimacy. These nodal points need orchestrating at times by controllers or power brokers (i.e., leaders), but equally, they exist within a single movement together partly because of the way in which they naturally belong together. There can be, for example, simple linear links in the power chain, such as a pathological approach to church growth theory being aligned with a concern for individual bodily health.[10] Or, there are more complex patterns, which link individual obedience with freedom, and in turn, link freedom with clearly marked boundaries, the crossing of which, it is said, represents the capitulation of freedom (i.e., usually to the devil, or sin). Thus, we have a framework in which obedience and resistance can coexist and compete, yet still retain adherents within a power network.

Central to our discussion of circuits is the concept of agency. Agency is something that is achieved: it is active operation, action and the instrumentality of organizations. It is something which is achieved by virtue of organization whether of a human being's dispositional capacities or of a collective nature. In short, agency, or the achievement of effective agency, is the stabilizing factor in circuits of power, and thus of organization; agents are invariably mechanisms for control. The incorporation of agencies within organizations is normally secured on the basis of contract,[11] although that contract need not be reciprocal, conflict-free or equal. An example of this from within our fundamentalist case-study may be of some help here, to illustrate my point. Wimber's organization, Vineyard Ministries International (VMI) is a body that orientates itself around its agencies, that is to say, around what it sets out to achieve. Members of his organization are both agents of signification, and agents of production: agents relate to the agency, which seeks significance and productivity. Both are inextricably interlinked: to separate them would be to focus on only one side of the conditions of organizational participation. Thus, we cannot view Wimber's network of churches as simple phenomenal expressions of some essentialist inner principle such as religious exploitation or a distorted form of biblicism and idealism. An organization is, like any other locus for the accomplishment of agency, a place of individual and multi-participative decision and action.[12] (This echoes our earlier observation in Chapter One, concerning fundamentalism being a complete cultural-linguistic system.) General theories of power do not explain the politics of organizations such as Wimber's. Organizational action is an indeterminate outcome arising from competing agencies: people who deploy different resources or spiritual gifts; people whose organizational identities will be shaped by the way in which disciplinary and membership constraints work through and on them; people who seek to control and decide the nature of organizational action and identity. Consequently, the interests of actors in organizations and the decisions they make depend upon the various forms of organization calculation. Thus, organizational action is not the expression of some essentialist inner principle: claims to such principles necessarily neglect the complex conditions under which organizational action occurs.[13]

However, if a theory of agency is pressed too far, with too much emphasis placed on liquidity, the search for some of the essences within Wimber's work and works could easily be lost in a sea of relativity. Without wishing to contradict the earlier argument, although it is not possible to locate a fundamental inner principle at the heart of an organization, it is possible to suggest the points by which Wimber might orientate himself. This observation leads us to suggest that within the concept of agency, there is room for some 'strategic agencies' which will necessarily involve those agencies establishing a primacy within an organization. As Clegg points out: 'To achieve strategic agency requires a disciplining of the discretion of other agencies: at best, from the strategist's point of view, such other agencies will become merely authoritative relays, extensions of strategic agency.'[14]

As Weber is well aware, an army is the ideal form of this. The troops, as relay-agencies, subordinate themselves to the strategically subordinating agency. In the same way, P. D. Anthony has observed that 'soldiers of God'[15] have often been the highest expression of obedient organization membership. In the thinking of Wimber, with 'church growth' and demonstrating the power of God in the community as the supreme targets, it is not difficult strategically to subordinate almost every aspect of Christian life and witness to this goal. 'Signs and wonders' have to connect with church growth, as does healing, deliverance and prophecy. And behind the stratagem of church growth is a cluster of nodal points whose locus centres around a belief that the Church should be powerful (as it is said, God is), both as a sign that God is with the organization and inhabiting the strategies, and also because of the explicit connection between power and productivity.

The connection between agency and (dominant) strategic agency actually raises the central paradox at the base of power relations. The power of an agency is increased in principle by that agency delegating either tasks or authority. The delegation can only proceed by rules, and rules necessarily entail judgement (by both parties), which, potentially at least, empowers the delegates. From this, arises the tacit and taken-for-granted basis of organizationally negotiated order, and on occasion, its fragility and instability.[16] Thus, to operate in this paradox, there is a vested interest on the part of the leaders in 'normalizing' the agencies concerned, and in particular, the dominant strategic agencies. We will see in Chapter Four how the peculiar use of ideological language in worship contributes to this goal, in helping to establish the agencies and orientations of Wimber as routinizing affairs within the organization or church concerned. And such adherence to the now established normal goals on the part of those being led, although resulting in a kind of subordination, also brings with it a form of space. As Barnes puts it, such agencies 'must recognize that the output of appropriate action which they produce is what minimizes the input of coercion and sanctioning which they receive'.[17]

Power is thus implicated in the form of authority, and framed within rules. The interpretation of rules within an organization must be disciplined and regulated if new powers are not to be produced, and existing powers eroded. In the case of Wimber's Vineyards, it is in the permanent interests of the strategists to promote the primacy of organization. Failure to do this, to establish authority and limited subjugation, could only in the end result in the overturning of the structures that mediate power, and the powers that mediate structure.

It has been implied from the start of this section that an appropriate point of departure for the analysis of power is not pure agency, but rather the social relations (power as the expression of community) which constitute effective agency, particularly where it is organizational in form. In fact, the field is somewhat broader than this: consideration of the relational field of force in which power is configured is required, recognizing that one aspect of this configuration is the social relations in which agency is constituted. Thus, the key to our understanding is to grasp the fact that power as a phenomenon can only be comprehended relationally. Power is not a 'thing'; pure energy may exist, but it may (usually) only be known and held as it is relationally constituted. The relational conditions which constitute power are reproduced through the fixing of obligatory points, channels and boundaries. Only then can power be fixed and 'reified' in form.

The greatest achievement of power is its reification. We have already suggested, following Adams,[18] that leaders within fundamentalist groups like Wimber's are types of 'power brokers'. But they are more than that. They are reifiers, energy converters whose task it is to turn mass (e.g., the congregation) into energy, and energy into mass (e.g., concrete results). The very act of rationalizing the congregational process and animating the social will is in itself an act of reification. And it is precisely because of this process that we can say that power and resistance always stand in relation to one another. Power always involves power over another, and thus at least two agencies, and therefore resistance. This resistance, like the power itself, provides frameworks or circuits in which the power is processed or reified. Because resistance necessarily involves relationship, there is a consequent field or structure within which energy can flow.

We have reached a point in our discussion now when we can say with some confidence that to speak of 'power-centredness' or talk of a 'dominant power paradigm' as a way of reading fundamentalism is actually an over-simplification. Certainly, in our preliminary theological and historical analysis, it was possible to locate a general interest in maximum power. However, as we have seen in this discussion, power as such is really only a word that describes a series of relational processes. As a concept, it has no meaning on its own. Concern for power is an agency in itself, a dogmatic nodal point within the circuit of Wimber's work and works, relating to other fixed points such as productivity, effective mechanism, defined exclusivism and a series of linked dualities. The ordering of these axiomatic relationships is done by a socialization of 'rules' that maintains energy flow. Yet although power may only exist relationally, we cannot agree with Daudi who claims that 'power as such may not exist'.[19] Equally, it is vital to move from the facile assertion of Wrong that power is simply(!) a capacity.[20]

Power is inextricably linked to structure and is represented in the circuits of framework in a number of ways. Power is evidently present as each specified modality of episodic, dispositional and facilitative power. It is also present in the overall flow of action through the circuits of power, the relational articulation which will constitute the calibration of this flow. Power can be contained within circuits, or flow through it, and it is the strategic agencies that determine the rate and direction of flow.

In conclusion, because no power or form of power is an island, entire of itself, the framework of circuits of power can be used effectively to discuss the emergence and state of Wimber's thinking and communities that does not leave us hostage to formulae of dimensions, faces, dialectics or levels. The model of circuits of power is capable of carrying analysis in ways that other models are not, with the additional advantage that secondary materials within a coherent framework can be incorporated in order to address some of the central issues at the heart of fundamentalism. It also allows us to see that the inductive model for addressing divine power, as suggested by Berger, is in fact a way of understanding the power-flow in fundamentalist thinking, as well as being a nodal point in its own right in the overall circuit of power that is operating.

Reflections on Charismatic Authority as an Agent of Power

We have already made reference to power being something that arises out of a complex series of circuits. If this is true sociologically for fundamentalism, it is also true historically and theologically. Various types of fundamentalism occur precisely because of the complex interactions in a given community between belief and society, plurality and identity, culture and tradition, to name but a few. Take, for example, the rise of contemporary charismatic renewal in the British Isles. Its own theology and history are traceable initially to Pietism and Quakerism, then to Wesleyan holiness and revivalism, through to early twentieth century Pentecostalism, and finally to the work of Bennett, Du Plessis and the Fountain Trust in the late 1950s.[21] Of course, each of the individual movements that have combined to cause modern British charismatic renewal had their own distinctive emphasis, yet they nevertheless form part of a new matrix or circuit for the present, through which power is now partly understood for those inside the movement.

It is thus possible to speak of historical or theological 'nodal points', which offer places where participants in a given movement might locate power. As we have noted before, the nodal points themselves may function chiefly to affect rationality or efficiency in the circuit. Sometimes, however, it can be both, and it is upon such a nodal point as an agent of power that we shall focus here. Because we are concerned with the conflation of divine and human power in fundamentalism, it seems appropriate to centre on a key area where this is particularly evident: that of the office of leader or guru – the *person* (or persons) who ultimately controls or guides a given fundamentalist group. In the case of Wimber, we shall see that his charismatic authority is a *necessary* power agent that funds the inductive power circuit that defines his particular form of fundamentalist belief and practice. Without the agency of charismatic authority, the control issued to the power circuit would break down, and as such, we can speak of Wimber's charisma as being a nodal point of power conflation, in which God's power and human power are merged to the extent that Wimber's charisma cannot easily be distinguished from that of the Spirit.

Max Weber's work is perhaps the most important in explaining the sociological implications of charisma.[22] Weber is largely responsible for introducing the term to the literature of sociology, although its origin was religious. Weber applied the word to his sociological treatment of types of authority. For him, there were three types: rational-legal, traditional, and charismatic authority. In so doing, Weber set apart the charismatic leader as having a personality unlike 'ordinary men and treated as endowed with supernatural, superhuman, or at least specifically exceptional powers or qualities'. Weber states that these properties are not accessible to the common leader; they have a 'divine origin'. Such a 'divine' power source needs recognition by those subject to this authority. In other words, the charismatic leader's claim needs to be validated by faithful followers or disciples who see in their leader 'proof' of supernatural qualities.[23]

Consequently, Weber indicates that charisma is an unstable phenomenon: 'The charismatic leader gains and maintains authority solely by proving his strength'. Followers will soon depart from the charismatic leader who cannot 'perform miracles' or 'heroic deeds'. Continued charismatic domination therefore often requires the audience to reject 'all ties to any external order' and to break with 'traditional or rational norms'. In effect, the charismatic leader says 'It is written, but I say unto you . . .', thus lending a revolutionary dimension to charismatic leadership.

Although Weber recognizes the subversive character of charisma, in the sense that it usually attacks or transcends the routinization of structures, he nevertheless believes that its residual power could be transformed and applied to roles, offices and institutions. A charismatic impulse could develop into a stable 'movement' in its own right. Provided there is continuity in tradition and succession, coupled with new phenomena that could be appreciated for their own dynamic and charismatic power, a charismatic leader could spawn a charismatic movement that would flourish. The conditions for such a leader arising (with a following), are, in Weber's view, 'subjective or internal reorientation born out of suffering, conflicts or enthusiasm'.[24] Thus, for Weber, charisma is essentially a supernatural gift that has originated from beyond the personality of the leader; it is a religious phenomenon, though with political ramifications because of its link with authority. Charismatic leaders need devoted followers to validate their calling, and that validating process needs constant maintenance in the form of miracles or works of power if leadership is to be maintained. Eventually, therefore, charisma becomes routinized in offices or roles, in organizations that have a strong identity focused around the importance of power and performance. Another way of expressing this would be to speak of charisma being a nodal point in a power circuit, though Weber himself would not have expressed his theory like this.

Towards a Framework for Understanding Charisma as an Agent of Power

No theory of charisma formulated to date has adequately described the dimensions and process of charisma. The purpose of this section is to formulate a framework that sees charisma as a 'process', not simply an 'act'. A process reveals the integral interrelationships that exist between leader and led. Alluding to this relationship, Thomas Dow states that 'obviously, people must recognize, accept, and follow the pretender before he can be spoken of as truly charismatic. The question is why do they do so?'[25] What follows is an attempt to answer Dow's question, by proposing a framework that offers explanations of 'how' and 'why' charisma operates as a nodal point.

(i) MESSAGE ELEMENTS
Potential followers may be attracted to a leader by a variety of means. One of these means is a charismatic message. However, the 'charismatic message' itself contains a number of sub-ingredients. First, for example, the message is usually revolutionary in character. That is not to say that a concrete ideology is being proposed that is violent or extreme. It does suggest, however, an alternative to the status quo, an alleviant from the present stress or climate. The charismatic message, in order to dominate, and therefore be truly charismatic, must require a 'rejection of all ties to any external order (or message)',[26] so that the *message itself* becomes the only route of escape from a perceived crisis. In considering Wimber, one is faced with a radical, revolutionary message, that purports to be able to rescue the Church from its alleged (i) powerlessness, (ii) numerical decline (by 'power evangelism'), (iii) inability to manifest 'signs and wonders' in its midst (by 'power healing'), and (iv) distance from a powerful, immediate and accessible God (through the 'Third Wave'). These revolutionary ideals are set out in most of his works, and expounded at length in conferences: 'while programme evangelism is, to a limited degree, effectual, power evangelism has always been, and still is, the best means of church growth'.[27]

Second, resulting from this revolutionary element, it follows that the message must be simplistic. Charismatic communication is frequently characterized by 'grammatical and content simplicity'. The grammatical and linguistic simplicity of Wimber's message cannot be doubted. True, there is a sophisticated web of simple truths interrelating in Wimber's work, but this is not the same as complexity grappling with reality, even though, to some, they appear to be indistinguishable. Themes that lack complexity in message often reduce the probability of choosing alternative perspectives. In turn, such perspectives facilitate the charismatic leader's following, who alone is in possession of the 'basic master plan' – the only way to escape the crisis.

Third, a charismatic message usually contains 'figures of presence'. Charisma, as an agent of power, is often dependent on creating an aura of pertinency, apart from the argument itself. 'Presence' may also serve to reduce the breadth of perspective, and orient the charismatic follower to become attracted to the inherent aura of the message. Louise Karon, in her essay on *The New Rhetoric*, highlights the effects of presence in charismatic persuasion:

> First, it [presence] is a felt quality in the auditor's consciousness. This quality, created by the rhetor's 'verbal magic', enables him to impress upon the audience whatever he deems important. Second, presence fixes the audience's attention while alerting its perceptions and perspectives. Third, its strongest agent is the imagination. Fourth, its purpose is judgement. Fifth, it is created chiefly through techniques traditionally studied under the headings of style, delivery, and disposition.[28]

Fourth, a charismatic message is dependent on the promulgation of collective identity. A follower who identifies with a message must ultimately fuse their identity with that of the charismatic messenger. Eric Hoffer points out that the true charismatic leader must evoke 'the enthusiasm of the communion – the sense of liberation from a petty and meaningless individual existence'.[29] The articulated message must say 'what people want to hear, but do not know how to say themselves'.[30] Shared identity in the charismatic situation is vital if the audience are to be persuaded, and not just thrilled.

This leads to a fifth dimension in message elements, namely 'polarized aggression' in the message. This term, employed by

Schiffer,[31] highlights the charismatic communicator's ability to argue *for* something, *against* something. Such a construct requires a characterization of opposing viewpoints, and in the work of Wimber, it is common to find inertia or opposing viewpoints gently ridiculed. He is persuading people to act, to 'do the stuff' (his phrase for *literally* fulfilling Mark 16.15–18), and anything that interferes with the centrality of foundational commissions is 'dubbed' alien, corrupt or divisive to the common task he feels Christians should be employed in. Such an approach often requires the opposition to be simplified, so its (alleged) falsity can be understood and rejected by the followers. Examples of this include the separating of that which is deemed 'dead' and 'alive', good and evil, or the humanizing of Satan as a personal adversary, anxious to disrupt and destroy the work of the charismatic communicator and the followers.[32]

The undue attention paid to Satan by Wimber is no accident. A charismatic leader needs an adversary, who can be called to account when the charismatic message appears to fail in concrete terms, and there is a power failure: a break in the circuit. For Wimber, a strong believer in effective prayer for healing, subject to employing the right techniques, Satan or sin are often the cause of sin or sickness, or contribute to the failure of the healing prayers offered; for example, in the case of David Watson, Wimber's friend and companion. Watson had contracted cancer of the liver. Despite prayers for healing from Wimber and his associate, Watson died. Wimber's explanation of this is that 'Satan murdered him'.[33]

The five characteristics mentioned in this section on message cannot obviously be the only ingredients in a systematic understanding of charisma and message elements. However, each ingredient cited appears with regularity in various theories of charisma. The leader who creates a message with these elements increases its potential in the overall charismatic situation.

(ii) PERSONALITY ELEMENTS

It was probably the work of Weber that first highlighted the element of personality in charisma. Although charismatic leaders emerge from different cultures and different situational crises, some common personality traits are identifiable. A charismatic leader need not exhibit each trait, but (usually) the more traits expressed, the greater the leader's appeal.

The first is 'high status'. This can be achieved either through routine ways (office, role or position), or through the ability to demonstrate miracles, signs and wonders. In either process, 'charisma routinization' takes place, which moves the leader to a position which is exalted above that of the group. A second trait directly emerges from the first: the leader has a 'stranger quality' about himself or herself. To maintain high status, it is necessary to have some distance from the group, though too much could be alienating. Perhaps the proverb 'familiarity breeds contempt' has a corollary: something strange yet familiar breeds charisma. Certainly, in the case of Wimber, both traits are exhibited. His charisma is dependent on his total control of conferences (he is always billed as the main speaker), and tight, but limited, control of his network of churches (Vineyards). However, he keeps some distance from the ordinary affairs of his churches and conferences, thus heightening his mystique and charisma in the eyes of the audience.

In contrast to these remarks, a third trait is the exhibition of 'conquerable imperfection'. Wimber, in spite of consciously or unconsciously building his charismatic image, is at pains to stress his ordinariness: 'I'm just a fat man trying to get to heaven', he proclaims. But this is not a 'truth claim', although he is a large man. Rather, it is a device that helps endear the audience to the man. Similarly, he speaks movingly of his own illness, whilst encouraging others to engage in a ministry of healing. In the words of one of his own songs, he is the 'wounded soldier'.[34] This is conquerable imperfection. The third trait is balanced, indeed made tolerable, by a fourth trait: that of a 'special calling'. A leader can 'cause an effectively internalized response because he can generate ecstasy, euphoria, resentment, and politically relevant passions in his followers who feel united ... by an emotional bond'.[35] This trait can be further endorsed by a fifth, namely sexual mystique. Jimmy Bakker and Jimmy Swaggart have both shown this; that the sexuality of the charismatic leader is of absorbing interest to immediate followers, not just the general media. Whilst Wimber has a stable sexual identity (wife, children, grandchildren), many of his personal prophecies for others (often called 'words of knowledge') concern adultery or fornication; these 'words' are shared with large audiences, or written about, despite their personal nature. Within the leadership team of Wimber, however, there is considerable variety in sexual mystique, ranging from Paul Cain (an angel appeared to him in his youth, told him God was jealous of his girlfriend, and he must now remain pure: 'From that day on, he has experienced no erotic thought'[36]), to Blane Cook,

Wimber's deputy and heir-apparent, dismissed from his pastorate in 1988 for alleged sexual misconduct.

A sixth quality is the ability to act, and behave in a dramatic, professional way. Wimber's conferences, although relaxed, are 'slick'. There is an order about the drama that feeds the charismatic situation, aiding the persuasive process. Seventh, an innovative lifestyle or approach is required, which operates out of this ordered drama. Wimber's principles operate out of these personality traits which are visibly incarnate in the conferences themselves. His teaching calls for an innovative way of life that leads to numerical church growth. The final two traits to mention are 'miracle working' and 'myth-making', or symbolizing. Attention has already been drawn to the fact that miracles are essential for Wimber in his understanding of evangelism. No matter how good the communication, miracles and results will be demanded of the leader who functions in the charismatic situation; the production of success – the reification of power from the circuit – validates the message. To compensate for the possible lack of success, it is therefore necessary to provide a mythical or symbolic 'backdrop' to the charismatic situation, which will provide a framework for constructing reality. Myths, when properly established, can be a rhetorical means of creating oneness with an audience. These traits, of course, are not exhaustive.

(iii) DELIVERY ELEMENTS

Ann R. Willner claims that 'nearly all leaders for whom charisma has been claimed have also been described as eloquent, or spell-binding orators. Charismatic appeal involves investigating not so much what a leader says, as how he says it, i.e., the style of his verbal communication'.[37] The three categories of speech delivery considered here represent elements that many theorists have mentioned as aiding charismatic perception. Each category has sub-characteristics that have been observed in speech delivery amongst charismatic leaders. The three to be discussed are vocal force, vocal inflexion, and non-verbal language – 'body language' and other gestures.

Vocal force is a general term that describes such delivery techniques as volume variety, pitch variables, stress on words, and so on. Erwin Bettinghaus' study of political campaigners and revivalists in *Persuasive Communication*[38] notes that a bond is often developed between audience and leader by means of vocal cues. Speaking softly, in a concerned voice, invites the audience to listen more attentively, and share the concern. Shouting or ranting can often be a vocal cue that suggests imminent action, outrage, or condemnation. The vocal force of the leader has an impact on the reception of the words that are being spoken, facilitating the charismatic process. In this respect, Wimber is a marvellous rhetorician. His use of vocal force is nearly always appropriate to the desired goal of his rhetorical output. Stories that illustrate healing, for example, move in a typical vocal pattern. Usually, the condition of the person and the sickness is articulated in a depressed, resigned, hopeless sort of way, helping to underline the helplessness of the sick person. The healing process is described tentatively, exemplifying the risk or faith involved. The result (success) is described in excited tones, with the pitch and speed of speech delivery rising all the time. The effect of the vocal force is to move the audience, from resignation to faith, and from faith to excitement and expectancy.

Vocal force is complemented by vocal inflexion: rapid responses, pauses and repetition. These devices often forestall critical analysis, preventing the construction of alternative perspectives. Repetition of theme, phrases and slogans (e.g., 'Keep on doin' the stuff!') reduces alternative thought patterns; the audience is sucked into the logical coherence (or power flow of the circuit) of the 'neat phrase' that seems to be widely applicable and appealing. Emotional states can be aroused in an audience by the use of pace in speech. Slow talking conveys seriousness, methodic teaching, 'the main message' to remember. Rapid talking can convey a variety of things: emotion, excitement, 'fresh news', and so on. Again, Wimber is no stranger to these techniques. Stories and testimonies, or narrative renderings of portions of the Bible, are spoken with speed. The more systematic aspects of his principles are spoken with more care, and in a slower fashion. In both cases, variation of pace assists the overall process of charismatic persuasion.

Third, situational non-verbal cues can arouse emotional responses as well. Audiences seeking a charismatic figure respond to the 'body-language' of leader-communicators. For example, physical attractiveness can aid charismatic perception. Mark Knapp states that 'it is not at all unusual to find physically attractive persons outstripping unattractive ones on a wide range of socially desirable evaluations, such as success, personality, popularity, sociability, sexuality, persuasiveness ....'.[39]

Wimber is neither attractive nor unattractive. A man in his

sixties with grey hair, and overweight, he nevertheless manages to convey an aura of 'cuddliness' (is there a better word?), a man who hugs his grandchildren, but large enough to look imposing if displeased. Charismatic figures like Wimber use hand and body gestures to emphasize dramatic qualities: jabbing, pointing, pounding and fist-like patterns with the hand, linked with facial expressions and overall body posture. Clothes can also make a statement about the charismatic leader. Rosenfeld and Civikly note that 'we select fabric and colour to help us conform to our self-image'.[40] Swaggart and Bakker wear expensive suits (suggestion: successful, sincere), Aimee Semple McPherson a white shroud (suggestion: pure, angelic). Wimber wears casual clothes; usually a shirt and sweater, and plain trousers and shoes. The suggestion is that this person is relaxed, friendly, possibly even neighbourly. The audience can therefore also relax; most people attending his conferences, I have observed, dress casually.

Touch is also part of the process of non-verbal communication, and is often a vital element in the charismatic persuasion process. Touch is the 'language of love and acceptance', according to Sidney Jourard,[41] in which intimate mutual identification can take place. In the charismatic situation, this can be especially so. Throngs of people yearned to touch Jesus Christ, so that miracles of healing might 'flow' from him. This phenomenon is widespread today in Pentecostal circles, or in 'faith healing' services. In the case of Wimber's churches, due to a peculiar accident of history, people who are praying for healing often do not touch.[42] Nevertheless, close proximity, gathering round a sick person, hugging and affirming by touch are all encouraged.

It should be repeated that these messages, personality and delivery characteristics of the charismatic communication situation are not prescriptive for every charismatic situation. All sorts of variables in cultural settings and environmental crises create unique exhibitions of charismatic phenomena. But charismatic impact and persuasion are increased with the presence of each identifiable characteristic.

4
Power and Ideology

Introduction: Worship as Ideology

Much has been written about the ideology of certain movements in order to explain their power and appeal. There is no doubt that familiarity with the theology or the ideological formulations of a specific movement is essential to an understanding of it, especially in the study of fundamentalism. The question therefore necessarily arises: how might we locate an ideology, particularly if it is hidden? Most studies of fundamentalism (including this one at present) tend to suggest that the ideology of a given group can be located in the dogmatic creeds, principles and formulations that it advances to the world. At least one consequence of this 'reading' is a tendency to perceive fundamentalist ideology as either a reductive or deductive theological stratagem.

Whilst this might be partly correct, it cannot be wholly true. If fundamentalism is to be correctly understood as primarily inductive, then the ideology needs to be traced to the actual religious experience itself, not to the principles or dogmas derived from it. It is my contention that 'core' ideology can be located in the *worship* of fundamentalist groups: it is the worship of a community that provides it with its primary religious experience, and thus its certainty and ideology. As Eric Hoffer remarks, 'the effectiveness of a doctrine does not come from its meaning but from its certitude'.[1] Nowhere is that certitude more keenly expressed than in the arena of worship, where God is both met and meets, is addressed and addresses.[2] It is here that core ideology and its power can be principally located in fundamentalist groups: the God who is known and can direct when properly encountered.

The worship songs of John Wimber (by which I mean the words and the music in a particular piece, and their relation to each other) are a good example of the power of ideology within fundamentalism. Beyond asking how the rhetoric of worship is both powerful and persuasive, there lies a deeper question about what or who is being addressed. For Wimber, the answer is of course simple: God. But there is more to worship, even simple worship, than this. Lionel Adey in his *Hymns and the Christian 'Myth'* observes that most hymnographers focus on a single person of the Trinity, and in doing so, create 'mutations of God'. Such mutations result in convergence of the identity between the person of the Trinity and the worshippers, and a consequent belief that a mutual cleaving process takes place.[3] This may seem obvious to some, and indeed, perhaps unavoidable. Yet Wimber and his song-writing colleagues are perhaps peculiar in addressing all three persons of the Trinity; in fact, no one person appears to be substantially more preferred to another. But what does emerge from even the most casual analysis of *Songs of the Vineyard* is that the individuality and corporate nature of Trinitarian personhood (which might include distinctiveness in identity, functionality, space and time, yet mutuality and relationship), is dissolved. God as Father, Son and Holy Spirit assumes the same dissolved character throughout: intimate, loving, precious, refreshing, fulfilling, mighty and omnipotent, all without qualification. The data suggests that it is not so much God who is being addressed, but rather favourable concepts of God – an ideology – that has rooted itself in the individual and corporate identity of the worshippers. This will be discussed more fully later on, in an attempt to disclose the direction as well as the effect of Wimber's worship. Social and systematic theorists have often noted that worship fixes axioms and paradigms, and moves and persuades people in a way that few forms of communication can hope to match.[4]

Authors and speakers are not always fully conscious of the techniques they are using and why they might be effective. Certainly, in the case of Vineyard worship materials, this may well be the case, although the selection of approved material for public use usually only includes their own material, even excluding material from similar traditions. Furthermore, in accord with Berger, we must note that some texts, especially those deriving from ritual performances (i.e., worship), provide a strategy for participation. The songs of Wimber's Vineyards are most obviously an example of this: they encourage participation by singing, as well as inviting the audience to become a congregation, sharing in the general description of the world encountered in the text. These texts do not offer an abstract philosophical system, yet they do operate at a distance from everyday activities and issues. As such they represent strategies for solving problems about the relations between human beings to each other and to the spiritual forces or beings of their universe. So, the power of ideology lies in a strategy that is sociologically transcendent: the songs raise the participants above the lesser subjects and objects of this world, so that they may actually touch God, and he them; overall, a 'community of feeling' is created by the worship.[5]

The Power of Emotion: Passion, Passivity and Power in Vineyard Worship

In order to assess the emotive capacity of Vineyard worship in its core ideological role, it is necessary to begin by describing the actual structure of the worship. Unlike many conventional hymn books, *Songs of The Vineyard* reflects no liturgical or seasonal scheme in its ordering. There is no plan of rotation as one might have encountered in the New England Puritan or Shaker communities, which often sung metrical psalms. There is no topical arrangement of the sort once employed by John Wesley.[6] The songs are simply arranged in alphabetical order by the first line, with the occasional 'titled' song appearing in italics in the index if it is known by a name other than its first line. There are contextual reasons for structuring the book like this. Firstly, most participants at a Wimber conference learn the songs by heart; they are sung over and over again consecutively – sometimes up to seven or eight times. Repetition is an important structural device, that can serve and underscore core ideology. One hour of pure singing may only contain five or six songs in total; the songs and the structure in which they operate are designed to be 'picked up easily', to be learnt.[7] Secondly, the song book is a reference book for musicians, and for those who are unfamiliar with the style of worship. Seasoned participants do not use the books – their hands and arms are usually occupied in worship (either raised, in dancing, or in a 'blessing gesture').[8]

We are tackling an area where exact boundaries are hard to fix. Worship in Vineyard churches and conferences covers a great range of activity, but some territory markers are needed to keep the discussion within manageable limits. Here I will only be considering songs that have originated from Vineyard sources, although much of what I say will be capable of wider applications to other forms of fundamentalism, especially those groups that can be identified with charismatic renewal or 'Restorationism'. Most of the songs to be discussed have been written since 1980. The material is of a homogenous nature: most authors are male, and from urban backgrounds, with a familiarity with contemporary popular music and culture. Furthermore, they are fundamentalists in the revival tradition, distinctively influenced by Wimber. He has written about one-fifth of the songs himself, and all the other authors are members of one of his churches.

It is clear that the worship songs are typically constructed around a series of metaphors in poetic form: God as 'Potter', his people to be 'moulded', the individual as the 'child' of God. The overall theme is 'dwelling' on the God who has power over his (malleable) materials – people. Careful sifting of the texts reveals that only a few of the songs frame metaphors in contrasting relationships with others (light/dark, captivity/freedom). Yet most of the songs do not escape being sharply dualistic: the world and its woes are not to be compared to the bliss of heaven, God's love and the beauty of Jesus:

> Lord, we ask that You would come right now.
> Jesus, come and heal us now.
> Spirit, come and fill us now.
> We love You, we love You,
> We love You, yes we do.[9]
>
> *Bill Dobrenen*

Although the structure of the song is typically monotonous (verse 2 just substitutes 'I' and 'me' for 'we' and 'us'), the before-and-after pattern established by the song should be noted. Presence, filling and healing are requested, and the anticipatory response to fulfilment ('We love You') articulated. As will be shown later, the dualistic metaphors are typical of Wimber: presence (of the Lord) versus absence, healing versus sickness, and filling versus emptiness. As is often the case with Wimber, the song is couched in terms of 'love for God', thus preventing the requests articulated in the song appearing to be purely self-indulgent.

An inquiry into the theme of a song is to simply ask the question, 'What is this song about?' The answers might be Christ's sacrifice, the beauty of Jesus, or the Christian life, or any number of other topics. Although Wimber does use some Christian 'battle songs' in his collection, most of them concentrate on a loose cluster of themes that interconnect. Such themes can be divided into four basic categories: (1) songs of the love, closeness, beauty and might of God, (2) songs focusing on the power and dominion of God, (3) holiness, and (4) songs of and about praise and worship.[10] Though my analysis does not use these categories, they are generally applicable.

Another dimension to consider in analysis is that of form. Not only what is said in the songs, but the way they express it, reveals something about the way in which relationships between human beings and deities are conceived. One especially important aspect of form is the mode of address. In volume 1 of *Songs of the Vineyard*, just under half the songs are distinctly personal, with the word 'I' appearing in the first line; the 'I/You' relationship is the dominating form or mode of address in Wimber's worship. Other songs tend to be credal, calls to corporate worship, or songs of love.

If it were possible to simulate a debate between Wimber and Wesley (or some of the other more established hymn writers of the past), differences would quickly emerge. Wesley's hymns are essentially *didactic* – to help unread people learn theology; whereas Wimber's are *existential* – to help people experience God in new ways. For Wesley, and others of his type, there is a stress on the sin of mankind, and the need for salvation; on Christ's atonement, and the power of the cross; on the need for holiness, discipline and order. Although, as we have noted earlier, Wimber claims to be an heir of Wesley, Whitefield and others, the stress is quite different. Songs focus on the power and love of God; the Christian is not so much sinful, as unfulfilled, and in need of healing; the cross of Christ is almost absent, replaced by an emphasis on the majesty and closeness of God:

> I receive You, O Spirit of love,
> How I need Your healing from above,
> I receive You, I receive You,
> I receive Your healing from above,
> I receive Your healing from above.

> I can feel You, touching me right now,
> Come reveal Your power on me now,
> I can feel You, I can feel You,
> I can feel Your power on me now,
> I can feel Your power on me now.[11]
>
> *John Lai*

The text is suggestive in its approach to God.[12] In its use of the personal pronoun, the song is an invitation to commune with God, who can provide the power and healing that (it is suggested) is lacking. The onus on the singer is simply to be receptive to the power available. Thus, the worship presents a kind of 'power asymmetry': the worshipper is 'cast' as being outside the 'power circuit', yet is being implicitly invited to connect up within it.

The song cited above is typical of the passivity present in Vineyard worship songs. The unresisting and submissive character desired of the worshipper is a common denominator in almost all of the songs in *Songs of the Vineyard*. Yet it is a passivity that does not include sufferance, abstinence or pain; the worship songs operate at a level where, if

> I surrender all my love and I rejoice,
> You suddenly appear and wipe away the tears
> And fill me with Your love and tender mercy,
> And fill me with Your love and tender mercy.[13]
> *Peggy Wagner*

Tears, fears, pain and misery are resolved in the songs, provided the worshipper has surrendered to the love and power of God. Significantly, the source of such malaises (personal responsibility, Satan, or whatever), is seldom mentioned. This is a vital strategy in the advancement of ideology. Reflecting Wimber's belief that the Church simply needs to receive power, the worshipper is portrayed as a passive victim of emotional, physical or spiritual affliction. The solution to the problem is equally passive: to receive and reside in a counterbalancing flow of power and love.

Although there is a sense in which God is the focus of the songs – 'Lord' is the most commonly used title to address God in Vineyard worship, after 'You'[14] – any distance between God and humanity has been eroded. The secret of knowing him lies in the inductive strategy, an inward movement, not only towards power and healing, but ultimately to a realm of intimacy where God is experienced. The following two songs exemplify this:

> Hold me Lord, in Your arms,
> Fill me Lord, with Your Spirit,
> Touch my heart, with Your love,
> Let my life glorify Your name.[15]
> *Danny Daniels*

As Your Spirit moves upon me now
You meet my deepest need,
And I lift my hands up to Your throne,
Your mercy, I've received.[16]

Carl Tuttle

It is a realm not only of passivity but of passion; the emotions
and feelings that are surrendered to God result in an inward order
(control) that can counter the external forces (chaos) of sickness,
evil, dissipation and impotence. This is the emotive power of the
ideology: suggesting in metaphor, theme and form that surrender
of self (especially the emotions and passions), and focusing them
on the Lord, will result in the self being accepted by God, and
turned into a positive force that can combat harmful outside
pressures.

Wimber's core ideology is thus manifest in the dominant strategic
foci of Vineyard worship songs. In metaphor, theme and form, a
clear stress on submission to power emerges, in the wider pursuit
of fulfilment and power for the individual Christian, the Church,
and ultimately, the human race. Why are Vineyard worship songs
like this? The rhetoric of passion and passivity employed in the
worship songs of Wimber is not nearly so present in his teaching.[17]
Could it be that the songs simply serve the purpose of getting
audiences into a happy, secure yet submissive frame of mind,
before teaching takes place? Perhaps, but I suspect the answer is
more complex than this, and has something to do with the place
of passion in the rhetoric of 'Revivalism'. As has already been
observed in earlier chapters, Wimber's principles depend heavily
on the tradition of Revivalism, providing an ideal vehicle for his
contemporary teachings. Given this, it is important to look more
deeply at the place of passion in this kind of ideology.

Analysis of ideology always needs to take account of the social
situation in which language functions, and a history of such social
situations may provide clues as to the origins of such rhetoric.
Space does not permit the charting of the history of revivals here,
but most scholars of revivals appear to hold to the view that the
place of feelings and affections in social or public religion was
prevalent in America by the early nineteenth century.[18] The roots of
the ideology may lie in many places: Puritan stress on 'conversionist
language' or Methodist emphasis on 'personal testimony' may all
have contributed to the new phenomenon that Sandra Sizer
describes as a 'community of intense feeling' in the context of

revivals.[19] Individuals underwent similar experiences that tended
to centre on conversion, and thereafter united with others in
matters of moral and social orientation. The language adopted
and employed in such contexts created and sustained both the
community and the feelings of it.

With respect to Wimber, similar concerns are at stake over the
place of emotions in his worship meetings. It is people's feelings
that are to be changed first (by worship), before their minds are
changed (by teaching). This may function in a variety of ways,
but the following example will serve as a model. Wimber declares
that the essence of the 'prayer of faith' is that it achieves its object,
yet is originally within the divine will. Thus, a prayer for healing,
for example, must come from the right motives, be in accordance
with God's promises and providence and the guidance of the Holy
Spirit, and be presented by a person who has renounced all sin or
other 'blockages' to God. Yet the prayer may fail, God being free
to act or not as he wills. Wimber's response to this is that the
prayer of faith may have the effect of changing the petitioners'
feelings, so that they do begin to desire and feel what God feels.
The logic of this, even in a moderately predestinarian framework,
is somewhat tortuous, but logic is not the point. Wimber is
dealing with changing feelings, or the 'state of mind', rather than
cause-effect relationships. His descriptions of the practice of prayer
emphasize the intensity of experience, the 'boldness' of the
petitioner, the strength or power of the 'encounter'. The mind and
emotions are to be fixed on the object of prayer until an answer
(or relief) is found. All this is framed within the context of a God
whose heart can be touched by our own yearnings:

> Your prayers are very precious,
> They reach the heart of Jesus,
> Like a sweet, sweet perfume.[20]

The stress on feeling leads to a stress on unity of feeling
('agreement'). If worship is to 'flow' (in the Spirit), and prayer is
to be rewarded, it is vital that the affections and minds of
the audience are as united as possible. Under these ideological
conditions, further fundamentalist principles may then emerge.
Emotion can therefore be described as a primary nodal point in
the inductive power circuit we are examining. Its ideological status
is beyond doubt: it fixes the initial 'power asymmetry' for the

believer, and then inductively induces them to adopt the preliminary
power principles outlined in Wimber's worship.

The Empowered Community

The forms of the Vineyard songs reveal the fundamental importance
of articulating emotion and passion in Wimber's meetings. Prayer,
testimony and exhortation, all proceeding from the ideology
expressed in worship, combine to create a community of feeling.
The words and music in the worship setting operate as basic 'lines
of influence', as models for the experience of others. The worship
songs articulate emotions which can be shared, creating an ethos
of unity and sacredness in which God is intimately experienced:

> You are the Vine, we are the branches,
> keep us abiding in You.
> You are the Vine, we are the branches,
> keep us abiding in You.
> Then we'll go in Your love,
> then we'll go in Your name,
> that the world will surely know
> that You have power to heal and to save.[21]
>
> *Danny Daniels, Randy Rigby*

An analysis of Vineyard songs also shows that the community
of feeling could be anywhere, at any time, and could extend over
any distance. The songs do not borrow from domestic, war/battle
or substantial biblical imagery, and appear to offer little in the
way of structure or hierarchy. Yet this is an ideological strategy
in itself. Externally, the community appears structureless, united
only in spirit. Internally, however, the community of feeling is the
community of the fulfilled. And this fulfilment arises out of the
community's self-reflection of their closeness to God, and his
closeness to them. There is thus a conflation between the agency
of Vineyard worship and God's own self-involvement with the
world. It is because the community is so close to God that issues
like sin, the cross and conversion are seldom dealt with in song;
such things are deemed to be peripheral. They are for those who
are approaching God, not those who are already with him; the
immediacy of God is gently pressed in worship, virtually to its
limit. In all this, the worship songs of Wimber seem to reduce
significant knowledge of God to testimony about transformed

emotional states, and stress how the individual believer has been affected.

Most importantly, the creation of a community of feeling which perceives itself as purely religious and beyond the mundane can disguise the use to which ideology is put. The metaphors, themes and forms employed in Vineyard worship offer a construction of reality to the worshippers that transcends normal life, and has little in the way of structural or political identity. Yet the Vineyards of Wimber can be deeply implicated in such matters. Their employment of suggestive metaphors is profoundly narrow and exclusive, leading to the individual worshippers becoming a community of people who have learnt to locate their affection carefully, and who have transferred their (redeemed) passions to God, and thereby purified their lives:

> Lord, I love You,
> You alone did hear my cry,
> Only You can mend this broken heart of mine,
> Yes, I love You, and there is no doubt,
> Lord, You've touch'd me from the inside out.[22]
> *Eddie Espinosa*

The metaphors present in Vineyard worship are crucial to the operating ideological strategy that creates and magnifies the community of feeling. Vineyard worship songs are unlike traditional nineteenth century gospel hymns, which paired positive and negative metaphors in their own way.[23] The subtlety of the ideology present in Wimber's worship songs lies in their failure to specifically articulate anything negative, which might be put against the positive. Now, this needs some clarification. Certainly, singing about the healing, power, love and touch of God implies in some way that these things are to come, and thus the present is less than perfect. Interestingly, however, even the present tense (and sometimes the past) is often ambiguously portrayed in the core ideology:

> As Your Spirit moves upon me now,
> You meet my deepest need,
> And I lift my hands up to Your throne,
> Your mercy I've received.[24]
> *Carl Tuttle*

Yet exactly what one might be delivered from is mostly left unsuggested. The present situation is described (the Spirit is moving on the subject), a response to this articulated (raised hands), and a reward for accepting these metaphors declared (mercy *has* been received). Thus, the ideological function of the metaphors in the worship songs is to draw the audience into love and submission; their individual pasts are negated by not being specifically articulated or precisely expressed in worship.

The community is thus empowered via a matrix of metaphors, themes and forms in worship that create an ideological 'community of feeling' that is ultra-receptive to God's power, concerns and intentions. The ideology, helped by the music, establishes and fixes a relationship between God and the believers that is intimate, at times passive, passionate and sensual, and occasionally, almost sexual. The ideology of the worship functions in the community at many levels. Primarily, it acts as a primer; preparing hearts to receive teaching. Yet it also acts as a harmonizer, stressing unity and solidarity of experience and purpose. As ideology, its empowering capacity lies both in what it suggests and fails to suggest. Its empowering possibilities also lie in the songs being inductively simple, and then endlessly repeated in practice, accompanied by flowing melodies that reduce the horizon of mental and aesthetic reflection.[25] In this sense, we might agree with Wayne Booth and his assertion that this (Vineyard worship) is a modern ideology, with a complementary language of assent: 'it shows the characteristics of many religious systems – most important for our purposes, the capacity for self-validation by internal reference from one dogma to another'.[26] Herein lies the certitude of the inductive strategy.

The worship songs of John Wimber and his Vineyards, therefore, are undoubtedly a fundamental vehicle for their ideology. In fact, this is true of the whole charismatic 'worship situation' that believers find themselves participating in when subscribing to Wimber's distinctive form of fundamentalist-revivalism. Yet in spite of much criticism of Wimber's style – 'individualistic', 'full of mindless repetition', 'introspective', 'manipulative' – serious theological engagement with this method of conveying fundamentalist ideology is virtually unknown.[27] We have already noted that theologians have often failed to deal with fundamentalism in a satisfactory manner, and ignorance of its worshipping tradition is primary evidence of this.

Given that fact, a study of Wimber and fundamentalist-revivalist worship is important for a number of reasons. First, the immense

and increasing popularity of this form of worship needs noting
and explaining, even though other Christians may find its style
and ambience abhorrent.[28] Second, sung music plays a significant
role in communicating the ideology of a movement and in shaping
theological awareness, a dynamic that is not often inculcated into
mainstream church consciousness.[29] Composers in the renewal or
'Restorationalist' movement are acutely aware that a good song
is often more memorable than a good sermon, and this in itself is
significant. The songs as ideology are intended to be remembered
'in the head and in the heart', so that the believers' closeness to
God and the community of faith has a constancy about it, arising
out of an inward communion with one's own recall of the dynamic
worship in which God is encountered.[30] Thus, if we ask 'who
benefits from this ideology?', the answer would primarily lie in
the area of leadership and control. A homogenous worship culture
issues stability and unity, and also enables the leadership
consistently to offer favourable concepts of God to the
congregation. (The fact that the office of 'worship leader' is so
highly prized in charismatic and revivalist groups is no accident.)
Third, worship songs are powerful indicators of the concerns and
character of a community. As A. P. Merriman comments in *The
Anthropology of Music*: 'Music is a human phenomenon produced
by people and existing and functioning in a social situation ...
Songs provide the student of human behaviour with some of the
richest material he has for analysis, but their full potential remains
to be exploited'.[31]

Bearing in mind this outline of the ideology contained within
Wimber's worship songs, the next task is to probe how that
ideology is constructed, and to particularly press what is implied
about the nature, quality and character of God, and the relationship
of believers to the person of God. What will emerge from this
analysis is an understanding of the kind of power that funds the
ideology.

Some Structures in Hegemonic Ideology

If it can be said that the social construction of reality in Wimber's
theology and churches arises, at least in part, from a form of
emotion, then the structure behind that emotion must be examined.
It is being suggested that Wimber subscribes – especially in his
worship materials – to a hegemonic ideology that 'fixes' the basic
capacity of that emotion. This fixing is essentially executed through

the careful selection (possibly unconscious?) of two dominant metaphors in the songs themselves, to which we shall turn in a moment. However, there are three more basic considerations to ponder first, which relate to the structuredness of ideology in all fundamentalist groups.

First, attention needs to be paid to the distinction between using a *word* and using a *name*. With a word, the speaker places the referent in their world to the extent that the referent is amenable to their cognitive structuring capacity. With a name, however, an independent 'reality' is addressed, which can interact with and affect the speaker. What is named can vary from being a person to a disease, to a food or God. When God is addressed by a name, two things take place: (i) the worshipper is brought into a relationship with God, and (ii) God, once appropriately named, is deemed to preside over the concerns of the believer. As we shall see with Wimber, the titles ascribed to God in worship are primarily 'You' and 'Lord', the first connoting love and immediacy, the second power and authority. In these titles, hegemonic ideology is fixed.

Second, looking at the actual structure of worship can reveal something about its strategy. Worship, as an emotive force, has both a God-ward and communal goal. For example, Wimber's song 'Here We Are' suggests to the singers assembled that,

> Here we are, gathered together as a family;
> bound as one, lifting up our voices to the King of Kings.
> We cry 'Abba, Father, worthy is Your name.
> Abba, Father, worthy is Your name'.[32]
>
> *Steve Hampton*

The song creates a relationship of obligation between the believers, and alludes to the relationship between God and the worshippers. The metaphors 'family', 'bound' and 'lifting' ideologically define the identity, purpose and activity of the singers, knitting them into a like-minded unit, in which further hegemonic ideology can be fixed.

Third, attention needs to be paid to the actual structure of the music and words, and especially the way in which *emphasis* is achieved. For example, repetition of a sequence of words and notes in Wimber's worship is a common device:

More love, more power, more of You in my life.
More love, more power, more of You in my life.[33]

Jude Del Hierro

The music lingers over the words 'love' and 'power', teasing them out, with the line then repeated, turning this part of the song into a kind of liturgical mantra. In the example above, the musical and textual structures provide a framework in which the hegemonic ideology can operate with effect. This is done via two pivotal metaphors.

Two Ascriptive Metaphors of Power

The notion that metaphors communicate a core ideology of God is not a new one. For example, Sallie McFague's *Metaphorical Theology: Models of God in Religious Language* (London, SCM, 1983) outlines a shift in theology, in which dogmatic propositions about metaphysical realities have given way to exploring the way in which narratives and metaphors function in religion as vehicles of meaning. McFague shows how religious language with all its images and metaphors actually becomes theological language, offering ideological concepts of God, life and the cosmos. Her approach to narrative, like mine to fundamentalism, attempts to illuminate how language motivates and shapes the lives of believers; in short, how the social and theological construction of reality comes to be. The metaphors of 'You' and 'Lord' are both models of God, as well as ideological tools in Vineyard worship, that mediate a ready-made framework of power to the worshipper.

The immediacy is achieved, at least in part, by an uncritical but relentless emphasis in the worship on the power of love. Niklas Luhmann, in his provocative book *Trust and Power*, identifies love as a 'generalized symbolic medium of communication'.[34] By this Luhmann means that metaphors – such as 'You' and 'Lord' – are general symbols in communication that are designed to solve problems, by offering a web of meaning that is intimately connected with reality. As such, these metaphors may be used to refer to specific problems when employed by worshippers, since they are communicative instructions which can be manipulated according to circumstances. In other words, the names for God are often ascriptive rather than descriptive. Of course, the metaphors of 'You' and 'Lord' themselves are codes for a range of concepts: love, power, authority and immediacy, to name but a few. Although

there is sometimes overlap between the meanings of the two
metaphors in Vineyard worship, these distinctive metaphors are
quite properly to be singled out for special treatment. They are
the most frequently occurring metaphors, and their ideological
function is traceable in most of Wimber's work. The 'You' of
Wimber is the source of 'signs'; the signs are signs of love; 'You'
is the subject of intimate, direct speech, as was noted in the
previous section. 'Lord' is the source of 'wonders'; the wonders
are displays of power (miracles, prophecy); the approach to the
'Lord' is usually made by more indirect speech, affording the
believer less risk of failure.

Understood thus, 'You' is a kind of metaphor for the love of
God, 'Lord' for the power of God. But love itself, when spoken
of directly in Vineyard worship songs, is not simply a description
of a feeling or a state of affairs. It is a code of communication
itself, a form of ideology, according to the rules of which feelings
can be formed and simulated, denied or imputed, used or abused.
The songs offer a pattern of behaviour to the worshipper; the
meaning of love or the immediacy of God as 'You' is enhanced
by small signs, from any source, that validate the code. Thus, even
if a high stress on love and 'You' appears to imply that Vineyard
worship is somehow 'total communication' ('songs not just about
God, but to him'), it is not actually quite the case:

> Lord, I ask that You would come right now.
> Jesus, come and heal me now.
> Spirit, come and fill me now,
> I love You, I love You,
> I love You, yes I do.[35]
>
> *Bill Dobrenen*

The implication of the metaphor 'You' is that the content of all
Vineyard communication to God is centred on love for God. In
fact, 'You' is a code that signifies that God is close to the needs
of the worshippers, and that their desires are consistent with their
love for God. 'You' is ultimately a code for empowerment, via
personal intimacy with God.

Given this connection between 'love' and 'You', how do these
metaphors function as ideology in the context of worship? Three
considerations arise. First, God as 'You', connoting love, can
receive information from the worshipper, since love is receptive.
As such, God described as 'You' assists a process whereby ordinary

occurrences can be transferred by the worshipper onto another horizon of possibilities. Often, these are signified by Wimber in only the most general terms: healing, filling or touching. The horizon of possibility offered in Vineyard worship is one of love, but a love that can transform situations by personal adoration of 'You'. Second therefore, and somewhat paradoxically, metaphors of 'love' and 'You' enhance communication by not truly communicating. The metaphors hold their value for worshippers in their vagueness, by perhaps suggesting God is already anticipating the worshippers, or that they already are understood, without having to actually articulate their desires. Third, the communicative medium of love offers stability of understanding. The metaphor 'You' fixes an ideological image of God in the mind of the worshipper. God is personal, known, intimate and present, forever ready to show his love by meeting the needs of those who communicate with him by 'love'. 'You' portrays a God of love and passion, whose desires are centred on demonstrating his love for people with 'signs' that betoken this aspect of his nature. As a dominating, focused metaphor, 'You' is effective because it binds the community of feeling together, harmonizes its desires, and permits little in the way of contradiction or paradox. Since all is subjugated to giving and receiving within this framework, the scope of communication and behaviour is actually quite limited.

Working alongside the metaphor 'You' is the metaphor 'Lord'. Naturally, they interconnect at many levels, yet they offer distinctive portrayals of God in the ideological process, and contribute to the presiding model of God at work in Wimber's theology. The metaphor 'Lord' connotes power and omnipotence, and is an obvious semantic 'problem-solving' device. Naming God as 'Lord' in Vineyard songs seems to function ideologically in three ways. First, there is a considerable overstatement present where God is invoked as 'Lord'. There is nothing that God cannot do; his unlimited power is a cause for praise:

> You are the Mighty King, the living Word;
> Master of everything, You are the Lord.[36]
> *Eddie Espinosa*

This type of praise ties in with much of the testimony and teaching that follows worship. God's superabundance and complete power cannot be limited. Therefore God can do small or great things for his people, that display his love (signs) and power (wonders). Second, 'Lord' is a code for obedience and submission, but of a particularly interesting type. If the desires of the worshippers are to be met, then submission must be offered to God. 'Lord' then, as a metaphor, operates as an exchange mechanism; for submitting to God's power and Lordship, worshippers are rewarded with having their problems solved by power:

> I give You all the honour and praise that's due Your name,
> for You are the King of Glory, the Creator of all things ...
> As Your Spirit moves upon me now,
> You meet my deepest need.[37]
>
> *Carl Tuttle*

A third ideological aspect in using the name 'Lord' is to encourage trust. That is to say, trust of one another in the community who know one Lord, who is the same for them all. And also trust of the Lord himself, whose power alone can save and heal. 'Lift Jesus higher'[38] proclaims that there is 'power in His name': the more Jesus is trusted (lifted), the more likely it is that the power and healing in his name can be experienced by the worshipper. Fourth, the metaphor 'Lord' also serves to reduce complexity. Just as 'You', signifying love, negates the necessity to be specific about problems, 'Lord' operates as a device that removes God from ordinary life. The metaphor 'Lord' places Jesus high above the problems and difficulties of the believer, yet draws the individual into worship, by suggesting that submission to Christ's Lordship and engagement in worshipful communion will help negate the problems even before they are specifically identified:

> Lord, I'll seek after You,
> 'cause You're the only one that satisfies,
> Turn t'ward to kiss Your face,
> And as I draw near to You,
> I will give You all my love,
> I will give You my self,
> I will give You my life.[39]
>
> *Eddie Espinosa*

By focusing on the metaphors of 'You' and 'Lord' in worship, Wimber has created a social and theological hegemonic ideology that guides the communication of selected essentials, via a fixation on concepts of love and power. The ideology consists of symbols and metaphors that connect their selection with emotion, and offer a framework in which individuals can find identity and power, and see it magnified in their own language about God.

In citing the songs above, I have attempted to show how the worship songs of Wimber are 'an [ideological] strategy for encompassing a situation'.[40] That strategy, as can now be seen, does not just encompass situations: it actually creates them. There is a real sense in which the worship songs of the Vineyard are themselves a construction of reality, that offers forms of love and power to the worshipper that are transcendent. Through passion, passivity and power, the emotivated fundamentalist community stands over and against the world, by articulating ideological states of being, in which full love and full power become realized. Worship is not a matter of the mind for Wimber; it is a 'matter of the heart', in which the worshipper's reality is transformed by praise. Songs like 'Praise the Lord with all your heart' are a primary source of ideological instruction to the worshipper, that suggest that reality will be changed by love and power in the activity of praise.

This Chapter began by noting Adey's observation that focused worship may produce 'mutations of God' in attempting to represent God in praise and supplication. Granted, this may be true of all worship to some extent. However, questions remain over the picture of God that emerges in Vineyard worship. A few remarks seem pertinent here, that will be relevant to later discussion. First, the twin emphases by Wimber on an all-powerful and all-loving God bear some resemblance to the teaching of Mary Baker Eddy, founder of the Christian Science Movement (see Chapter Seven). God's sovereignty (inherent in her Calvinist upbringing), and God as pure love (a New Testament doctrine she felt Calvin had neglected), are combined strategically to encompass basic problems in theodicy. As with Wimber, there is an inward and outward response called for on the part of the believer, to defeat the problems caused by evil. The inward spiritual journey must ultimately connect with an experience of God's power, which must then (necessarily) be expressed via outward demonstrable signs. The worship of both Wimber's churches and Christian Science churches is an important prerequisite in this process.[41] Second, although the immediacy of God is celebrated in Vineyard worship, it is a nearness that does not permit worshippers to be fully human; in this sense, the portrayal of God, although loving and powerful, is nevertheless coercive and exclusive, since the operating power is *force*. Thus, the worshippers are ultimately instructed to become *not* what they are, and be transformed into a 'power-replica' of Christ or the Spirit.[42] Third, and arising out of the previous two points, the absence of various aspects of Christian doctrine appropriated in the worship should be noted: the incarnation, life and death of Christ, the Church, the Christian life as 'journey', are just a few examples. Fourth, the worship itself, as a core ideology, along with the music, might be said to function emotively. In the words of Raymond Warren, it is there to 'relax and reassure the congregation, which may have the effect of helping them to accept the meaning of the song, or perhaps lull them into not thinking about it at all'.[43]

So, who benefits from this ideology? The hegemonic ideology present in Wimber's worship ultimately fixes a federation of concepts based around love and power. These function both sociologically and theologically. God is both immediate ('You'), yet also the holder and purveyor of absolute authority over all things ('Lord'). The community itself is also constructed around this model. Wimber's 'kinship groups' – a key core element in his Vineyard network – establish congregational immediacy: personal closeness and accountability characterize the inter-relationships within Vineyards. This ideology also permits the leaders to be closely involved with the ordinary affairs of their congregation. If God is immediate, then his leaders are at the forefront of that immediacy. Like the 'shepherding movement' of British Restorationism, Wimber and his leaders can involve themselves in every small detail of the life of a believer, through prophecy, words of knowledge, exhortation and encouragement. Equally, an emphasis on God's Lordship has sociological consequences. Leaders have authority: they represent the interests, view and power of the Lord, which is held by leader and led mutually within the wider power network. They are the ultimate beneficiaries from the ideology: their power to control is inevitably increased. The hegemonic ideology established here accounts for, at least in part, the refusal of Wimber (and other fundamentalists) to dialogue seriously with opponents and critics. A dialogue can never really be appropriate, since any agreed 'results' by the two groups would either weaken the power of the leader or signal to the group that the power of God can somehow be shared in a plural coalition. This in itself would deny fundamentalists the exclusivity and certainty they seek, via a controlling core ideology, which is central to the inductive power strategy.

Evaluation

In examining Wimber's worship, we need to avoid the common trap of treating his songs as simply texts. The music, as has been suggested previously, is not incidental, but integral. To ignore the theological impact of music is surely a mistake. The melodic, harmonic and rhythmic dimensions of music are all value-laden. Music imprints its own ideological meaning, no matter how hard this is to articulate.[44] Moreover, in a song, the words and music bear upon each other: they interact in subtle and profound ways. In the case of Wimber, the combination of 'soft contemporary rock' and 'romantic/intimate' tunes clearly help 'carry' the textual ideology of the songs.[45] The songs are agents of ideological power and this has several implications.

First, in many of Wimber's songs there is the conviction that God himself is the primary agent in worship, and that a profoundly personal relationship with God is possible for the worshipping believer. This is the inductive strategy in its basic form: encountering God through 'energizing [worship] from within, and no less responding in it, alluring one again, inviting one into a continuing adventure'.[46] Some of Wimber's songs have a tendency to suggest that worship must somehow be engineered before God can be encountered, but behind this lies a deeper commitment: to be caught up in God's own dynamic life and pulled into a deeper knowledge of his love and experience of his power, both privately and corporately.

Second, the concept of divine power operating in many of these songs is distorted. I suspect this proceeds from a kind of quasi-Monarchian doctrine: Christ the King, enthroned in glory with the reigning Father is emphasized, at the expense of Christ in his risen humanity, who has known weakness. As T. F. Torrance and others have commented, there is a chronic tendency to thrust Christ into the majesty of God and neglect his continuing ministry in our humanity. The self-giving love of Christ on the cross – surely the very acme of God's power – does not feature significantly in Wimber's canon of worship songs. The power that is therefore portrayed is usually that of supernatural brute force, rather than the ambiguous power of Calvary. At least one consequence of this is occasional condoning of naked self-assertion and the pursuit of power in the interests of the Church militant: the establishment of a mighty kingdom *prior to the return of Christ*.[47]

Third, this focused attention on divine and human power means

that other aspects of the Christian life receive scant attention.
Human weakness is an obvious example. Those songs of Wimber
that deal with 'spiritual warfare' are strongly success-orientated,
showing little awareness of our inherent frailty and limitations,
and still less that such weakness can itself be an agent for the grace
of God. Some songs actually adopt polemic *against* weakness.[48] And
what of sin? The concept is almost entirely absent in Wimber's
songs, and when it does surface, it is usually only as a defeated
power rather than a serious or persistent problem. The cost of
discipleship is another major theme to be neglected. Although
Wimber's 'I am the wounded soldier' implies difficulties in the
Christian life,[49] concepts such as frustration, perseverance,
endurance and patience in the midst of opposition are hardly
mentioned. There seems little recognition of the possibility that
the Spirit may lead us into a sharing of Christ's suffering and at
the same time be that in which God spans the gulf between
desolation and triumph. Too many of Wimber's songs lead the
believer into only encountering God through either intimate or
'victorious' words, rhythms and melodies.

Fourth, if human weakness is down-played in this way,
something similar may also be said of God's divine power 'made
perfect' in weakness (2 Cor. 12.9). Although Wimber addresses the
cross in both his teachings and his songs, few songs focus on the
death and sufferings of Christ. Where this is done, it is usually
bracketed together with the resurrection and ascension, and used
to communicate God's supremacy over sin, death and sickness.
The notion of the cross as a place where God bears the full reality
of evil is absent. And there is hardly a hint that the cross might
give one a glimpse into God's participation in human suffering.
The relationship between the Spirit and the crucified Christ is also
distorted in Wimber's songs. The Spirit is either like a lover bearing
gifts or a brute supernatural force: but both are unrelated to Christ
as a role-model of power. Yet life in the Spirit within the body of
Christ does relate: Christians share both the glory of Easter and
the death of Christ. The Spirit was given to the disciples, after all,
with nail-marked hands (John 20.22–3).

Fifth, we must note the treatment of the Church and world in
Wimber's songs. In common with other Restorationists, Wimber's
songs portray the Church as a powerful body – like a 'mighty army',
for example – which tends to stress the gathered congregation as
an agent of God's power. Those songs of Wimber that do deal
with the Church are particularly prone to conflating divine and

human power in a distinctive manner: what we again find missing
is a sense that authentic *koinonia* involves pain and hardship.
Where pain or division is referred to, it is firmly in the context of
'spiritual warfare', where the Church is treated as an object of
Satan's focus, in order to limit the power of God. Equally, there
is nothing in Vineyard worship to suggest that God's power is at
work beyond the gathered worshipping congregation, an indication
of the monopoly fundamentalist worshippers think that they have
on God's power.

Lastly, we note that although Wimber's songs tend to exalt the
universal power of God, actual concern for social justice and for
the needs of others outside the gathered congregation is rare. (This
could be said of many more established hymn compilations.) Songs
expressing suffering in solidarity with victims of human hurt
appear to be completely absent. This is of particular significance
for the next chapter. Wimber, in justifying his programme of
fundamentalist charismatic renewal, claims to be an heir of
Pentecostalism. Yet the roots of Pentecostalism lie firmly in the
appalling suffering of the American black slave trade. Those
songs of faith arose in the midst of unspeakable hardship and
powerlessness, quite unlike those of Wimber.

5

The Power of God

It has been suggested above that Wimber's fundamental(ist) strategy for affirming Christian tradition in the face of modern religious pluralism and contemporary secularism is an inductive one. He validates historical or biblical analysis by seeking direct religious experience at first-hand. Wimber's brief discussion of the virgin birth in *The Cross* amply demonstrates this approach:

> Taking [the birth narratives] at face value and regarding the virgin birth as a historical fact will result in certain consequences. Among the most obvious is that it strongly suggests that miracles are possible. If one believes in the virgin birth of Jesus it should not be too difficult to believe that God can and does perform other miracles.[1]

This pattern of interpretation – taking a historical text at face value, locating a primary experience of power within it, and then attempting to imitate or validate that same power in the present – is one that Wimber uses, with some variation and abridgements, many times. Other examples might include his treatment of prophecy as a form of judgement, a 'word of knowledge' being a word of power, since it places the subject under the authority of the word and speaker. Or, perhaps more commonly, the inductive strategy can be traced in the treatment of demon-possession, a form of oppression that continues today in precisely the same way that it was said to have done in Jesus' day: the power of darkness must be overcome by a greater force – the power of light.

As was noted in Chapter One, it is important to conceive of fundamentalism as something which is not simply concerned with propositions, but also in terms of experiences and relationships, that offer a more complete universe to the believer. (It is a key weakness in Barr's work on fundamentalism that he takes a narrow view.) This necessarily means that Wimber's work – in common with other fundamentalists – often defies accurate definition. To ask what Wimber means by 'the gospel', for example, is to invite a plurality of answers. True, Wimber is capable of exact and sophisticated expression, but to try and 'boil down' much of his theology would be to miss the point. For Wimber, the heart of the Christian faith resides in an experience of the power and love of God, not in a creed. Any 'articles of faith' or ideology that might be uncovered can only be there precisely because they have the power to induce this experience, in order that the forces of darkness might be overcome, and the believer be set free to become a child of God.[2] The question therefore necessarily arises: how is the power of God known today, and what evidence is there for it, as far as Wimber is concerned? Further still, how does that power empower individuals, and what are the effects? Indeed, is the power of God as demonstrable as Wimber would suggest?

Power in the Present: Riding the 'Third Wave'

Wimber believes that he is just one operator in a more general 'power movement' of God (a 'nodal point in an ever-expanding power circuit' would be Clegg's terminology), generally known as the 'Third Wave' of the Spirit.[3] The term 'Third Wave' is symbolic, used by those within the late twentieth century charismatic movement to describe the activity or movement of God in which they are participating. The 'First Wave' is generally regarded as early twentieth century Pentecostalism, and the 'Second Wave' the emerging post-Second World War charismatic renewal movement, amongst which trends such as 'Restorationism' in Britain or the 'Jesus People' in the USA might be included. There are a variety of differing opinions within the movement as to what exactly it constitutes, but broad consensus could be reached on one factor at least, namely that the 'Third Wave' is intended to renew, revive and equip *existing* congregations and denominations not create new ones, although this may be a by-product.[4] Healings, prophecies, deliverance and 'signs and wonders' are treated as normative, and therefore as phenomena that can be placed within existing patterns of denominational governance, and adapted to 'fit' as necessary. However, Wimber has effectively begun his own network of churches, to carry forward the programme of the 'Third Wave'.

Other distinctive elements within the movement might also include a belief in 'baptism in the Holy Spirit' at conversion, rather than as a second work of grace subsequent to being 'born again'. (Traditional adherents to Pentecostalism and some Assemblies of God churches would generally reject this possibility.) However, 'multiple fillings' of the Spirit subsequent to being born again are expected, which might resemble what some would call 'baptism'. Phenomena such as speaking in tongues are not necessarily highly prized. Although Wimber has run seminars on speaking in tongues, he does not, in common with other operators within the 'Third Wave', see it as a physical validation of spirit baptism, but rather as a language for intimate prayer, spiritual warfare or other ministries. Lastly, but of particular interest here, ministry under (or in) the power of the Spirit is the 'portal entrance'[5] into the 'Third Wave', rather than a spiritual experience for individuals, which typified the first two waves. To be in the 'Third Wave' is thus a code that validates the existing inductive approach, confirming that God is at work (in a distinctively powerful way) in the present, which authenticates the truth claims made about God by the charismatic-fundamentalist group concerned.

Jesus: Supreme Model of Divine Power

If Wimber and his Vineyards generally regard themselves as moving within the 'Third Wave', the question naturally arises: which role models are available to induce that movement? It is in the person of Jesus that Wimber finds the ultimate evidence of divine power. Throughout Wimber's works, Jesus is consistently presented as a powerful personality who can take hold of and transform the inner life of others. He is the 'God–Man', an archetype or model who demonstrates God's actual supremacy over sickness, death and defeat. Jesus acted and taught as one with a divine power and authority who is unlike anyone else; further still, because Christ lives, an encounter with him now leads to a radical transformation. Believers can become or have 'a new prince/princess in the Kingdom, a joint heir with Jesus, a privilege of power, authority, and access ... a dual citizenship, a victorious living experience – not just a saved sinner' (*Power Points*, manual, p. 13). For Wimber, the very essence of Christianity is the continuing experience of divine empowering through contact with Jesus or the Spirit. Thus, a demonstration of a relationship with God on the part of the believer must usually be a demonstration of empowerment in the present.

It is Wimber's handling of Jesus, and most especially the

significance of his death, that has attracted the fiercest criticism
from evangelicals and other fundamentalists. Most of these
critiques tend towards accusing Wimber of inattention to the
redemptive work of Christ. Whilst this might be partly true, it
misses the actual distinctiveness of Wimber's Christology. Wimber
is not primarily concerned with the mystery of how Christ is two
natures, although he does address this. Instead, Wimber places the
works of Christ firmly as the basis for our Christian life, although
the speculations about his person also have a place. Some of
Wimber's earliest writing on Jesus illustrates precisely this. The
seminal *Signs, Wonders and Church Growth* treats Jesus as both
a model of ministry and a power transformer:

> Jesus came not only to bring the Kingdom of God, to save and
> heal people, but also to impart to others this healing ministry that
> they might share in bringing people under the Rule of God. We,
> as the Church, were commissioned by Jesus almost 2,000 years ago
> to announce the good news to all creation through the healing 'signs'
> that would accompany and authenticate the message wherever it
> was preached ... the transference of Jesus' healing ministry to
> others ... and the powerful exercise of it today is of the utmost
> importance if we hope to see the Kingdom of God reach the ends
> of the earth.

For Wimber, one of the primary tasks of Jesus was to be a
model of divine power for the disciples. They were to observe
Jesus' power over sickness and demons, copy the 'model' that
Jesus used, and then attempt to emulate (rather than simply
imitate) the process in the wider interests of expanding the work
of God: 'Jesus' method was clearly to minister while his disciples
watched, then to have them minister with him watching them or
receiving their reports, and then to leave them doing it on their
own'. Jesus is thus a kind of power broker, demonstrating power,
and then sharing it, before giving it away to a small group of
prepared and committed disciples.

In offering this perspective on Jesus, Wimber is standing within
a broad fundamentalist tradition, especially championed by
Pentecostals, that views Jesus as the pre-eminent model for spiritual
experience. In this tradition, Christ encompasses the Christian
faith as its pioneer and perfecter, an *example* for believers (John
13.15; 1 Peter 2.21), who teaches followers to become like the
teacher himself (Luke 6.40). But Jesus is a role model not only for

Christian character, but also for Christian experience – specifically
spiritual experiences analogous to the ones preserved in the Gospels
about him. In other words, Jesus as a holy human being, conceived
by the Spirit and therefore uniquely a temple of the Holy Spirit,
becomes a prototype for those created in his image (born again).

The notion of Jesus as a pre-eminent model or demonstration
of divine power is offered by Wimber in the context of his
understanding of the establishment of the Kingdom of God. For
Wimber, this Kingdom is one that is set up in opposition to the
rule of Satan. The sharp dualism that this involves will be discussed
in more detail later, but for the moment we should note that
Wimber's commitment to the establishing of the Kingdom of God
in the present leads to Jesus being assigned a role more functional
than dynamic. Of course, Wimber does assert that Jesus is alive
now. But his treatment of Jesus' earthly life appears to provide a
rationale for confirming the trend of his inductive power
framework. For example, his summaries of the life of Jesus usually
focus on his works, and how they can be repeated today: there is
far too little stress on aspects of Christ's life that (apparently)
cannot be imitated, not least the atonement. Writing in *The
Kingdom of God*, he notes that Jesus offers a pattern for working
against demon-possession, disease, aspects of nature, and
ultimately, death. Jesus performed these works as necessary
demonstrations of power, since believers themselves will have to
deploy this same power if they are to further the work that Jesus
began, namely defeating Satan:

> The Kingdom will arrive on a worldwide basis when the worldwide
> power of Satan is broken at the Second Coming of Jesus. Until
> then the battles go on, even though the decisive battle has been
> won at the cross. The call of the army is to rout Satan and his
> demons.[6]

Whilst this treatment of Jesus to some extent explains some of
the more basic ways in which divine power is wielded in Vineyard
communities, it does not tell us much about how this in itself
forms the basis for relating to God. Again, as with our observations
on the ideology of worship, we are given a perspective on God by
Wimber that allows for a degree of intimacy and interiority
(connoted by the metaphor 'You' in worship), that acts as a
counterbalance to the outward and exterior stress on power as a
work, that affects the world and the believer (connoted by the

metaphor 'Lord' in worship). This is achieved quite simply, by stressing Jesus' relationship to God and the Spirit as a source of power:

> The secret of the sinless life of Jesus and his miraculous ministry is grounded in his relationship to the Father. Even though he was God, Jesus drew his power from an intimate, childlike relationship with the Father in heaven. The ability to hear what God is saying, to see what God is doing, and to move in the realm of the miraculous comes as an individual develops the same intimacy with and dependence upon the Father.[7]

So, the key to the effective exercise of the divine power of Jesus in the life of the believer is not just copying Jesus, but also developing 'the same relationship of intimacy, simplicity and obedience' (*Signs, Wonders and Church Growth I*, sec. 5, p. 8). Equally, however, Wimber is careful to point out that the Holy Spirit is alone the 'key to Jesus' power and effectiveness in his ministry'. Wimber sees the Spirit as the *primary* source of power in the life of God: God alone can give the power, which is the Spirit; Jesus alone can demonstrate its most effective use, which is gained via his intimacy and subordination to the Father. Thus, Wimber writes: '[the] indispensable reason for [the Holy Spirit's] presence in the Christian's life is to give power ... The Spirit is the Christian's sole resource for supernatural power in doing the work of God'.[8]

Wimber's thinking on the person of Christ may therefore be summarized as follows. First, Jesus is a 'nodal point' who knew and communicated the power of God in a particular time and context, and still offers a pattern for today which believers can imitate. Jesus is alive as 'Lord' for the believer, but that Lordship is something that must be acted upon, via the power of the Spirit. Second, Jesus' divinity itself is confirmed in experiential terms: for those who follow him now, Jesus is a power model, through whom the power of the Spirit may be obtained. Third, Jesus' power is in opposition to the power of Satan: the function of Jesus and his works of power is to undo those of Satan. Last, the power of Jesus is actually the power of the Spirit, given by the Father, working through the most effective agent possible: the person of Christ. In other words, there is a latent doctrine of subordination present in Wimber's thinking, which is explicitly exposed when the theme of power is used as an interpretative key to his theology.[9]

However, in the light of these observations, we must now turn to look briefly at the theme of power in Wimber's view of the Spirit.

Wimber's Doctrine of the Holy Spirit

It is perhaps not surprising that Wimber's Christology is essentially subordinationist. In common with other fundamentalists, Wimber has an inadequate doctrine of the Trinity, which must be partly traced to the dominant ideology of most fundamentalist communities. A premium is placed on authority, hierarchy, certainty and power structures, that compete with and confront the pluralist outside world. A relational and mutual doctrine of power, such as might be found in a Trinitarian doctrine, is too ambiguous and threatening to form the ideological basis for a fundamentalist community. Thus, it is not untypical to find the Father, the Bible (as an infallible work or power) or the Spirit (understood as brute supernatural force) dominating. Jesus functions only as a figure or example that testifies to a higher power. Although 'Lord' is a key metaphor in Vineyard worship, it is important to read 'Lord' as a code for conveying power and authority, not as a literal description of Jesus in relation to the Father or the Spirit. In this sense, Wimber stands within a long tradition of fundamentalists who have stressed the name (or names) of Jesus as primarily active agents that reify divine power, rather than truly describing it.[10] Indeed, we can go further here, and suggest that Jesus' Lordship in Wimber's theology is a pure agent (nodal point) that communicates power, yet is not the real power in itself. Thus, on the one hand, Jesus' Lordship as emphasized by Wimber tends to deny the real humanity of Jesus in the life of the Trinity,[11] and on the other, fails to give Jesus himself the same 'level' of power that the Father or the Spirit possess. Jesus is subordinate both to the will of the Father and the power of the Spirit.

Although Wimber notionally assents to a Trinity, he, in common with other fundamentalists, finds little real place for it, because it does not feature significantly in the Bible, or in experience. There are some direct sociological consequences as a result. The qualities of interdependence, equality and openness are undervalued, and a hierarchical structure put in their place. Leaders have control over power, and give it to whom they choose. However, Wimber's reading of John's Gospel and the relationship between Jesus and the Father suggests that 'their relationship is the ideal, the pattern, the *basis for our experience of the Father*' (*The Dynamics of Spiritual Growth*, p. 77). Fundamentalists like Wimber are generally more concerned about works (as a tool against pluralism, or as a nodal point that 'feeds' the fundamentalist community) than about 'persons', human or divine. Thus, the question naturally arises: how does the Holy Spirit operate in Wimber's thinking, given that it is, at least to him, the way in which God reveals himself, empowers and effects individuals, and leaves demonstrable 'signs' or evidence of God's activity?

Some preliminary observations are necessary. First, the Spirit for Wimber is clearly a form of 'transformative power': it changes that which is alien to God, conforming it to his plan or likeness. Second, a number of Vineyard–Wimber worship songs explicitly address the Holy Spirit, usually as an intimate, loving force, that is waiting to settle upon the believer, rather than already being there.[12] Third, this passivity in worship can be very different in Wimber's 'clinics', where he often refers to the Holy Spirit 'falling' on believers with some degree of force, and certainly acting on some without their consent: indeed, he traces the genesis of Vineyard growth to precisely such a brute display of God's power.[13] This activity usually follows a simple invocation from Wimber or another Vineyard pastor: 'Come, Holy Spirit'. This may be repeated loudly and often, until there is a measureable impact on the congregation (sometimes the words 'More power Lord, more power', are used instead). Fourth, further evidence for Wimber's 'brute force' view of the Spirit lies in the metaphors sometimes used to describe it. For example, it is not uncommon for some exponents in Wimber's genre to speak of the Holy Spirit as a gun: 'It does not kill, however, but converts'! So the power of the Spirit can be 'turned on others', compelling them to believe in God by demonstrable 'signs or wonders' (miracles). This is certainly how Wimber interprets the Acts of the Apostles.[14] So, Wimber portrays the Spirit as an 'unstoppable force' in exactly the same way that some other Protestant fundamentalists describe the word of God: too powerful for anyone to resist.

For Wimber, however, the primary evidence for God's power is its *expression* in spiritual gifts: 'spiritual gifts are the expression of God's power at work in the world'.[15] These gifts – ranging from prophecy to evangelism, and from healing to teaching – are given *only* to the waiting Church. They are imparted by God and received by the elect, and are to be used as 'tools which enable one to fulfil the ministry required'. The gifts also energize the individuals and communities who receive them, so that 'as they are used, service is effected by the power of God'.[16] Wimber has an extensive list of what might pass as a spiritual gift, and with the exception of tongues,[17] all the gifts are deemed to be tools that either directly demonstrate the power of God to unbelievers, or build up the believing community to a point where it is more able to do the same. We must also remember that Wimber's doctrine of the Spirit must be set squarely in the context of his notion of the 'Third Wave': the Spirit can energize any congregation now, provided they are open to the new order receptivity will bring.

For Wimber, receptivity by individuals and communities to the energizing possibilities of the Holy Spirit is the key to empowerment. Wimber basically advances a modern form of Pentecostalism, that stresses the 'need' for the Spirit, by pointing out that it is the active power behind Jesus in all his miraculous, authoritative and proclamatory activity: without the Spirit, Jesus would have been rendered powerless. Thus, the task of the Church is to be filled with that same power, with Jesus as the role model, and to be 'equipped saints', in order that others might also know the power of God, as Jesus made it known, in 'signs and wonders'.

Opposition to Divine Power: Anti-receptivity, Satan, Principalities and Powers

In considering Wimber's view of the Spirit, his treatment of Jesus, and his overall commitment to affirming the power of God, we must now consider how these 'powers' engage with the modern world. Wimber locates the power of God primarily in the miraculous: demonstrable 'signs' of God's supremacy over all existing powers. Occasionally, however, power can also be located in teaching or in acts of service, but only in so far as they function as a 'sign' of power. So, the power of God is known in activity, not in personality or symbol. This is an important starting-point for assessing the dualism of Wimber, alluded to earlier. Wimber treats power as a property that is in some sense relational in character: receiving divine power bestows properties upon the believer, who in turn can relate to the exterior powers/forces of the world in a new way. The gospel, according to Wimber, is believers finding God as *their* God and as the source of power to overcome the opposing forces of Satan, sickness and the world.

In separating divine power from all other powers so clearly, Wimber has to ensure that it is exercised in a distinctive manner. This is vital to the maintenance of the hegemonic ideology, as well as the functioning of the 'inductive power circuit' that constitutes the community of believers. In a sense, some form of dualism is inevitable for most fundamentalists. The vigorous modernism and pluralism of contemporary society require a response from a community whose power ideology is under threat, and that response is nearly always divisive.

Wimber emphasizes both 'the power' itself and the dynamic quality of what it accomplishes. The question arises, however, what happens when there is no 'evidence', either of 'the power' or its reification? In other words, what if there is a 'power failure': a 'break' in the inductive circuit that mediates and reifies power? Wimber, in common with other charismatic fundamentalists, resorts to dualism, although his is of a fairly sophisticated kind. Four primary ways of dealing with this failure can be traced in his work.

The first strategy is to deny that proper induction has taken place. It is in Wimber's treatment of healing and the believer that this is primarily found. Although he acknowledges that there are people who are not healed – including four people in Scripture 'not healed at the time' – power failure is explicitly blamed on the individual or community: insufficient faith, unconfessed sin, corporate disunity in the body of Christ which weakens its power, an incomplete or incorrect diagnosis, or a lack of persistence in prayer.[18] This mechanistic attitude is not surprising. Wimber grasps 'signs' to validate the power of God in the present, in order to subvert the mechanisms of an unbelieving world: if no 'sign' appears, the methods for inducing those 'signs' must be checked, and made to work.

A second strategy of interest is that of 'inner healing'. This is an area of 'ministry' specifically devoted to the inner life of the believer, and it focuses on a loose cluster of concepts such as 'wholeness', 'fullness' and 'memory healing' – delivering the individual from the grip of painful memories (conscious or unconscious) that inhibit the free movement of the Spirit in the person's life. It is used as a technique for 'removing blockages' that prevent the natural flow of the power of the Holy Spirit. The very nature of its inward, personal context, however, guarantees that it will have some degree of effectiveness. This whole process is aided and abetted by the worship offered, which tends to make intimacy with God an *internal*, personal event. Reification can therefore be said to have taken place spiritually, internally or psychologically, as a hostage against the absence of a tangible, observable 'sign'.[19]

Third, we must consider the strategy of recourse to Satan. Addressing Satan, demons and the spirit world is a prominent feature of Wimber's work, and 'deliverance' from demonic oppression or possession plays a significant part in his ministry. Demonology in Wimber's work, however, does not just emerge when there is a need to find a scapegoat. Wimber, looking to Jesus as a model, notes that 'the manifest presence of God always causes the demons to show themselves ... demons will shriek loudly and do many other things, sometimes in sheer terror, and sometimes as evasionary tactics' (*Signs, Wonders and Church Growth II*, sec. 6, p. 3). Wimber more generally describes this as a 'power encounter': the forces of darkness being met by the power of God. Christ is the supreme master of the 'power encounter' since in all his dealings with the demonic, he appears to have triumphed. For Wimber, Satan is still active, opposing God's power by spreading sin, sickness and misery in order to weaken the effectiveness of believers.

According to Wimber, it appears that anyone can actually be demonized. Clearly those outside the community of believers are most at risk. Wimber consistently refers to 'entry points', moments, events, traumas or sins through which demons can gain access into the soul and body of a person, and 'bind' them. Wimber goes further than most fundamentalists here, however, in asserting that even spirit-filled believers are not immune from such demonic oppression or possession. In 'Deliverance: Can a Christian be Demonised?' (*Signs, Wonders and Church Growth II*, sec. 7), Wimber suggests a 'grid', ranging from no demonic control to total demonic control. Believers can be sifted by Satan, tempted and then finally attacked, resulting in the believer becoming possessed to a greater or lesser degree by an agent of Satan (demon). Thus, it is possible for a believer to both minister in the power of the Holy Spirit *and* be afflicted by a demon, both at the same time.

Clearly, in this third strategy, what Wimber is describing is an alternative inductive power circuit, which can account for failure, defeat, sickness and setbacks. It exists, at least in part, due to Wimber's inability to recognize the dualist element present in his dominant ideology. Since sin, struggle, perseverance and 'ordinary reality' are not common features of Vineyard worship, power failure inevitably gets attributed to a Satanic circuit. In saying this, I am not denying the reality of evil itself, nor even the possibility that Satan might exist. I am simply maintaining that this third strategy of Wimber's is definitively dualist, and can therefore be justifiably called neurotic. For Wimber, one of the primary tasks of the gospel is to deliver people out of bondage: non-believers are subject to the power of Satan, until being delivered, via a power encounter, by Christ.[20] In other words, individuals are subject to either one kind of power or another: as with Wimber's view of the Spirit, the stress on force allows little space for personal responsibility and freedom. This kind of dualism places a great weight on the agents of power: demons or exorcists. In Wimber's view, we are locked into the same sort of struggle Jesus had. Consequently, if a believer – especially a prominent one – fails to be an effective agent, or more seriously, is found to be 'afflicted' themselves, the source of their power must be checked. In some cases it must be removed by Wimber or others, in case it is abused and distorts the power flow in the community. For example, two prominent Vineyard pastors have been dismissed for sexual misconduct in the last five years ('Satan entered them'): one had his prophetic office 'stripped' from him, the other allegedly took part in a public 'laying off of hands' performed by Wimber. (Both still remain part of the Vineyard however.)[21]

A fourth and final strategy is Wimber's referral to the more general category of 'powers and principalities'. Sometimes, a natural phenomenon such as a storm can be 'demonic' in origin: this is certainly how Wimber reads Jesus' 'calming of the storm' at the Sea of Galilee. Wimber maintains that Jesus addresses the malign spirit *causing* the storm: only then is there calm (Spring Harvest Address, Easter Day, 1992). More usually, however, Wimber speaks of general malign spiritual forces that are said to influence cultural trends and localized tendencies (e.g., 'a spirit of apathy reigning over a city'). Wimber has made some use of this strategy, although he was sceptical about their existence as late as 1986.[22] However, granting their existence does give believers a specifically generalized account for why they might not be 'breaking through' in a certain place. The Vineyard–Wimber response to the problem is usually to engage in some type of 'spiritual warfare', and attempt to remove the 'blockage' by powerful, accurate prayer.[23] Again, we must note Wimber's extended use of the violent 'shooting' and 'gun' metaphors used to describe this spiritual activity: territorial spirits reigning over places are to be 'brought down'.[24]

In analysing Wimber's fundamentalist theology thus far, a number of distinctive ideas are becoming clear. First, Wimber's assertion that the power of God is known today is advanced in two different ways. On the one hand, the power of God is known in the inner life of the believer, either via an experience of intimacy with the Father, or via a more specific claim such as 'inner healing', in which the hidden or inner parts of one's life are 'touched' by God.[25] On the other hand, the power of God is known in tangible, observable 'signs' or 'wonders': miracles that occur in the midst of the believing community that can be used as testimony or evidence to demonstrate God's power to unbelievers. These are both primary *results* of power for Wimber's followers. Second, the spiritual or numerical growth of the affected or witnessing congregation is further testimony to God's demonstrable power. Third, Jesus himself offers a 'model' of both the property of power and its relational capacities. Jesus, obedient to the Father and filled by the power of the Holy Spirit, offers a pattern for believers. Submitting to God and being open to the Spirit – as Jesus was – means believers can not only mimic Jesus' works, but also be conformed to his likeness, becoming like him. It is at this point, amongst others, that some identification of divine with human activity can take place in the Vineyard community, since Wimber's theology ultimately points to a blurring of these distinctions. Thus, the power of God is known through his present agents: those, like Wimber, committed to a 'signs and wonders ministry'. This leads to a hierarchy of powers in the Vineyard, which is partly due to its core ideology and the absence of any real Trinitarian doctrine that stresses mutuality or finds a place for the person or humanity of Jesus.

Wimber's explicit dualism can be primarily located in his explanations for power failure. Although sin and personal responsibility play their part in his theology, they receive nothing like the emphasis that demons, powers and principalities receive. An alternative inductive power circuit is thus suggested by Wimber, with a different direction ending in powerlessness. The inward life is subjected to bondage; the outward 'signs' for the individual are 'sickness', or perhaps even death, rather than empowerment; the communal 'signs' become disunity, numerical and spiritual decline, rather than growth. In all this, Satan is presented as the prototype of destruction, who would counter demonstrations of God's power with demonstrations of his own. In Wimber's writing, Satan has virtually become incarnate, as tangible a person as Jesus was.[26] Of course, this emphasis serves the alternative (demonic) power circuit very well, and the focus on works rather than persons keeps alive the possibility of validating the power of God today by repeating works. Given these observations, however, it is now appropriate to take a closer look at *how* it is said divine power empowers believers.

How Divine Energy Empowers Individuals

Wimber's teaching on the power of God for today rests on his core ideology, which includes a stress on the Fatherhood of God, the power of the Spirit, and Jesus as a 'model' for successful power encounters. However, even Wimber acknowledges that divine power can only be truly experienced when encountered through agents that embody such power. At the same time, Wimber does not rule out God acting decisively beyond his agents – the 'Third Wave' theology implicitly accepts this – yet, receptivity by the individual remains an important key as to *how* empowerment is achieved.

According to Clegg, divine power might empower human beings via a network involving the operation of charismatic and competent authority upon 'nutrient power',[27] which in turn is attributed to or projected onto the character of God. The operation of these powers produces predictably beneficial effects for the individual and fundamentalist community, who become convinced of the truth of their gospel, and then allow themselves to be further influenced by agents or leaders whose charismatic and competent authority produces similar trends.

As far as fundamentalist communities like the Vineyard are concerned, the receiving of divine power comes in two particular ways. The first is an initial 'accepting' of the historicity and consequences of 'the cross', Christ's death for the individual, that secures their place in the life of God. The second is a stress on the ongoing need to be 'moving in the Spirit', accepting empowerment daily. In both cases, Wimber stresses the flow of power that comes through these agents (cross and Spirit), and that they can flow through the believer, provided they are in intimate touch with God, and therefore within the overall power circuit.

Receptivity is therefore an active dynamic, especially within fundamentalist groups. The requirement – indeed necessity – of confirming and supplementing historical analysis by seeking direct religious experience at first hand is a primary feature of the inductive strategy. Traditional truth claims about God (e.g., 'He died for my sins') must be authenticated by a demonstration of the power of God in the present (e.g., 'I feel born again'). The sections that follow explore the link between the cross and the Spirit in Wimber's theology, as it relates to individuals being empowered by divine energy. Wimber himself does not explicitly make any real link between the two, but the one cannot be understood without the other. Both are individual yet interconnected agents of divine power that demonstrate themselves in the life of the believer.

The Cross: Christ's Redemptive Work

Given the explicit dualism of Wimber's theology and doctrine of the Spirit, we must now examine the place and weight that Wimber assigns to the death of Christ. He addresses the power of the cross in most of his works, but has also produced a thesis (tapes plus manual) that specifically deals with the subject (*The Cross*, 1986). This particular work must be seen, at least in part, as a response to some evangelicals, who, dissatisfied with his charismatic emphasis, accused him of not being 'cross-centred'.[28] Wimber's response on this matter appears, at first sight, to contain a number of 'fundaments' about the cross that would appeal to both classical Pentecostal and evangelical believers. For example, Wimber affirms the traditional Pentecostal claim that 'by his stripes we are healed', taken by many to mean that physical healing comes via the power of Christ's sacrifice and suffering. Equally, Wimber stresses that 'sins are forgiven' because of Calvary: the cross means spiritual salvation for those who believe. Wimber also affirms a doctrine present in many charismatic movements, namely that the cross was a turning-point in the war between Satan and God. In this view, Satan attempts – via Judas, the Jews or the Romans – to kill Jesus, and succeeds in doing so at Calvary, only to find (unwittingly) that the cross is a victory for God, and Satan has accidentally pressed his own 'self-destruct button' (*The Cross*, manual, p. 55): 'At the cross, where the devil had planned to parade himself as victor, he was, instead, conquered with all his forces and powers. The enemy's plan back fired! He thought he had won when in fact he had lost.'

There are, of course, perfectly respectable antecedents in classical

Christian spirituality for all the above views. What then, is distinctive about Wimber's vision of the cross? Certainly, whichever doctrine Wimber affirms in his theology of redemption, one thing is consistently clear throughout his thinking. The cross is a victory. This victory is for individual Christians to realize in their lives, and it brings benefits to the believer who understands and practises its power. But there is more to Wimber's theology of the cross than this, namely the explicit power themes present therein.

In the first place, Wimber affirms that the death of Christ brings salvation. That salvation is from 'the power of sin', 'the curse of the law' and 'from wrath' (*The Cross*, manual, p. 66). However, the actual saving event of Calvary belongs to a wider context: 'The purpose of God to bring man back to him is demonstrated in the Christ-Event. This event includes the whole of his redemptive life . . . his sacrificial death, his powerful resurrection, his ascension back to the Father. All of these separate parts are one event.'[29]

Wimber explicitly states that no one part of Christ's life has significance over another: each individual event in the total Christ-Event is an invitation from God to humanity. The underlying substance of that invitation is that believers may each know the redemptive power of God personally. The fruits of redemption – knowing the power of God – are universally available, but only made concrete in the lives of believers: those who have accepted their need of it, and have been regenerated or 'born again'.[30]

Beyond this, Wimber's remarks about the effects of salvation, although many and diverse, can be reasonably divided into four distinctive categories. First, the saving Christ-Event makes spiritual, moral and physical regeneration possible, but only after repentance has taken place. Believers must begin by recognizing their own weakness, vulnerability and handicap (of whatever kind), and renounce their own powers. Only then can regeneration take place, in which the believer is 'impregnated by the very seed of God' (*The Cross*, manual, p. 77), and then deemed to be a new creation. Second, Wimber also stresses that salvation is 'justification', in which the sins of believers are forgiven, following Christ's atonement. Further still, Wimber maintains that justification also confers acquittal by God from the punishment due for sin and graciously reconciles believers to God. Third, salvation is also adoption, in which the believer is conformed by a combination of grace and submission into the image of Christ: 'Sonship implies responsibility. . .It is inconceivable that we should enjoy a relationship with God as his child without accepting the obligation to imitate the Father and cultivate the family likeness' (*The Cross*, manual, p. 80). Fourth, Wimber claims that salvation brings sanctification. On the one hand, believers are already sanctified by Christ's atonement. Yet on the other, sanctification is an ongoing process, requiring a dependence on the 'power of the Holy Spirit' as transformation continues.

In Wimber's doctrine of salvation, therefore, we find a primary assertion about the power of God. In Christ's redemptive life and work, the believer is regenerated, justified, adopted and sanctified. In each of these events or states the believer 'plugs' into a knowledge and experience of God's power, which gives freedom from the powers that previously held the individual, be they sickness, sin or whatever. So, the Christ-Event is a victory in its entirety: a show of God's strength and power. Wimber does not see the life of Christ (or his death) as a sharing in weakness or defeat with humanity. The power themes in Wimber's view of salvation are therefore at their strongest when he describes the effects of the Christ-Event. He conceptualizes it in terms of conflict, of bondage and liberation. There are struggles – between the flesh and Spirit, Satan and God, between heavenly and demonic powers – which the power of God alone can, has and does overcome. The ultimate function of Christ's death was, therefore, to 'release power'. The power of God becomes accessible to believers, provided they find the courage to trust in it and to enact it.

It is clear from analysing Wimber that regeneration, justification, adoption and sanctification are themselves power terms. In turn, each of them is used inductively by Wimber: their historical truthfulness must necessarily be confirmed by the believer somehow seeking a direct experience of the power first-hand. Such an observation partly explains why Wimber devotes so much time to 'testimony' when dealing with salvation. Wimber's use of story, the actual narrative account of how a believer 'came to be saved', is extensive. The more abstract theology of how one is saved, and from what, is not of primary interest to Wimber. His concern is to see the power of God active in the life of believers, which for him more than adequately supplements any historical or theological analysis.

In summary, Wimber's view of salvation contains four distinct power themes. First, there is a contradiction in his theology. On the one hand, Wimber invests a great dependence in 'signs and wonders' as agents. He consistently argues that 'signs and wonders' are more likely to impress non-believers and convert them. Wimber derides what he calls 'programme evangelism', yet proposes his own version: if believers initiate a programme of signs and wonders, this will be more effective than other programmes. So, in common with other fundamentalists, Wimber explicitly places his faith in an infallible or inerrant agent. (For Wimber, it is 'signs and wonders', for others it might be the Pope, or the Bible.) Yet Wimber also states that the initiative and effective power in redemption is God's: he repeatedly insists there is no self-redemption of any kind. Further still, redemption is only for those who consciously choose to opt into God's power and out of the powers that presently bind them. Believers are thus those who chose, and are now the chosen. Second, Wimber does not differentiate between the atonement and incarnation: the whole Christ-Event is seen as having redemptive value. However, any discussion by Wimber of the incarnation usually focuses on the embodiment of power (the Spirit in the human–divine Jesus), and ignores, more or less totally, any real stress on the actual weakness or suffering of Jesus. The cross itself was a key power encounter, in which Satan unwittingly released the power of God by killing Jesus, so believers may now have access to the resurrection power.[31] Third, we must note the dualistic and dramatic elements present in his views of salvation: triumph, victory and deliverance are concepts extensively deployed in Wimber's presentation of redemption – the struggle with dark forces (sin, demons, etc.) is ended ultimately in the victory of Christ. Fourth, this redemption brings power to believers, in the specific forms of regeneration, justification, adoption and sanctification, enabling the Holy War against Satan to continue.

The Coming of the Holy Spirit

Although Wimber asserts that it is Christ's life, death and example that make victory possible for the believer, there is a sense in which the Christ-Event is interior and personal to the individual respondent. Regeneration, justification, adoption and sanctification are all states that may or may not influence the actual community seeking corporate empowerment. We have already indicated that Wimber's Christology is probably subordinationist in character, and most especially in relation to the Spirit. Wimber's problem with 'ordinary' commitment to Christ is that it does not necessarily produce any transformation in the Church or in the world. In particular, Wimber is often critical of other fundamentalists who stress personal commitment to Christ, yet do not work to see the power of God demonstrated in the body of the congregation.[32] It is for this reason that Wimber places a high stress on the exterior and corporate properties of the Holy Spirit. Following Jesus can be almost a private affair, but an encounter with the Spirit – according to Wimber – is nearly always public, and therefore the Spirit and the encounter itself are agents of empowerment for the body of Christ.

We have already noted that Wimber's interest in the Holy Spirit extends well beyond the traditional Pentecostal beliefs of baptism in the Spirit followed by speaking in tongues. Wimber's focus lies in 'signs and wonders' which empower and motivate believers in their faith. Further still, these works of the Spirit provide a demonstration of God's power to non-believers, causing a reaction that leads to numerical and spiritual 'church growth'. As has already been stated, for Wimber the Spirit is a brute, supernatural force, that allows little space or freedom or individuality. Also, the Spirit is characteristically dominant, which necessarily links with the hegemonic ideology already identified: those who can most effectively wield the power of God's Spirit are, necessarily, the leaders and apostles of the Vineyard churches. How though, does an individual believer become empowered? There are essentially two stages in the process.

The first stage is to be overcome by the Spirit. Blane Cook, a former Vineyard pastor, speaks of individuals being 'overloaded' with the Spirit's power.[33] This is a metaphor that is explicitly intended to convey the idea of overloaded electrical circuits, such that fuses blow, or components temporarily over-react to the power surge. The phenomena that accompany the Spirit's settling on an individual are enormously varied, and according to Vineyard understanding can indicate slightly different things. For example, a person shaking (apparently) uncontrollably or involuntarily is deemed to suggest either resistance to the Spirit, or unusual openness, resulting in 'overload'. The increased respiration, falling over (being 'slain in the Spirit'), laughter or weeping, which can take place during Wimber's clinics, are said to be responsive signs to the powerful action of the Spirit on the individual. Fluttering eyelids and excessive perspiration may indicate the same. Occasionally, believers who are praying for a particular person will locate a 'hot spot', an area on the person's body that is giving off unusual heat: believers are directed to 'minister' to such place, although a 'hot spot' does not necessarily indicate a physical problem – it could be spiritual or emotional.

The phenomenon of being 'slain in the Spirit' has already been mentioned: a happening in which an individual is knocked down and collapses under the force or weight of the Spirit's settling on that person. Sometimes it is held to be a form of admonishment, laying low those who oppose the Spirit (or the Vineyard leaders) through pride, sin or resistance. At other times, it is held to be gentler, such that the believer is simply overcome with bliss and rapture. Yet whichever way this phenomenon occurs, it is always orientated towards reducing the autonomy and control of the individual, in order to ultimately empower them. It is thus a form of domination, in which the Spirit forces itself on the believer, in order to transform them. Of course, this activity is underpinned by the ideology present in the Vineyard worship: as discussed earlier, both 'You' and 'Lord' are metaphors of force and domination in themselves, which necessarily imply a reduction in capacity for the believer to resist God.

Empowerment for the believer arises directly out of such experiences, since they are held to be deep encounters with God, and the individual is often convinced of some kind of inner transformation. But empowerment can also result from observing more exterior, public phenomena. This is the second stage of empowerment. For example, 'words of knowledge' are often given out at Wimber's clinics. These are personal insights about an individual that are held to be a specific revelation from God, that could not have been revealed in any other way except by the Spirit. Sometimes they are very general (e.g., 'There are some deaf people here tonight, who want to be healed'), but on other occasions, they may be most particular (e.g., 'There is a woman here having an affair – she knows she must repent -- the Lord says you must stop seeing Martyn'). Wimber himself claims to have such words of knowledge, as do many of his followers, although at his clinics, it is usually only Wimber who actually broadcasts such things. These words of knowledge, however, could easily be dubbed 'words of power', for that is what they are.[34] They indicate to the believers that God is powerfully present; they establish those who give such words as men of power; they establish a form of domination, since under these conditions, nothing can ultimately be hidden from God or the leadership. As with the other phenomena associated with the activity of the Spirit, empowerment arises out of the individual being possessed and controlled by the Holy Spirit in such a way that it is useless for the true believer to try and resist. The only path open is to submit to the power, to be filled with it, and then to be animated by it.

Evaluation

The inductive power circuit, into which Wimber is locked as a strategy to counter the effects of modernity, demands a close relationship between theology and proof, between faith and action. In all the areas we have touched on, the kind of power Wimber believes in appears to be one of dominance – a dominance that is present in the heart and character of God, that is intended to empower human beings. Where the Spirit is present, signs and wonders follow, and church growth occurs. The operation of the power, even if forced by God or his agents, always produces beneficial effects upon the receivers, who become convinced of the truth of the gospel, and of the divine character (love and power) that bestowed the blessing. In turn, the charismatic and competent authority of the agent is also validated. For Wimber, this is supremely Jesus: the ultimate power agent, who was best able to demonstrate God's power, either by his total obedience to God, or by his consistently victorious power encounters with Satan. The task of the ordinary believer is to be an imitator of Christ: to be a person of total obedience, total commitment, and of great faith. Empowerment for individuals and the congregations will come to all who see Jesus and his works as an ideal role model for today.

Clearly, in the type of power structure encountered in the Vineyard, there are going to be problems arising directly from this inductive theological strategy. These problems, I would hold, are common to most fundamentalist groups. For example, it will always be difficult for human agents of God's power who perform miracles or prophesy to differentiate themselves from the actual power. The power of personality and individual charisma in the task of persuading people to accept God's power is a vital issue, yet one that is often left unacknowledged. The stress on obedience and submission as a precondition to empowerment, again with Jesus serving as a role model, sets up a potentially damaging understanding of the Church, in which the ordinary believers might be abused. Equally, the weight given to the power of God as an unstoppable force, both in theology and in practice, can leave little room for individual freedom, for choice and for debate.

Lastly, the whole question of agency is largely unresolved in Wimber's works. For example, on the one hand, 'signs and wonders' are divine agents for congregational growth. On the other, Wimber sees these phenomena as agents to be introduced as a stimulant to growth. In reading Wimber, it is sometimes very difficult to know if he is talking about divine or human agency when he discusses instruments of power, or both. The confusion, no doubt, arises out of the confusion that already takes place over power in the Vineyard network: believers do not seem to be able to distinguish between Wimber's power and the power of God. This is, in fact, a fairly common problem in fundamentalist groups. For example, believers sometimes have trouble distinguishing between the (inerrant) text and the (guru or infallible) interpreter. In their minds, there will be a notional clarity about the difference between divine and human power, and divine and human agency. However, in practice the belief tends to be much more blurred.[35] All of this has rich implications for studying the Vineyard churches themselves.

6

Power in the Church

Chapters Four and Five assessed the ideology and then the theology of Wimber. In this chapter, I investigate Wimber's doctrine of the Church, how power is demonstrated in the Church's inner life, and in its witness to the world, and how it organizes its power. Wimber, in common with many charismatic fundamentalists, controls his own network of churches. At present, there are about six hundred 'Vineyards', about half of those being in South America. The remainder are mostly in North America, although there are Vineyards in Britain, Australia and South Africa. In addition to these official Vineyards, there are also a number of 'Vineyard-friendly' churches or groups, that will 'front' or host Vineyard meetings. In Britain, for example, the Anglican Bishop David Pytches (now vicar of St Andrew's, Chorleywood) has close connections with Wimber.[1] Pytches organizes a Vineyard-style conference annually ('New Wine'), which attracts thousands of visitors, and Vineyard Pastors address those present. In Oxford, an informal Vineyard 'kinship group' exists, run by another Anglican, Teddy Saunders. Beyond the Anglican Church, Wimber enjoys support from modern Restorationist churches such as 'New Frontiers' (Terry Virgo), 'Ichthus' (Roger Forster), as well as more old-fashioned revivalists such as Colin Urquhart. In short, Wimber's support power-base primarily consists of conservative evangelicals who have had some experience of charismatic renewal, or who are Restorationist.[2]

In the early stages of his ministry, Wimber appeared to have little interest in fathering churches: he was content at the time of writing *Signs, Wonders and Church Growth I* to let denominations use and adapt his material as they wished for their own ends. Those that deployed his church growth principles were not required to become Vineyards themselves nor, indeed, to even join a network. Yet this has gradually changed, as Wimber's commitment to a more precise form of power reification has grown stronger. Internal struggles within his own churches in the mid-80s forced him to consolidate his grip on them: he now enjoys the status of 'apostolic authority'. From this position of strength, he has begun an intense period of expansion, although he still remains prepared to aid other churches in their efforts to increase numerical growth.[3]

The theological key to this expansion can be found in Wimber's *The Kingdom of God* (1985). In this volume, he closely approximates the 'Kingdom of God' with the Church, although is careful to ultimately distinguish them. What in effect is presented here, however, is something not unlike British Restorationism. In this school of thought, the Church is the agent of the Kingdom of God, with Kingdom authority and power. The Church must therefore witness to and display all the power and authority of the Kingdom, and function, as of old, apostolically. So, in Wimber's view, we are to 'invade the Present Age with the Age to Come' (*KOG*, p. 13). There is an inevitable feel of 'over-realized eschatology' in such approaches. The present Church becomes synonymous with the power of the Kingdom in an age to come, and apostles seek to adopt a first century world-view and replicate the kind of signs, wonders and experiences that might have occurred then.

However, the fact that Wimber presses for repetition of the apostolic age so that the Church may become (again) a purer 'power-body' only really accounts for how he thinks the Church should witness to the world – its outer life. But what of its inner life? Here, the inductive power strategy is much less obvious, as the focus of empowerment shifts from power to intimacy. *Church Planting: God's Heart for Expansion I* and *II*, and *The Church in the 90s* (1990) show that an intimate relationship or experience with God will ultimately lead to numerical church growth, and, further still, the founding of new churches, or church-plants. These plants will be, by their very nature, expansive, and agents of the same power that brought them to life. The source of this empowerment as being 'intimacy with the Father' is not without significance. Intimacy, unity and obedience to the Father are pointed to as the source of growth, yet it is Wimber himself, father of the Vineyard, and head (apostle) of the 'kinship groups' who is the mediator of authority and blessing. As we shall see later, the conflation over 'fatherhood' in the Vineyard has implications for the tight 'family' organization that is present. (As is so common with fundamentalist groups, it is nearly impossible to repudiate the 'father' of the Church if you are a member of the family.)

Evangelism in the Church

Peter Berger rightly identifies that part of the core of the inductive strategy is to turn to *experience* as the ground of all religious affirmations. Of course, this can be one's own experience, to whatever extent this is possible, as well as the experiences that are enshrined in a particular history or tradition. In making this observation, Berger is pointing us to a view of induction, where, it is said, religious tradition or history is to be understood as a body of evidence concerning religious experience and the insights derived from those experiences. He goes on to state, however, that the inductive strategy often entails taking 'a deliberately naive attitude' towards accounts of human experiences: this is especially so in more dogmatic (or fundamentalist) communities, where social control and ideology are constructed out of the 'core contents' of these experiences. To question the experience would be to raise doubts over the governing conclusions drawn from them. This is why the inductive strategy sometimes appears similar to that of the reductive. Yet the two are to be distinguished quite sharply. The inductive strategy regards modernity as part of its evidence and experience. It need neither condemn nor celebrate it, yet it must be detached from it, in order to protect the sanctity, certainty and uniqueness of its own experiences, for the sake of ecclesial identity.

Wimber practises the inductive strategy with regard to evangelism in two distinctive ways: an appeal to the (unique) experience of the present, and then to the past. In each case, the appeal requires an uncritical 'face value' reading of the account of the experience. A typical account is described below, illustrating this simple directness:

> In London recently, two young American girls (Vineyard) came upon a Japanese man sitting on a bench. They asked him if he knew Jesus. When he replied he did not and was a Buddhist, they asked if they could 'pray on him'. He said yes so they laid hands on him and asked the Holy Spirit to come upon him. He immediately began to weep and they asked, 'Do you feel that?' 'Yes, oh yes,' he replied. 'That's Jesus,' they said. 'Would you like to know him?' He said, 'yes', and was converted. Only *after* he had received the

touch of God and responded to him did they tell of the claims of Christ.[4]

Wimber's seminars on evangelism and church growth are laced with such illustrations. They serve to remind believers that the power of God is immediate, available, effective, and, under the right conditions, demonstrable. Indeed, what Wimber effectively offers through 'power evangelism' is a greater and more life-enhancing experience than the person who is receiving it has previously known: this is the 'proof' of the power and truth of God.[5]

However, effective evangelism need not occur through a dramatic 'power encounter'. If experience is the key to power and empowerment, there will necessarily be a limited range of opportunities for observing and receiving power that are less confrontational. One of these contexts, for Wimber, is worship. Wimber regards the experience of the Vineyard community at praise and celebration as a 'sign' in its own right.[6] Of course, 'worship' for the Vineyard is more than just praise and celebration: it includes many manifestations of power that others may experience: prophecy, words of knowledge and healing, to name but a few. Indeed, for Wimber, the evangelistic task of the Church is to allow it to experience the power of God, and respond accordingly. Evangelism is always more than just preaching or teaching: it is the sharing of experience ('the empowered community'), in the hope that others may also share in this, and join the Church.

However, this stress on the individual and their experience of power belongs to a wider framework: church growth. Wimber believes that the Church of the 1990s will be one of 'unequalled power . . . unequalled purity . . . the most powerful army on earth during (these) times of divine judgement and revival'.[7] In making such appeals, of course, Wimber cannot (entirely) draw on the present record of the Church, nor even of the Vineyard. Tracing the experience of power in the past becomes vital in shaping the church doctrine of the future. Characteristically, this is done via an uncritical reading of biblical and historical texts.[8]

In The Dynamics of Spiritual Growth (1990, p. 209), works of power such as the healing of a cripple are specifically linked to numerical church growth. This strategy is practised elsewhere by Wimber in the wider interests of demonstrating that evangelism, even in the early Church, is a matter of demonstrating God's power, and non-believers experiencing it for themselves. Naturally, there are many problems with reading historical texts in this way. Harnack, for example, reckoned that such experiences of power were 'inner' manifestations, subjective confirmations of an insight into an encounter with the truth.[9] Wimber, however, reads the acts of God, both past and present, entirely in terms of experiences of power that might give rise to effective evangelism, and, later, church growth. Thus, the task of the Church as a social body is to be an expanding or self-multiplying agent of God's power, in order that non-believers might experience for themselves the certainty of God.

'Affirming the Body': 'Signs and Wonders' in the Vineyard

Wimber believes power is made real in the life of the Church, both in its inner life and its witness to the world, via the manifestation of 'signs and wonders'. These are miracles or particular demonstrations of God's power, which, according to Wimber, result in people being evangelized or converted, or drawn into a deeper relationship with the Father. The evangelistic potential that Wimber ascribes to such phenomena has already been noted. But do they benefit the Church, even if no numerical growth takes place as a result of their occurrence, for example, at a Vineyard conference? Three possibilities are suggested here, each of them pointing to the power-based identity of Wimber's churches.

First, miracles, or rather, stories of miracles, have a rhetorical function. They inspire fear and hope, identify enemies and friends, set boundaries for groups, and help sustain congregational momentum. Wimber's anecdotes about healings and deliverance play a crucial part in affirming the body of believers. Whether or not these miracles *really* happen, they clearly have *significance* for individuals and groups who are claiming to have witnessed them. In the case of Wimber, the stories or testimonies are always designed to underline the powerful dynamism of God that is prosecuted so forcefully in fundamentalist and revivalist groups.

In many respects, the stories mirror modern 'urban myths'. Second, third or fourth-hand testimony that cannot actually be verified, yet fits into an existing plausibility structure, and perhaps even expands it slightly, confirms latent suspicions and hopes in individuals and groups. The stories enable discussion of phenomena that might hitherto have been suppressed through fear or ignorance. Examples I have personally encountered from some Wimber followers which convey hope include the following: a man healed of AIDS; a genetic deformity 'wiped away'; miraculous feedings; dental cavities filled by 'the hand of God'; and eyeball, leg and hand replacement, where none existed before. There are a host of other 'myths' surrounding demons that warn, or instil a degree of fear. Blane Cook claims to have been 'slimed' by one (i.e., attacked, as depicted in the film *Ghostbusters*); Bill Surbritzky (not a colleague of Wimber's, but a 'signs and wonders' exponent nonetheless) claims that wives who engage in oral sex can become demonized; some Vineyard members claim to have 'seen' demons, in a variety of poses. As every child knows, a myth is a story that is not true on the outside, but true on the inside. The healing stories or myths propagated by Wimber are not intended for lengthy analysis to see if they really happened. They are intended to affirm and expand existing horizons of belief, as well as point to the possibility of an omnipotent-interventionist power beyond them. They are intended to communicate that God is able to do immeasurably more than we can ask or imagine.

Second, signs and wonders convey assurance of the presence of God to believers. The use of the word 'assurance' here is no accident. To understand the function of signs and wonders within the Vineyard network, it is necessary to have some grasp of the doctrine of assurance. Beginning with the Evangelical Revivals of the nineteenth century (Wesley, Whitefield, et al.), the doctrine of assurance has always been at the forefront of 'experimental' (i.e., experiential) Christianity.

Pentecostal groups and fundamentalist Protestants all have some kind of doctrine of assurance. Quite simply, it is as necessary as the hallmark that identifies a precious metal. The doctrine of assurance identifies true believers, and reassures them of the presence and favour of God. For Wimber, signs, wonders and healings function in this manner: the social body that fails to demonstrate the power of the Spirit is 'out of the will of God'. The church that manifests the fruit and gifts of the Spirit, however, is self-assured of God's immediate presence with it. Thus, signs and wonders assure the body that it has a distinct identity that sets it apart from the world, as the community of the redeemed.

Third, signs and wonders function mechanistically, within a mechanistic system. The use of the word 'mechanism' here is intended to indicate that Wimber's concerns for the Church

primarily lie in areas connected with its effectiveness and efficiency.
Wimber, steeped in the 'church growth' tradition of Donald
McGavran and Peter Wagner, regards the Church as the agent
that must *effectively* fulfil the (so-called) Great Commission: to
make disciples of all nations. Within church growth thinking, there
is a variety of opinion as to how this is to be done, ranging from
'programme evangelism', 'tele-evangelism', through to Wimber's
own distinctive neo-Pentecostal emphasis. Yet the common thread
that unites the church growth thinkers is a mechanistic approach
to basic beliefs. As James Hopewell says: 'Mechanist approaches
focus on programme effectiveness...Churches that are growing
in size both signify and accomplish the work of the Lord...
"Bigness" is, moreover, a "powerful evangelistic tool" and provides
the resources necessary for effective programmes of worship and
ministry.'[10]

Wimber, in common with other church growth thinkers, sees
the Church as little more than a mechanism or agent (with a stress
on efficiency), as it attempts to do the work of God. In Wimber's
case, of central interest are the works of either Christ or the
Church, and their capacity to convert individuals, leading to church
growth. Wimber's rhetoric is often packed with mechanistic words
like 'tools', 'effective', 'priority', 'mobilize' and 'control'.
Mechanistic approaches to the Church ensure that power is
received, distributed and held both economically and effectively.
In the inductive power circuit, efficient mechanisms are vital for
transferring and demonstrating power. Such mechanisms might be
a method of prayer, an evangelistic technique, or a 'key insight'.
If power is not demonstrated, mechanisms can be checked, altered
or discarded, in favour of more efficient ones. Naturally of course,
this can lead to pragmatism becoming consecrated, possibly leading
to a slide into morphological fundamentalism. Indeed, within the
inductive power circuit, this trend is virtually unavoidable. This
can be traced historically in Wimber's theological emphasis. Since
the early 1980s, his search for efficient forms of belief that
demonstrate power most effectively has taken him from signs and
wonders to healing, then to worship, then to prophecy, and finally
to eschatology and holiness.[11] Yet in each phase of emphasis, the
stress on signs and wonders within the Church has been primarily
twofold. First, to assure believers of the presence of God, and,
second, to ensure the effective and efficient demonstration of God's
power, that will lead to growth of the same.[12] There is a sense
then, in which the mechanistic approach to the Church and to

signs and wonders simply treats them as agents or as rather vacuous channels for God's power. Whilst this is partly true, these agents also have a role as transformers: converting the original power into something effective and appropriate for growth. However, given the virtually limitless ideas on what is deemed effective or appropriate, how can a power-based Christian community maintain an identity?

Fear, Obedience and Purity: Power in the Church

Wimber's view of the Church suffers from an inordinately high stress on the power, rule and reign of God in the present, at the expense of valuing the freedom and respect that God gives to all creatures – what some would call an 'over-realized eschatology'. This touches many aspects of Wimber's thinking, but can be most easily traced in his teaching on healing. Wimber stands within a fundamentalist Pentecostal tradition that speaks easily of the dead being raised, teeth being filled, bones being re-formed or growing anew, and eyeballs re-forming in their sockets, where once there had been nothing.[13] For Wimber, such events are 'indicators' that the Kingdom of God, in the form of the 'Third Wave', has arrived with greater force now than since the time of the Apostles. This book cannot examine the truth of such testimonies, although personally, I think the stories have a rhetorical function (i.e., persuasive) in Wimber's gatherings, and are very probably exaggerations or 'hearsay', and in some cases, mistakes.[14]

Yet the stories themselves also have a deeper purpose that is common to many fundamentalist groups. Fundamentalists are at odds with the pressures of modernity and plurality, and are actively engaged in the work of persuading non-believers to become disciples. Fundamentalists distrust 'the world', and fear its malign influence on their order. Thus, evangelism that is inductively based may point non-believers to the (alternative) power of God, but it can also point to the non-believers' experience of the world as grounds for fear and trembling. Again, the 'core experiences' of the world's problems need to be grasped, and only then can openness to an alternative power structure begin. (A good example of this within the Vineyard would be the treatment offered to AIDS patients.[15]) Stirring up fear about the events in the world, cultural trends and alternative belief systems in society is standard fundamentalist practice, and, according to Caplan, Gerlach, Hines and others, it affects the community of believers in at least three ways.[16]

First, it binds the community together against the world, in a tighter type of relationship than before. If 'gaps' appear in the 'defences', the community will risk disintegration, so personal freedom and differences of opinion are often compromised for the sake of defensive unity at such times. Second, the existing hierarchy of leadership *and* basic beliefs is often restated with greater force, so that there is a pattern of order for resisting the threat. Third, and consequently, the identity of the community as a church often becomes concretized. In Wimber's case, this often takes the form of resorting to 'family-type' metaphors, which appear to offer the best hope of protecting basic beliefs vested in hierarchy and intimacy.

If fear of the world forms part of the basis for ecclesial identity, an equally strong ingredient is that of the necessity of obedience. In the case of the Vineyard, this has taken a remarkable form. In 1989, Wimber met with a North American called Paul Cain, who claimed to be a prophet. He brought with him some associates from a church in Kansas, and the group subsequently became known as the 'Kansas Six'. Cain, a former associate of (the discredited) William Branham,[17] claimed that God was restoring prophetic gifts to the Church on a par with Old Testament prophecy: to prove this, he is alleged to have predicted the Armenian earthquake, which was a sign to John Wimber that Paul Cain was from God. Cain was convinced that God had called the 'Kansas Six' to work with the Vineyard, and they subsequently submitted to Wimber's apostolic authority.[18]

Cain left the Vineyard in late 1991, and with Bob Jones, another of the prophets dismissed at around the same time for sexual impropriety, the 'Kansas Six' no longer enjoy the same status they once had. In spite of the brief sojourn of the 'Kansas Six' at the Vineyard, their presence there illustrates how power-related phenomena induce obedience amongst fellow believers. Cain implicitly claimed to be a new breed of disciple. He referred to the Apostle Paul as his 'great predecessor', *implied* that he was the product of a miraculous conception, and that he was free from any sexual desires (i.e., a pure 'channel' for God's power).[19] Early on in his ministry with Wimber, he suggested that God would create a new breed of children – an 'elected seed generation' – who would be more empowered in the work of the Spirit than ever before. His ministry seems to have had an extraordinary impact on the Vineyard, and beyond. British church leaders sympathetic to Wimber attended a conference on prophecy at Holy Trinity, Brompton, in 1990. After listening to Cain, and weighing his prophecy and words of knowledge, they signed a statement affirming his ministry, and the authority of the prophets.[20] All this prophetic activity occurred at a significant time for Wimber: Vineyard pastors were divided, amongst other things, on the issue of planting churches in Britain, and Wimber's authority over the whole Vineyard network was being questioned by some. The prophets, having submitted to Wimber (with their words and works of power), went some way to restoring that authority.

This was in part achieved by Cain's own ministry and teaching. Like Wimber, Cain appeared to be able to publicly give out words of knowledge (personal details about illness, secret sins, etc.), with remarkable accuracy. He also prophesied that revival would break out in Britain (in 1991),[21] and that the Vineyard would be an instrument of 'great blessing'. In his teaching, he reintroduced the Ananias and Sapphira 'syndrome', which encouraged unwavering obedience to Wimber and himself. In one recording, he explicitly states that those who judge, criticize or oppose either himself or Wimber would be opening themselves to 'a lot of judgement and the severity of God': their families and friends may also be affected, and those who consistently oppose the prophetic word will be 'taken by God' (i.e., die).[22] Wimber himself endorses this type of teaching, and in his comments on Cain, impresses on the audience the need for intimacy with God to be connected to obedience: for Wimber, part of the function of Cain's signs and wonders was to engender a greater degree of acquiescence amongst Vineyard members.

The example of the 'Kansas Six' helps us to understand a third dynamic at work in the empowered Church. Fear and obedience – either of God or those agents who represent him – often leads to an emphasis on holiness. 'Holiness' here, as in other fundamentalist and revival movements, is generally a withdrawal from 'the world', and focuses on personal morality, especially sexual, as the best means for countering spiritual ineffectiveness. Thus, Paul Cain's alleged sexual purity – probably a cause for deep suspicion in any other context – is lauded by some Vineyard members. Equally, the sexual failings of Vineyard pastors cannot

be tolerated, and usually result in apostolic or prophetic powers
being stripped.[23]

The stress on holiness as an emerging trend within the Vineyard
need not surprise us. Many revival movements find a move towards
bodily and spiritual purity unavoidable. It is ironic that movements
that often begin by 'embodying' joy, celebration and love in
community life, end up finishing with disembodiment and legalism.
Some 'house churches' in the British Restoration movement can
be seen to have done this, even in their brief history. The reasons
for this are manifold, but are connected at a deep level to the
community's need to preserve the purity of their power. This
necessarily involves exorcizing any impurities in agents or channels
of God's power, as a means of preventing distortion or power
failure. A stress on purity also enables a mechanistically orientated
church community to 'evolve', in the full Darwinian sense. If the
Church is to be a powerful body, and therefore pure, there is
little room for the weak, or for those who cannot reach certain
'standards' of spirituality. True, they can be ministered to in the
body, but they are unlikely to feel equal to, or as valued as, those
who can demonstrate God's power in their lives.

Thus, Wimber's view of the Church mirrors his theology.
The Church is to be a power-body, an agent, like Jesus, who
enacts God's power. Entry or initiation into the Church is via
an experiential power encounter, and continuation in the
Christian life is being affirmed in the body by more signs and
wonders. Such phenomena bring assurance of salvation to the
believer, and also confirm the validity of the mechanisms that
are able to best demonstrate the power of God. In turn, a
believer is induced to remain within this fundamentalism by a
complex form of socialization. Fear of the world and its
alienating properties is exposed, and the haven of a 'family'
and a 'father' offered as an alternative. This 'family' has power
to deal with the malign forces at work in the world, but power
can only be truly assessed by individual believers if they are
obedient to the (godly) structured hierarchy of truths and
leaders, and live pure lives that are free from properties that
might distort or interrupt the flow of power.

Reflections on Authority

From a sociological perspective, 'the phenomenon of authority is
basic to human behaviour'.[24] Part of what keeps a power structure

in place is the exercise of authority, which must be one that is appropriate to the overall power complex. In Wimber's churches it is the *use* of power that is of interest, and not so much the substance or source of power. For example, money is a power-base or resource, but until it is put to use in some way, it is not actually a power in itself. More pertinently, if we consider the gifts of the Spirit as power resources (as Wimber does), it is the stewardship of such gifts that is the focus of our ecclesiological interest. Is power used for personal gain, or for the good of those beyond the community? Are 'gifts' exercised publicly or privately, and for what ends?

Equally, within organizations such as churches, it is not the occasional or incidental use of power which is crucial, but its structured use. In fact, the structure of power is a major form of stewardship itself, since how we use power may be largely determined by its structure. Thus, where there is regularly patterned activity, whether intended or not, we can see structure.

If we think of power as analogous to physical energy, we can think of organizational structures as the ways we channel, focus, impede, transform, store and transport power; structure makes power useful or at least more predictable in its effects. Such a view of power certainly 'fits' Wimber's mechanistic approach to power.

Structure is a gift of or to the Church, enabling it to be a formed and distinctive community: the organization itself is a power resource. Of course, like all gifts or resources 'given' to the Church, examples of good and bad use abound. But in fundamentalist communities, there is a particular interest in the formation of communities whose immediate direction lies in perfectedness, dynamic empowerment, or measurable effectiveness. Clearly, any appeal to ideological or theological essentials by fundamentalists must be supported by 'proof'. Usually this is a community of faith (numerical size need not be an issue), who can demonstrate that the essentials themselves do at least both reflect a vision of God, and 'work' in the world, if practised.

The stress placed on structure in Wimber's churches has its origins in what Wimber supposes the Kingdom of God should be like. This often materializes in the expectation that there is no limit at all to what God can do. So, the Church is expected to 'mirror' a state of affairs that has only ever existed hypothetically. As we noted in an earlier chapter, part of the problem for the inductive strategy is that it produces a view of the Church that can sometimes amount to little more than looking to the past to legitimate present practice. This is certainly so in the case of Wimber's Vineyards. But what is so often looked back to is not what the first century was actually like, but what it should or could have been like. Thus, just as the community of the past is imagined, so the present structure of the community is constructed around inductive imagination.

Further, a stress on 'kinship' in the Vineyard network implies a structure of intimacy. As was noted earlier, love as a source of power is appealed to in Vineyard worship. In the Vineyard churches themselves, the structure fosters closeness and 'ideal' family ties. Wimber's 'fathering' role in the Church is often conflated with that of the Fatherhood of God, such that the quality of being 'child-like' is more valued than, say, the more mutual term 'brother' or 'sister'. I shall return to the use of the metaphor 'family' as a structural device shortly.

Vineyards are also structured for growth. Their historical and church roots lie firmly in the 'church growth' tradition, which insists that the community of faith must be built around formulae or structures that directly result in the numerical growth of the congregation. This necessarily means that the stewardship of gifts, including the gift of structure, is subjected to the wider goal of demonstrating power in the life of the community, with that power itself being both an initial 'sign' of growth, and an agent for further increase.

Structure as an Expression of Value

Ideology or theology provides the core outline for church structure. The fundamental value commitments – power, intimacy, mechanism, the Kingdom – make Wimber's way of doing things not only right, but even natural. To those outside a fundamentalist community of faith, the structure may look inegalitarian, unfair or wrong (e.g., keeping women out of leadership, and encouraging female submission in the context of marriage). But to those inside the community, this way of doing things seems natural, desirable and godly.

Clearly, however, the most effective way of assessing values and structure is by analysing their outcomes. If we consider all the products of a system, we can see how the structure is itself a positive conveyor of values. A chemical works may produce a selection of marketable products, employ many people gainfully, and make a profit for its shareholders; it may thus achieve its stated aims, and be evaluated as a good company. However, any systematic analysis would also have to point out other things that might be produced by the company. Perhaps redundancies are enforced to protect profits, harmful chemicals released into the environment as 'by-products', or there are few safety or recreational facilities for employees. These observations might reveal another value system in operation: a negligent attitude to workers perhaps, or excessive pursuit of profit at the expense of safety or environmental considerations.

It is not that the Church is to be compared to a production line – although mechanist or church growth approaches to Christian communities are very exposed to this comparison. What is being suggested, however, is that fundamentalists are usually very clear about what their value commitments are. It might simply begin by being a defence of biblical inerrancy, gravitating to the more complex agenda of Wimber's Vineyard network: yet whatever the fundaments are, they form the basis for structure. A first step is to differentiate between types of power at work although we must acknowledge that they are, in fact, completely interrelated, forming a kind of social 'web'.

For a community to be governable, it must give its consent to be governed. Most commonly, the base of this type of power is the group's sense of solidarity. In Wimber's case, this sense of solidarity and identity is achieved by the establishment of common goals and shared fundaments, but also, at a deeper level, by appealing to believers as a 'family'. A constant theological and ideological appeal to the Fatherhood of God, coupled with establishing believers as his chosen children, binds the community of faith together as a special family, favoured by God. Coupled with this, we must acknowledge the real dynamic of Wimber's own 'fatherhood' of the Vineyard being confused with that of God's. Rhetorical anecdotes about ideal families, especially fathers and grandfathers, are frequently used by Wimber in theological illustration. (As an observer at Wimber conferences, I have sometimes wondered if Wimber sees his own attitude to his grandchildren as anything different from God's attitude to humanity.) Thus, the power of consent becomes doubly important, since it confers status on leader and led alike, yet within a sharply defined ideological context.

Another kind of structured power is that of 'orders', a word familiar in theological and sociological contexts. 'Orders' are sub-groups that have differing functions and values. For example, prophets, evangelists and teachers might all wield power within a given community, each offering expertise or specialized knowledge to others. 'Orders' help resource the power-base, and can also be responsible for specific areas of local power. Consequently, the 'orders' of a given community often indicate the kind of power interests a group might have. Priests and bishops may be fine for the Church of England, but fundamentalist groups, such as we are studying, are more interested in offices or 'orders' where there is 'anointing' with power, such as prophets, apostles, exorcists or evangelists.

Related to the above is a type of power that can be termed 'competent'. (Wrong identifies this with authority.) Competent authority can be established by knowledge. This can be knowledge of strategies (how to grow a church), mysteries (spiritual warfare), or of people (words of knowledge). Competent power is grounded in the ability of the leader to demonstrate authority or expertise with particular areas of inquiry, which the community has a mutual interest in.

Lastly, there is idiosyncratic power. Often this is called charisma, charm or leadership ability. (Wrong calls this type of power 'personal authority'.) This type of power within the structure of fundamentalism must never be underestimated. Frequently, the 'force' of this power may depend deeply on the charisma of the leader who is custodian of the basic beliefs. Perhaps the principal function of idiosyncratic power is to provide a type of 'spirit', style or character that supports and encourages the group's tenacious pursuit of its goals.

The focus on these different types of structural power necessarily points to the phenomena that are valued by fundamentalist groups like Wimber's. The Vineyard organizes its power around those goals and objects that are valued by members, such that the structure reflects the values, and the values reflect structures. For church communities, there is no escape from such narcissism. For example, if hierarchy is an ideological focus, it will inevitably pass through the theology of a community into its very view of the Church. Exactly the same will be true for an emphasis on 'words', 'works', 'sacraments' or 'tradition': in each case, the community of faith will be required to reflect and protect the values it upholds, and, generally, attempt to export them. Thus, we can say that the only way of securing a sound church structure is to begin with a good theology or ideology. Therefore, it is not unfair to suggest that fundamentalist communities will always attract criticism for their church practice at a variety of levels, in direct proportion to the criticisms levelled at their theology and ideology. Clearly, 'power' is a vital 'key' in unlocking aspects of church theory and practice.

Power and Networking

The structure of Wimber's churches can be said to resemble a web-like network.[25] There are linkages between the personal and the organizational, and ties of various types at different levels of social organization.

In the first place, there are personal ties made between members. In the Vineyard network this is formally structured through 'kinship groups', and in Vineyard-friendly churches, the same end is achieved through 'home groups' or 'cell groups'. These groups tend to meet weekly in the home of a member, with group size usually limited to around twelve people, in order to encourage intimacy, close support and mutual accountability. There is usually a leader of the group, who will be an appointee of the more senior leaders. A typical Vineyard 'kinship group' will meet in an evening for about three hours. Prayer, praise, exercising the gifts of the Spirit and teaching generally occupy this time, although the group will be encouraged to develop a 'family feel' by adopting a broader range of activities that lead to a deep level of bonding at social and interpersonal levels.[26]

Second, links are forged between leaders. In all fundamentalist groups, personal, theological and directional unity amongst the leadership is vital: any significant diversity would weaken the power network and threaten to 'devalue' the place of the fundaments. Wimber and his churches are no exception to this rule. Even a cursory glance at Vineyard history shows that theological diversity cannot really be tolerated; over the years, a number of leaders have left the Vineyard or been forced to abdicate leadership responsibility.[27] The key to maintaining a leadership group, be it apostolic or prophetic, is to ensure that all the leaders are closely bonded together personally (thus providing a model for kinship), and ideologically, so the power of the fundaments and the unity they bring is reinforced. The greatest threat to the network is loss of control, which will result in loss of power. Control and power are thus maintained by limiting the range and scope of theological and experiential diversity at work within the group.

A third factor to consider is that of ritual activity. In Wimber's case, ritual activity is most obviously encountered through the agency of revivalism. Revivals (sometimes called 'Celebrations' or 'Conferences') emphasize movement unity: they promote religious fervour and intensify commitment. Less obviously, they serve to report individual and group triumphs and trials (prayer 'victories' or requests), and communicate ideological refinements. Revivals strengthen movement unity by powerful dramatization: intense group prayer for individuals, enthusiastic singing and built-up expectations all play their part.[28]

Fourth, there is what might be called 'organized federalism'. How can the members of a relatively exclusive fundamentalist group be sure they are believing and behaving in an appropriate manner? Answer: by a limited form of external validation that is sympathetic to the group. Typically, this takes the form of a fundamentalist group being linked, yet remaining distinct from, other like-minded groups or individuals. On an individual level Wimber's use of established figures from the world of North American revivalism is especially significant. For Wimber, the services of men like Leonard Ravenhill, Mike Bickle, Paul Cain and Jack Deere convey the credibility of Vineyard fundaments to their members, as well as providing a support network for revivalists which could be classed as a loose federation. At a group level, the Vineyard churches may also link themselves to other churches, not just individuals. In Britain, for example, the Vineyard is supported by a network or federation of sympathetic churches, ranging from Restorationist to Anglican.[29]

A final factor to be mentioned is that of ideological linkage. Vineyard ideology is communicated through narrative, books, tapes and conferences, which serve individuals and groups. The ideology undergirds the Vineyard's ability both to control its diversity and to ensure its unity: it is the power of Wimber's appealing ideology that binds organizationally disparate groups together. Even in a highly dispersed network like the Vineyard, it is vital that there is a form of unifying 'centralism'. At the heart of that centralism is control itself, which is achieved through a common ideology. That ideology is the key to the infrastructure of the movement, and allows beliefs to be maintained in the face of diversity and plurality. In Britain, for example, Anglicans, Baptists and Restorationists may agree to differ about organizational factors, yet have a considerable measure of spiritual and ideological unity, because they are 'Wimberites' or have been

'Wimberized'. It is core beliefs that provide the solid basis for
unity, and any consideration of church structure cannot afford to
ignore this.[30]

These five factors are clearly not exhaustive. However, their
mention does demonstrate that social organization in Wimber's
churches and those churches that apply his principles is a complex
affair, not reducible to one single factor. Ideology is perhaps most
crucial, yet it is nevertheless only one factor amongst many that
enables the web-like power structure of Wimber's churches to
function. At the centre of the power structure is *control*. The
nature of that control must ensure a common language is spoken,
and common narratives shared, even amongst a highly dispersed
group like the Vineyard. Control remains vital, and it is held by
the leadership, who guard the principal fundaments and interpret
them for the believers. Only when control is certain can power
be communicated, mediated and distributed; control enables the
network to thrive, and restore itself when damaged, and more will
be said about this in the conclusion.

Evaluation

Fundamentalist movements are best understood within the contexts
of power and network: they tend to be decentralized, sectarian
and web-like in structure. The leadership tends to be charismatic
rather than bureaucratic in nature. The personal commitment that
is so often characteristic of believers is dependent on mutual,
communicable and transferable charisma, such that effective
leadership is not irrevocably tied to certain individuals. In Wimber's
case, a steady turnover of leaders may actually enhance social
growth rather than destabilize it, although Wimber necessarily
remains the common personal and ideological link for Vineyard
members.

The sectarian character of fundamentalist groups like the
Vineyard occurs for a variety of reasons. It is partly funded by the
ideology of personal access to power, which leads to what we
might call a federal stress on individualism. This sounds like a
contradiction in terms, but it is an accurate description of the
state of affairs. The 'Church' is a collection of people who are
individually saved, individually sanctified and individually blessed:
personal testimony and the validity of one's own experiences of
God are highly prized in such communities. Any 'catholic' notions
of corporate endeavour or experience are generally very secondary.

It is under these conditions that segmentation and hierarchy thrive, since personal and ideological differences will always threaten the fragile unity that a fundamentalist group might enjoy.

The various segments of any fundamentalist group are linked into one network by factors that produce bonding and unity. These might involve the fostering of close personal ties between members (kinship), refining the ideology, or validating the network by referring to a federation of like-minded groups. Such a structure is capable of a high degree of adaptiveness, which is at least in part the genius of fundamentalism in contemporary society. Fundamentalism is not easily suppressed, and its unwillingness to engage in dialogue means that it can often penetrate different socio-economic and cultural groups without (initially) being compromised. This in itself is achieved by an emphasis on unity, which is seen as the best means of receiving and exporting the power of God. The chief enemy for fundamentalists is therefore diversity, which parallels its ideological and theological enemies: plurality and liberalism. Social organization in Wimber's churches is thus based soundly on 'bonding' the believer, to a notion of unity, to ideology, or to a leader.

7

A Theology of Power

Intrinsic to Christianity's identity is the recognition of its missionary or evangelistic vocation. If this is the case, then some type of apologetics will always be at the centre of its task. For fundamentalists, this is especially true in the twentieth century, where apologetics have been consistently conducted in terms of power. The truth of a tradition or teaching, of experience or eschatology, are all intended to protect fundamentals concerning power: the providence of an almighty God, his total control of history, nature and super-nature, and the accessibility of that divine power to human individuals who are willing to yield to it. Such fundaments have been plainly articulated throughout the twentieth century by their advocates in the face of increasing pluralism, relativism or liberalism, all of which threaten to dilute and destroy. Further still, as in all difficult periods of history – be it political or ideological instability – the problem of affirming the unlimited power of God requires a special sharpness. This is one reason why Wimber is a good case to study. In periods of uncertainty, those who preach certainty often flourish: liberalism is a luxury for another time.[1] Wimber, as a particularly sophisticated fundamentalist, is ideally adapted to appeal to constituents who are troubled by the complex and bewildering circumstances of the world in the late twentieth century. His constructive theology offers a way of affirming God's 'almighty power' at a time when it might seriously be in danger of being limited by a range of ideas and experiences.

Wimber's distinctive and particularly effective handling of power makes analysis of him particularly valuable. Few besides Wimber have grasped with such clarity the nature of the apologetic task before fundamentalists at the present time. Namely, that an argument for beliefs must do more than simply appeal to orthodoxy or tradition. It must actually reflect and demonstrate God's almighty power in an age where this is in danger of being compromised.

Wimber addresses the problem of affirming divine power in a variety of ways. However, each strategy can be seen as a form of simple dualism in its own right. The most common to occur in Wimber's writing is the gap that he portrays between reality and possibility. This strategy cuts across his work on topics such as healing, deliverance, the Church and the Kingdom of God. In each case, it is usual for Wimber to suggest that the subject concerned is lacking in power ('wholeness', 'healing', 'freedom', 'strength', etc.), and that via an experience or the application of a particular formula, dynamic and counter-subversive power can be realized. Wimber systematically teaches that this lack of power is reality for most people, yet it need not be: new possibilities exist, provided one yields to the power of God.

This necessarily implies that Wimber teaches that the individual believer or community is to be delivered out of bondage from one form of power into another. Thus, one never moves from a position of 'nothingness' or freedom into a relationship with God or Satan: the believer or non-believer is bonded to and empowered by either one or the other. There is no middle ground. This, of course, has a significant impact on how human experience is understood and processed by believers. The world is effectively broken up into a series of divisions – divine–demonic, soul–flesh, interior–exterior, to name but a few – such that an excuse always exists if God's power apparently fails.

There is an ironic dualism present in Wimber's ideology. Although many of the Vineyard worship songs allude to the closeness of God and the immediacy of the Spirit, there is nevertheless a distance that exists between God and the world. This distance is increasingly emphasized in Wimber's more recent writings on holiness, and, to a lesser extent, on prophecy. This 'gap' is partly traceable to Wimber's evangelical emphasis on the justice and wrath of God.[2] However, the chief source is surely the result of his emphasis on revival. To enable and prepare for revival, believers must be holy and pure; to be holy, they must accept that they are presently unholy and unclean; acceptance of this implies God is distant, unable to move closer to the community of faith until it has repented, and purged and cleansed itself of sin and unbelief.

The virtue of Wimber's approach to the power of God is that within the community of faith it is both plausible and believable. It does acknowledge human reality, suffering, evil and futility. It also acknowledges the possibility of transformation and of empowerment, and ultimately offers the hope of being connected to a source of utterly irresistible and almighty power. However, there are substantial problems with Wimber's theology of power; his hard and sharp dualism is just the beginning.

Analysis of Wimber's System

Throughout Wimber's writings, his discussion of divine power assumes some basic characteristics. It is real and ultimate power, that can move within and around believers. It seeks their co-operation, but is not prevented from operating where there is passive or active resistance. It is a power that is moving towards imposing itself, on the basis that creation and humanity are already in bondage to darker powers.

There is no evidence that Wimber is versed in theories of power from either sociology or theology. Yet with regard to divine power, we must begin by noting that Wimber appears at first sight to regard power as a 'thing-in-itself', that is, an event of supernatural origin rather than an occurrence arising out of human interaction. This is at odds with the much more complex and interrelated way of understanding the place of power in fundamentalist communities adopted here. Along with other scholars, I believe that power-related phenomena occurring in the Vineyard may have little or nothing to do with the exterior activity of divine power, or, for that matter, Satanic power.[3] What then is the appropriate form for addressing power-related phenomena in Wimber's works and churches, given that some of it might be of divine origin, and some of it the product of other factors, such as auto-suggestion, psychosomatic responses, or the effect of a charismatic personality?

From a social science perspective, the term 'power' is really an umbrella word for various modes of organization; it is not in any way a thing in itself. I have suggested that Clegg's thesis is useful here, since the model of circuits of power, functioning inductively for Wimber, appears to be the most fruitful method for systematizing and analysing the tremendous variety of phenomena and theology that occurs within the Vineyard. Wimber himself appears to have a much simpler view of power, which does not sit easily with the complexity of Clegg's conceptual framework, yet in actual fact, this is not quite so. Wimber does implicitly acknowledge the relatedness of power, even if he is shy of owning it. His work on healing, for example, recognizes that the power of God operates through an assortment of physical and parapsychological mechanisms: indeed, mechanisms and formulas play a large part in Wimber's power theology. Wimber also speaks a great deal about 'empowering', and often devotes considerable space in books and lectures to criticizing existing mechanisms within the Church that fail to demonstrate power (e.g., programme evangelism). In some of his early conferences up until 1986, he was especially critical of stress placed on knowledge, creeds or doctrine. These, he argued, are no substitute for actually experiencing the power of God; this of course, as we have already seen, was argued for via an inductive theological strategy.

Then there is the question of authority. Sociologically speaking, charismatic authority may be said to exist because it is attributed to the charismatic figure by followers. Wimber would agree with this: Jesus' authority was partly derived from the respect and admiration he earned from performing 'signs and wonders'. Yet Wimber would also say Jesus had an authority independent of human attribution, resulting from his divinity, which simply needed acknowledging rather than attributing. In other words, Jesus has a power that is independent from any 'circuit' or relatedness, although he enjoys both. With Jesus as the 'model' for believers, this Christology finds its way into Vineyard ecclesiology. Power and authority relationships are readily acknowledged, and understood to be necessary. Yet each believer also has a 'personal' authority or power, just like Jesus, which can be exercised at will, only in relation to the Father. Thus, if Jesus possessed authority and power independent of human attribution, so can believers. Inevitably, this can lead to unrestrained individualism and particularity; believers can sometimes imagine that they are at the centre of God's attention, at the expense of any wider commitments that divine power might have.[4]

Wimber maintains that it was the exercise of 'signs and wonders' and Jesus' charismatic authority that provided a 'model' for the apostles to copy. They could only replicate this behaviour once they themselves had been empowered by the same force that enabled Jesus. It is Wimber's contention that the Church has consistently been distracted by less important issues throughout history up until the present, and has often failed to demonstrate the power of God to the world; its prime responsibility. For Wimber, an undue emphasis on correct doctrine, church structure or sheer disobedience has led to the potential of God's power being eclipsed from the Church. This accounts for Wimber's interest in revival, the 'Third Wave', and other movements of the

Holy Spirit. These occurrences shake the Church, forcing it to abandon strategies or doctrines that have become too comfortable or ineffective. The Church is now forced again, just as it was in the time of the first apostles, to depend utterly on the transcendent power of God for its source of life and witness. Consistently, throughout his works, Wimber points to groups such as Jansenists, Methodists or Pentecostals as examples of people who have, in Clegg's words, 'virtually achieved a totality of power'.

Wimber's view of church history resembles Harnack's belief that the Church underwent a kind of 'Fall' in its first three centuries, getting too caught up in authority, orders, doctrine and creeds, and ultimately losing touch with the divine transcendence. In other words, the source and type of power operating in the early church shifted imperceptibly from the divine to the human. This view of history presents the problem of what has happened to God's almighty power, if it only appears to be working intermittently? Wimber's answer to this is found in his sharp dualism. The past and present age are only being 'invaded' by God's power, the fullness of the Kingdom is yet to come. Until then, God is at war with Satan, although the final victory is assured to Christ and the Church. Thus, any movement that appears to be near to achieving a totality of power – in Wimber's view, this would have to be a 'revival' of some kind – points to the potential of the Church, the superiority of God's power, and, ultimately, to the end of history, when God's power will be fully established throughout creation.

For Wimber, this victory is begun and ended in Christ, although it operates in a peculiar way. On the one hand, Wimber affirms mainstream modern evangelical thinking, which interprets the atonement in the light of the doctrine of penal substitution. That is to say, God is essentially angry with the world, its sin and rebellion. As a God of justice, this sin cannot go unaccounted for, and the deserved penalty for humanity is death and damnation. However, God is also merciful, so instead of punishing humanity and allowing it to incur the wrath that is due, Jesus, as Son of God, is sacrificed and punished in place of humanity. Wimber tends to affirm this type of approach in his more dogmatic works, but it is really only a fraction of the story. Wimber also believes humanity, nature and creation to be under the power of Satan. Thus, a second atonement theory, more familiar to Pentecostal believers, also operates in Wimber's theology. If anything, this theory is the more dominant of the two. Christ invades the earth as a type of 'guerilla leader', leading a subversive band of individuals who will ultimately counter Satan and his allies. Christ acts as an example to his followers, leading them in a heavenly revolt against the powers of darkness, which are presently 'sitting tenants'. Victory is finally achieved when Jesus is killed, the cross, ironically, becoming a 'self-destruct button' which Satan is lured into pressing. The death of Jesus leads to hell being 'emptied', and allows God to raise Christ, signifying the end of death as an insuperable enemy. This atonement theory also carries a number of other benefits for believers. It brings victory, peace and salvation for the present life, which, crucially, can be experienced now: Christ's death is not just about eternal life, but about the present quality of the individual believer's life. Thus, for Wimber, Christ's atonement is a process as well as a goal.

However, the stress on the acts of Christ, including his death, hide a deep weakness in Wimber's theology. He completely ignores any attempt to deal with the incarnation. For Wimber, the virgin birth is only significant because it is a miracle, and because it 'proves' Jesus' divinity. But mention of Christ's 'self-emptying' (*kenosis*), and the significance of his adoption of weakness (cf. Phil. 2.1–11) is not to be found. One of the weaknesses of fundamentalism, it is often alleged, is its inability to cope with paradox. The incarnation, 'strength made perfect in weakness', is surely one of the most critical paradoxes at the heart of the New Testament, yet it is nowhere discussed in depth by Wimber. There are three key reasons for this.

First, an acknowledgement of God's conscious identification with weakness in Jesus threatens the recovery of a full omnipotence. If the enterprise of fundamentalism is to be partly understood in terms of defending omnipotence against pluralism and liberalism, the suggestion that God chooses to limit himself in Christ implies weakness. The traditional route out of this paradox for fundamentalists is to focus on Christ's works, rather than his being, since the works are at least recorded as being acts that point to omnipotence. Second, the incarnation confers a status on humanity and reality that does not sit easily with Wimber's dualism, particularly in the realm of healing. Wimber's theology invites believers to become more than what they are: healed, whole, fulfilled or empowered. The consequence of this is that Christ's identity with those who cannot or will not change is undervalued. In this respect, critics of Wimber often allege that he has no theology of death or illness. Those who are permanently disabled, for example, can quite rightly point out that Wimber's theology implies they are unacceptable as they are, both to God and to society. Third, Christ's willingness to suffer, and ultimately to succumb to torture and death, is essentially passed over. Wimber's interest lies in what the death of Christ achieves, and who it affects. The actual fact of the death itself is, however, a problem for him, since it is quite plain that Christ either lost his power here, or chose not to use it. Neither of these options is really acceptable to Wimber: he does not conceive of God not using his power, or of it being limited. This accounts for the 'self-destruct button' theory of atonement, at least in part. The cross is not Christ voluntarily resigning his powers, and willingly suffering as a sign of his solidarity with the most broken of humanity. It is instead a kind of trick, an 'ambush' that commits Satan to a path that ultimately results in victory for God.

Difficulties in Wimber's System, and the Emerging Theory of Power

(i) JESUS AS POWER

As has already been noted, the ideological focus of Vineyard worship tends towards pressing the theme of Christ the King, enthroned in glory. Christ is the glorious object of worship, the mediator of love and power to his people, but rarely the one who in his humanity exemplifies a way of life into the activity of God. Closely connected with this is a theology that believes divine power can be demonstrated not only in the life of Christ, but also in the life of the individual believer.[5] What suffers in this theology is the self-giving of Christ on the cross, the very abdication of omnipotence, in the wider interests of meeting creation in love, which necessarily includes risking rejection, and, ultimately, death.

Clearly, the power of Christ (and God) portrayed is a supernatural brute force, even though this is masked by Wimber through his ideological stress on love and intimacy. The widespread use of militaristic language in Vineyard worship discloses the fact that the programme envisaged by power evangelism will always place respect for humanity and loving relationship in subservience to a sharper spiritual agenda; an all too common feature of fundamentalist communities. In Wimber's case, this can partly be tracked in the selective appropriation of Old Testament texts, both in ideology and theology. In worship, for example, suggestive phrases about 'taking the promised land' or being 'led into victory' appear to imply a thirst for dominance and self-assertion. In theology, similar problems frequently emerge in a variety of places: evangelism, spiritual warfare and healing, to name but a few. Of course, there is a peculiar irony here. In the desire to recover the experience and conditions of the first apostles, which gave rise to substantial numerical church growth, charismatic fundamentalists often look to the Old Testament for guidance more than the New Testament (the first apostles had no New Testament), and are often just as selective in their choice of texts and application as their forebears.[6] Wimber places Christ at the head of a Church that is intended to imitate him, yet a number of cardinal problems arise directly out of this.

The first is the theme of weakness.[7] Many aspects of the Christian life (struggle, weakness, endurance, powerlessness, etc.), receive little attention from Wimber, except as episodes or patterns to be overcome. There seems to be little recognition of the possibility, as von Balthasar has suggested, that we may sometimes be led into a sharing of Christ's sufferings, and that God might be most expressive in the 'gap' that exists between desolation and triumph.[8] The relegation of real human weakness in the power evangelism programme is mirrored by the lack of focus on divine power being 'made perfect in weakness' (2 Cor. 12.9). Granted, the cross is a frequent topic, but only as a demonstration of power, to be seen in the light of the resurrection and the defeat of Satan.

In the interests of protecting the omnipotence of God in the face of modernity, the delicate balance between love and power is disturbed. What is lost is the realization that although God is omnipotent, power over creation has been renounced, and God instead only approaches his creatures with love. There is, too, some confusion over the actual *nature* of weakness. On the one hand, weakness is something to be emulated: Christ became weak, and those who follow him are invited to be weak, not powerful (2 Cor. 13.4, Heb. 5.12, 2 Cor. 1.27, etc.). Yet there is also the weakness that is to be overcome: moral or personal (1 Thess. 5.12), sickness, and lastly, economic (Acts 20.35).[9] Clearly, the burden of Wimber's power theology lies in acting upon the weakness that is to be overcome, rather than the weakness that is to be copied. The natural appeal of power evangelism is that it takes advantage of a modern condition in which power is greatly esteemed, and weakness is undervalued. This condition has itself arisen because of the perceived problems modernity and pluralism pose to Christianity. The inductive response, especially when practised by fundamentalists, is to renew their experience of God as omnipotent, and then to systematically reassert this in dogma that counters the influence of any prevailing power. Yet Jesus' incarnation is a deliberate abdication of total power and authority. Although he did perform acts that overcame various types of weakness, both in himself (e.g., temptation narratives) and others (e.g., healing, deliverance, etc.), his life was one of sharing and solidarity with a pathologically weak humanity. He did not just teach the value of weakness and utter dependence before God, but actually lived it, and raised its status in the life of the Godhead (Phil. 2.1–13). From his birth to his death, and even in resurrected glory, Jesus risked weakness against certainty, love against power.

Inextricably linked to weakness is the question of Christ's suffering. Here again, Wimber's power theology raises major problems. It is true that there is ample evidence in the ministry of Jesus that the God whom he reveals to us is the God who discloses himself with mighty signs of his presence and activity. God stands against evil and smites it with his power, and in parts of the New Testament followers of Christ are clearly expected to do likewise. Yet there is also a different perspective: Jesus begins 'to teach them that the Son of Man must suffer many things' (Mark 8.31). How is this so, if all Christ has to do is exercise his divine power against the weaker powers of Satan and the world? How does the suffering of Christ fit into power evangelism? The Gospels appear to offer a dynamic in which Jesus does not control and destroy the enemy, but rather, surrenders himself to the worst those enemies can actually do. The crucifixion of Jesus is the summary of God's respect for creation and its freedom. God expresses himself in suffering: people are allowed to be themselves, even to wrong and ignore God, and show disrespect to the point of killing. This is not met with counter-force, however, and neither is the cross a 'booby-trap' in which Satan accidentally destroys himself by meddling with a greater power. The suffering of God – supremely exemplified in Christ on the cross – shows a willingness to go through the final destructive experience, and so respect the power that is given to the world. Equally, the resurrection does not simply reverse this, responding to the taunt 'Come down from the cross' a few days later. It is the overcoming of evil and death in a way that affirms yet judges earthly powers, and exposes their limits.[10]

Proper attention to the suffering of Christ shows that Wimber's power theology presses omnipotence to a degree that eclipses God's self-giving love. It is in weakness, vulnerability, suffering and in death that Christ overcomes power, although his 'power encounters' do demonstrate that he can more than match the exercise and effect of Satan's power. Yet ultimately, he does not choose this way for himself: Christ gradually abandons 'signs and wonders', as his will and life converge with God's heart at the pinnacle of Golgotha. Thomas Smail comments:

> This is not the way of superior and coercing power; it is the way of self-giving love. In the New Testament, it is the cross that gives the love of God its meaning and definition ... He does not rescue people by bursting violently into the prison from the outside but by going into the prison himself with them, so that in the presence of his love the locks are turned and the doors swing open.[11]

So, divine self-giving, which expresses itself fully and decisively at the heart of human history at Calvary, is greater than all manifestations of coercive power, whether natural or supernatural.[12]

Many peculiar doctrines occur in Wimber's theology as a direct result of his not having an incarnational basis to his Christology.[13] One of the key weaknesses is the explicit divorce between the crucified Christ and the Holy Spirit. Life in the Spirit and in the Church is shaped by conformity to the image and likeness of Christ. This conformity, however, can be arrived at through suffering and weakness: to be 'sealed by the Spirit' is to be marked by the shame of Good Friday as well as the glory of Easter. In the Gospel of John, the Spirit is given with nail-marked hands to the disciples (John 20.22–3), in sharp contrast to the account in Acts.

(ii) THE SPIRIT AS FORCE
We have noted previously that Wimber's treatment of the Spirit often reduces him to a brute, supernatural force ('God is not a gentleman'). Just as some fundamentalists locate the prime source of their (and God's) power in a text or a particular tradition, so Wimber, in common with other charismatic fundamentalists, locates the evidence for God's omnipotence in the activity of the Spirit. The so-called 'Third Wave' is a reassertion of power over a world in need of convincing, convicting and saving, and as a movement of God, in Wimber's thinking, it gives the Church the resources to be an agent of God's power, establishing the conditions for the Kingdom of God to be built in the present.

However, as we have suggested in the previous section, the

works of power that Jesus performed – enabled by the Spirit – are not to be divorced from either the incarnation or the self-giving of Christ at the cross. The compartmentalism between 'power encounters' and suffering love is a false one. An example of this is Wimber's citation of various Gospel passages that show Jesus regularly healing people and casting out demons, as part of his daily work (e.g., Matt. 8.16). Yet Wimber often fails to acknowledge that the Jesus who performed these miracles did so in order to 'fulfil what was spoken by the prophet Isaiah, "He took up our infirmities and bore our diseases"' (Matt. 8.17). The Synoptic Gospels align Jesus' signs and wonders with his suffering: we are not intended to see Jesus' activity as the 'hurling of divine energy against demonic evil'.[14] The power at work in Jesus is the power of the servant of God, who shares our sufferings, carries diseases, and endures utter failure, rejection and death.

Similar problems exist with Wimber's reading of the Acts of the Apostles, and other parts of the New Testament. In Acts, Wimber's focus tends to be on particular episodes in which healings or deliverance took place, and the Church grew numerically as a result. Preferred accounts for Wimber, used extensively at the Vineyard and beyond, all validate present practice. For example, the story of Philip and the Ethiopian Eunuch (Acts 8) is interpreted as an exemplary use of words and knowledge for evangelistic purposes; the account of Ananias and Sapphira (Acts 5) serves to remind believers to submit to apostles and prophets; and the incident concerning the failure of Jewish exorcists (Acts 19) is used to demonstrate the superiority of genuine believers wielding the power of Jesus. What is generally absent from Wimber's reading of Acts is any mention of the disciples being called to suffer in the same way that Jesus did. Martyrdom, imprisonment, public beatings, conflict, disasters and rejection play little part in Wimber's inductive restructuring of the message of Acts. Wimber divorces 'signs and wonders', part of the work of the Spirit, from a leading into a life that involves sharing in Christ's pain, which is also part of the Spirit's work.

This is clearly one of the fundamental problems in Wimber's view of the Spirit. The power of the Spirit is deemed by Wimber to be a force that stands apart from the world, firing 'laser beams of divine energy'[15] against other powers, which must necessarily be defeated. It is not a subtle view of the Holy Spirit. There is no mention at all of one of the prime functions of the Spirit, namely to 'lead us [all] into all truth' (i.e., reality). In Wimber's view, the task of the Spirit is to move believers well beyond this goal: 'calling common people to move above and beyond natural laws and walk with him in the realm of the miraculous'.[16] If ordinary life is to be shunned because the Spirit is only truly available on a different plane, then God's genuine engagement with the world in Christ is reduced to a charade. Surely the realms of reality and the Spirit are the same? Of course, Wimber's view of the Spirit accounts in part for the agenda of the 'signs and wonders' programme. The Spirit can be coercive and brute, for an end is achieved through the means, and each justifies the other. If ordinary people can witness the Spirit at work in a way that is demonstrably powerful – as it was in the Book of Acts – then people will experience God's power for themselves, and the Church will grow.

We are entitled to ask at this point about the nature of the power funding this view of the Spirit. Essentially, it is a power that directs individuals to Jesus or the Father, and initiates them into the life of the Church. There is nothing necessarily at fault with this, namely the notion of the Spirit as a 'witness'. But what is lacking, is any concept of this power as being a power of love. This is ironic when one considers the attention Wimber pays to intimacy with God, a major feature of his ideology. Yet the power that leads individuals to this experience is seldom spoken of in terms of love by Wimber, except in connection with healing. However, the power of God, the Holy Spirit, *is* the power of love because, according to Christian tradition, the Spirit does not stand apart from the events of Good Friday and Easter (cf. 1 John 4.8, 16). God is love, and that love constitutes the very being of God as Father, Son and Holy Spirit: it is this power that creates and redeems, in active participation with the world and its creatures. The world is not made, saved or treated by a brute, coercive force, but by a self-emptying process that is at the heart of God's gift of himself to humanity. Consequently, the power of the Spirit can be nothing less than the power of love that is poured out on all flesh and into the hearts of believers. Gifts of the Spirit and fruits of the Spirit are agents of love, not power, intended for a deeper level of individual and communal relationality. All too often, fundamentalist groups treat gifts, be they tongues or texts, prophecy or tradition, as tools of God that assault creation, yet the gifts of the Spirit are not designed to be coercive by those who experience them. They are God's speech to a world in need of restoration, where signs of love are frequently eclipsed by demonstrations of power.

Wimber's distinctive views of the work and works of Christ, and the follow-up work of the Spirit, clearly point to God as an invading power, working from without. This has no doubt arisen, at least in part, because of the desire to re-establish a foundational base for omnipotence, which most fundamentalists think has been eroded. On one level, we might sympathize with this. Defending the possibilities of God's almighty power appears to be a noble task, particularly in the face of the modern situation. However, there are a number of casualties as a result of this stance.

The first problem to note is ironic; namely, that an insistence by Wimber on the omnipotence of the Spirit in the life of the Church leads to a dilution of omnipresence. The Spirit becomes privatized, the property of the faithful community that is in touch with the 'Third Wave'. Yet orthodox Christian tradition must surely assert that 'there are no longer any periods devoid of the Spirit', or indeed, places.[17] Wimber's defence of omnipotence ultimately leads to its weakening, since it is only really possible for him to speak of the Spirit working in specific episodic ways that connect with results, such as healing or church growth. A second problem arises from this observation: the ambiguity and risk of the Spirit's work is dissipated. A defensive view of the Spirit is over-protected by the community, so that it becomes withdrawn and tribal. This is a common feature of most fundamentalist groups, and it is maintained in such communities by believing that God's greatest power or revelation is only understood by a few, who must therefore act as guardians of the truth for the good of the world.

A third problem, and one to which we have already alluded, is the manufactured schism that exists between the power of the Spirit and the Spirit as love. Paul tells the Corinthians to 'Make love your aim, and earnestly desire the spiritual gifts', especially prophecy (1 Cor. 14.1). Yet as we have seen, the gifts are pursued as signs of power, not solely for love. This is true of prophecy and words of knowledge in particular, which may be used to coerce, shame, alarm and instil a sense of fear in the individual. All too often, prophecy witnesses not to love, but to the charisma and power of the prophet, and to the power of the community that witnesses its action.[18] Such problems are inevitable in a community where there is no working Trinitarian doctrine. Hierarchies of power remain in place, and the ideal of loving interdependence, mutuality and respect for both internal and external relationships is lost. Wimber's doctrine of the Spirit is a forceful presentation, but one which leaves little space for freedom and love in the life of God, as he relates to his creation.

(iii) THE CHURCH AS POWER BROKER

Many theologians in the twentieth century have, in their own particular way, differentiated between the 'form' and 'essence' of the Church. In practice, this distinction has approximated 'essence' with the transcendent and the Church that is to *be* when Christ returns. The 'form', however, is generally connected with how the Church organizes itself according to its historical tradition.[19] Of course, in making this somewhat sharp distinction, most theologians acknowledge that the two are intimately interrelated. Yet for the critique here, the distinctions are most helpful.

In the first place, for Wimber, the Church is to be an organization dedicated to promoting divine power in the material world. Yet his doctrine of the Church is not much more developed than this. In common with almost all other fundamentalists, Wimber lacks a theological estimate of what the Church is: he seems to show no interest in it as a catholic or corporate body, or even as the 'body of Christ'.[20] The practical necessity of visible communities is recognized, but their identity and existence is entirely subordinated to the task of individuals and communities holding and showing divine power. Effectively, the Church is simply a basic unit, a collection of people who can do more together if united than individuals who operate on their own. Second, the distinction between 'form' and 'essence' gives a further insight into Wimber's dualism. Many fundamentalists have appealed to the essence of the gospel in order to critique the present form of the Church, and Wimber is no exception. His power theology contributes most directly to his ecclesiology at this point. By contrasting the omnipotence of God (Father, Son and Holy Spirit) with the impotence of the Church, Wimber creates a gap between what the Church is and what it could be like. Appealing to the imminence of the last days has a similar effect, namely contrasting the (alleged) conditions of life under the Kingdom of God with those of the present Church.[21] Into this gap is placed Wimber's power theology, which forms the basis for church structure: equipping individuals and groups to be organized around demonstrating God's power through signs and wonders.

There are many problems with this approach. For one thing, there is little to prevent the community of believers from mapping their own desires for power and success onto the character of

God. Equally, any doctrine of the Church is clearly not taken seriously. More seriously perhaps, the absence of an incarnational theology leads to a situation in which the community of believers feels called to dominate and rule, not serve and suffer. Those theologians who have criticized the ideology or ecclesiology present in modern renewal songs are unanimous in their view that the Church presented in the worship is too triumphant, and too remote from real life.[22] Perhaps the most serious charge, however, is that there is no liberation from idols of power in such an ecclesiology. The Church which does not reveal the crucified Jesus but only the exalted Christ inevitably runs the risk of honouring exaltation itself, whilst rejecting the way of the cross. A number of considerations arise out of this. Believers identify Christianity too closely with power and success, and fail to find a place for the suffering Christ and the work of the Spirit in forming the Church around Good Friday and Easter Sunday. The full life of Jesus can only be manifested through the Church if its form is like the death of Jesus.[23] Where this dialectical process is broken, as in the 'signs and wonders' movement, there is little to prevent believers from idolizing power, or pursuing glory and exaltation either individually or communally, under the mistaken assumption that this is a sign or reflection of God's glory dwelling within their work and worship.

Some of the observations cited above are reflected in the work of Thomas Smail. Smail, a prominent critic of charismatic and revivalist theology, has also suggested that the thirst for power in communities like Wimber's has quenched love as a basis for ministry:

My own experience of charismatic renewal strongly suggests that if some of its leaders were as concerned with being men of love as they are with being men of power, because they saw that the only power the Spirit has is the power of love, it would be a more wholesome thing than it has sometimes been.[24]

Wimber's struggle with power and love in his theology is replayed, inevitably, in his view of the Church. The use of spiritual gifts in building up the Church, albeit healing, deliverance or prophecy, are often executed with insensitivity, and a degree of force. This approach has several costs. For instance, the expectation of believers is often that God will intervene on their behalf with power, enabling escape from calamity or dramatic rescue from evil. This is at the expense of appreciating that God sometimes takes us *through* evil, not *out* of it. Jesus himself was not rescued from death, even though he saved others from sickness and death: his way of life is exemplified by enduring sufferings, not transcending them. Equally, an ecclesiology of power often fails to understand the mission of the Church where no demonstrable power-related phenomena are occurring, only the power of love. What does the 'signs and wonders' movement have to say about Christian communities that simply offer love and acceptance, where perhaps no healings take place at all? Surely we must say that such places are as capable of showing God's power in its prime form (love), and that 'signs and wonders' look rather shallow by comparison.[25] There are individuals and communities too, that shun power altogether and choose to witness via a 'suffering presence', taking on board the conditions of others in a gesture of solidarity, love and friendship. This is the power of love incarnate, the body of Christ acting creatively and transformingly on suffering, offering only love in the face of whatever resistance.

Whilst all of the observations above tell of major weaknesses in Wimber's ecclesiology, the primary problem is this: his Christology and doctrine of the Spirit convert the Church (and its leaders) into God's power brokers. In spite of a simplistic, weak ecclesiology, Wimber's theology places the Church at the centre of God's attention, and locates God's power as coming *through* the Church to the world. Of course, this seriously weakens any doctrine of omnipresence, and ignores the reality of God being 'ahead of all evangelism, carrying on his mission in the world ... the abundance of God is poured out way beyond the boundaries of the Church, and [the] vital task is in discerning this abundance and accepting it with joy'.[26] This distortion has arisen in Wimber's theology as a direct result of his linking 'signs and wonders' to church growth, and then of elevating the concept to a status where it is deemed central to God's (successful) activity in modern society.

That criticism in itself might give the impression that with Wimber, as with other forms of fundamentalism, we are dealing with a distortion of something that is basically sound. Yet the very heart of Christian communication is being questioned: is the gospel primarily about power, or is it about love? An emphasis on power generally leads to the good news being presented in mechanistic or functional terms: it is useful for meeting needs, fulfilling, meeting crises or limitations or solving problems. It is a gospel that repairs things that have gone wrong (especially in healing ministries), or is essentially practical in a host of ways. The seductiveness of this is that it is partly true: there is indeed good news for problematic situations and persons. The flaw lies in the inability to appreciate the freedom and expansiveness of God, and the universality of his activity and love. Of course, recognizing the comprehensiveness of God's activity throughout creation leaves little room for 'monopolizing' God's power, and for the establishment of fundamentalist groups whose identity depends to some extent on believing that they have more insight into and more of God's power than other groups. An appreciation of the universality of God's love and power can therefore prevent the error that many fundamentalist groups commit; namely, acting as God's primary power broker, which in turn elevates the self-importance of the Church to the degree that God's own free activity is ignored.

Three final observations need making about how Wimber's ecclesiology relates to the world. First, as far as the church fellowship is concerned, hardship and suffering are things to be avoided. Even the recognition that *genuine* community involves pain and hard work, as well as celebration, is suppressed. This tends to encourage what I have called 'neurotic religion': believers subscribe to the Church to avoid pain, rather than deal with its reality. Second, the activity of God beyond the boundaries of the Church is seldom discussed. This does tend to fuel the arguments of those who accuse fundamentalists of being sectarian in character. The world beyond the Church – especially in worship songs – is only considered in so far as it is a stronghold of evil, and therefore the object of spiritual warfare. God's purposes for the non-human world are only obliquely implied in the affirmation of God's universal Kingship. As one commentator has put it, fundamentalist ecclesiology can be characterized as 'the Bride of Christ [spending] rather too long looking in the mirror'.[27] Third, and last, a fundamentalist ecclesiology like Wimber's takes little interest in social responsibility and issues of injustice. Costly acts of compassion or suffering in solidarity with victims of human hurt are rarely emphasized in worship or teaching. This directly echoes the root failure of most fundamentalists to grapple with the significance of the incarnation of Christ.

(iv) EVALUATION: DOCTRINES OF CHRIST, THE SPIRIT AND
THE CHURCH

I have attempted to show that Wimber's view of the Church can
only be understood in the light of his understandings of Christ
and the Spirit. Not only that, the weaknesses inherent in his
theology are necessarily imported into the ethos of the Vineyard.
For example, the emphasis on the works of Christ, at, say, the
expense of his incarnation, is often reflected in church life by the
gifts of the Spirit being valued more highly than the fruits of
the Spirit. Wimber's central concern in the 'signs and wonders'
programme, and in his power theology, is to argue for the
omnipotence of God. This is not just an abstract ideal, but a
radical concern to see the Church reflect and demonstrate the
power of God that is at its disposal, provided it is faithful.
Numerical church growth, following the witnessing of 'signs and
wonders', is simply confirmation of God's almightiness over all
other forms of power.

The weakness of his system is that God's universal love, which
respects creation and grants it freedom to respond in a myriad of
ways, is subjugated by the power theology. Not only that, the
power of God is taken into the Church, such that those who need
it may only receive it by witnessing its action, and then by opting
into a new community. In the interests of defending and exporting
the power of God, the dualism between Church and world becomes
too sharp. The omnipresence of the Spirit becomes meaningless,
and God (and the Church) are reduced to intervening power agents
in the world dominated by other powers. In such a theology, the
God (or Church) that is known in love, pain and redeeming
self-surrender is lost.

But why is love more important than power? Clearly, one of
the dangers of an over-simplistic appreciation of omnipotence is
that human freedom becomes meaningless. Yet, omnipotence can
be an agent of love, not in the sense of control, but in the sense
that the *capacity* for God to be fully involved in and fully willed
in creation as its sustainer remains. But it is not a *controlling*
power in the manipulative sense of the word. It is rather a *loving
capacity* that can enable creation to become fully what it is intended
to be through loving co-operation with God. The divine presence
should not *restrict* human activity, it should enable it. God's
primary being is love (1 John 4.7–12) not power, and those who
live in that love will live in God, and God will live with them.

This, rather than a naked assertion of power, is what will bring about redeeming transformation.

Thus, we hold that (in the memorable phrase of Barth), Wimber's theology makes God 'the prisoner of his own power'.[28] In place of this, I wish to propose a picture of God that involves making no denial of God's omnipotence, no reduction in the affirmation of divine power. What it does involve is a modification of the way in which the concept of that power is understood. That point has been well put in a recent book by Thomas Tracy. 'God', he writes,

> creates a field of other agents whose integrity he respects and so whose independent actions condition his choices. This amounts to a purposeful limitation of the scope of his own activity, but it does not represent a renunciation of omnipotence, but rather a renunciation of certain uses of power.[29]

This 'field of. . .agents', or network encourages freedom of response, relationships that are reciprocal, and, ultimately perhaps, love. This same fundamental point may be made in a slightly different way. I have been speaking so far in terms of a modification of the understanding of God's power. One could speak instead of a qualification of the concept of power by that of love. It is in this form that the point is made by another recent writer, Grace Jantzen. She states:

> The proper order of priority in understanding the attributes of God must be to take his love as central, and modify our ideas of omnipotence. . .in terms of it. . .Creative love is love which gives autonomy to that which it creates; and though omnipotence can be limited by nothing else, it is limited by love. . .If God's power is understood as the expression of his love, then God's power is his power to give independence, autonomy, even to creatures over whom, strictly speaking, he is sovereign.[30]

Conceptually there may be disadvantages in speaking of one attribute of God having priority over another. It runs the risk of suggesting some kind of tension within the being of God. Nevertheless there are compensating gains in the vividness with which the main point can be conveyed. This is powerfully expressed in some words of Søren Kierkegaard:

> O wonderful omnipotence and love! A man cannot bear that his 'creations' should be something directly over against him; they

should be nothing and therefore he calls them creations with contempt. But God, who creates out of nothing, who almightily takes from nothing and says 'Be!' lovingly adds 'Be something even over against me'. Wonderful love, even his omnipotence is under the power of love. Hence the reciprocal relationship. If God were only the Almighty, there would be no reciprocal relation; for the creation is nothing for the Almighty. But it is something for love.[31]

This is the understanding of God I wish to propose in the face of Wimber's theology. God is known supremely in love, not power. Attempts to reassert naked omnipotence via controlling agents will inevitably lead to a distorted view of God, with a community surrounding it that will consequently mirror the distortion.[32]

8

Further Reflections on Fundamentalism, Revivalism and Power

Reading Wimber's work in the light of power, as I have done, can indicate some possible directions which theology and sociology might take in dealing with the phenomena of fundamentalism generally.

First, an analysis of order and structure in fundamentalist groups or movements will always point to the location of power. Generally, this will be hierarchical, although there will be more than one type of hierarchy. For example, the elders may have power over the laity, and an inerrant Bible power over forms of worship. These hierarchies can work in harmony or competition, but communal progress takes place when power has been correctly appealed to and deployed. The order and structures of a fundamentalist group are generally designed for maximum demonstration of power, which in turn validates the authenticity of the approach.

Second, focusing on the inherent dualism within most fundamentalist movements can reveal the agenda of a group, as well as indicating the type of power being appealed to. For example, an appeal to an inerrant text or persons tends to locate power in certainty, rather than the (perceived) powerlessness that is suggested by the uncertainty of the modern situation. Wimber himself equates power with strength.

Third, we must accept that each fundamentalist group will have a different sociology and theology of power. Power is not a single concept, but a multiple reality. Understanding how fundamentalism functions will require certain questions to be asked of the agents of power, both human and divine. For example, what text or tradition has authority here? Which person has the gift or office or charisma to protect or interpret it? What are the common experiences of divine power that believers are expected to own if they are to be members? What is the divine power supposed to do, and to whom? How is that divine power mediated? How is it shown, and what is its effect?

Ultimately, as with most fundamentalists, crucial theological questions are raised by Wimber's distinctive charismatic fundamentalism. For example, is God all-powerful? Does he intervene dramatically, as 'signs and wonders' testifies? Is there any limit to what God can do? Wimber is susceptible to a common problem that can be located in most forms of fundamentalism. In attempting to defend the power of God via a power-centred theology, God's very being is presented in a distorted manner. Instead of God's omnipotence being an agent of his love (i.e., being), his love becomes an agent of his power. To ask 'Is God almighty and omnipotent?' is to ask a profound question. Wimber's answer would be 'yes'; God is the highest power. Yet Christian tradition primarily asserts that God *is* love; his all-powerfulness is an agent in the service of that being. Wimber puts God's love in the service of his power. Orthodoxy would insist that this should be reversed.

We see this distortion in Wimber's Christology. In Christ, Wimber sees an act of powerful intervention initiated by God. Jesus demonstrates 'signs and wonders' to signify the power of God. It is a mistake to take instances of 'power encounters' like the healing miracles of Jesus, and read these as though God were flexing his muscles against the powers of darkness. The healing miracles of Christ were often his particular response of love to needy individuals. Sometimes just a word would be spoken (cf. Luke 7.36–50; John 4.1–26, 8.1–11, etc.), rather than a physiological transformation brought about. Where physical healing does take place, it is often for individuals who are shunned by the prevailing religious institutions, or on the fringes of society. This could be because of the nature of their illness (e.g., leprosy, haemorrhaging, etc.), or their sin (e.g., the man born blind in John 9), or their social status (e.g., tax collector, gentile, servant of a soldier, etc.). The key to the healings in most cases is loving the unloved, blessing them in the midst of witnesses who had themselves often colluded with the alienating processes of society. Sometimes, this was true even of Jesus' followers. Again, Wimber fails to note this. Jesus seldom healed friends. Nor did he locate his healing ministry in a community of faith, in order to build up his congregation; it was more usually offered to those people who were explicitly or implicitly excluded from such gatherings. Christian tradition asserts that Christ is the embodiment of God's love, and not (primarily) his (brute) power or empowering capability. God risks all in being embodied in Christ for the sake of love and relationship, not for power and dominance. 'Signs and wonders' are tokens of love, not power, which converge at Calvary. At the cross, there are no miracles, for all the signs and wonders that went before are focused in the cross – love risking knowing and relationship, and thus even rejection – the way into God.

Provisional Postscript

Some points follow that might also hold good for other kinds of contemporary fundamentalism.

1. The type of faith that operates within fundamentalist or charismatic Christian communities is essentially private in nature. What is valued most is the experience of the individual, which authenticates the inductive strategy, and affirms the faith of community. One problem likely to arise from this approach is that of fragmentation or chaos. Theological and sociological scholars of fundamentalist and charismatic groups are constantly having to revise their categorization, since experience, the ground of belief, is always shifting.[1] Groups splinter, reform, re-align and then splinter again, with a regularity that is traceable to the foundational inductive power strategy. Wimber's churches will not be immune from these developments. If he manages to maintain unity amongst Vineyards in his own lifetime, he will be the exception, not the rule. History shows us that most if not all fundamentalist-charismatic groups split during or after the passing of the first generation of leaders.[2]

2. Wimber's teachings and appeal will survive him. Like Restorationism or Revivalism, Wimber's distinctive brand of charismatic fundamentalism has found its way into many mainline denominations, mostly via established evangelical groups that were already within. Many will adopt his 'signs and wonders' programme, as a viable means to church growth or for evangelism. As such, it is not unreasonable to suppose that his theology will outlast his churches, although Vineyards may not continue after his death.

3. Wimber's suggestion that there has been a series of fundamental discontinuities, historical and spiritual, between the Church as it is described in the New Testament and the Church as it is today (i.e., a 'Fall'), will almost certainly be challenged. The strategy that calls the Church back to experience the power

the first century church knew is always threatened by what Berger calls 'mellowness'. That is to say, there comes a point in the life of any church when it is realized that an attempt to live the past in the present has little appeal, and risks a disengagement from reality. The ultimate price to pay for this is marginalization. Wimber's Vineyards are not yet in danger of this, but neither are they immune from it. The lack of good theodicy and a realistic Christology are serious problems: without them, Wimber may not be able to prevent Vineyards from becoming charismatic or mystical sects, following his death.

4. The insistence on the immanence of God may become hard to sustain, especially if a prolonged period of decline takes place in the Vineyard. Proclaiming the Kingdom of God can itself become an agent for empowering. However, if eschatology is at first over-realized, what happens when it eventually becomes manifestly clear that it is in fact unrealized? Wimber has already had to face this in a limited way: the prophesied revivals for Britain have not occurred. Whilst a certain amount of 'cognitive dissonance' can be tolerated by a group, too many prophecies passing their 'sell-by date' does create problems.[3] It necessitates revision and reconstruction, and not all followers will subscribe to reinterpretation: some will leave as a direct result of promises not being fulfilled. This will no doubt be due in part to the conflation that takes place between the immanence of God and the charisma of the leader. As Bryan Wilson notes in *The Noble Savages*:

> Clearly the specific prophecies of the charismatic leader normally fail; the types and ranges of illnesses that he can miraculously cure are limited; the essential miracles are heard about rather than seen; the expectations of his followers are always eventually disappointed.[4]

5. The notion that the Church is fallen but is now being restored will prove problematic. Typically, groups that have claimed this in the past have prosecuted a new or apparently lost doctrine or programme for the Church. But the programme itself is seldom as comprehensive or as diverse as the body it is dealing with – the Church. In response to negativity, inaction or scepticism, fundamentalist groups tend to emphasize holiness and discipline, in order to counter the menace of mellow liberalism. But the emphasis on holiness and discipline is not without cost: some within the community of believers will refuse tighter strictures, or

an increase in the power of leaders. Pursuing high quality discipleship often comes at the expense of quantity – of people.

6. The leaders within the Vineyard will find their apostolic and prophetic offices hard to sustain, especially during periods of decline. Generally, it was their charisma and the charismatic situation that established the basis for the office. Competition from other groups, even similar ones, tends to increase choice, break monopolies, and ultimately dissipate the power of leaders. This process has already begun for Wimber: once the major exponent of 'signs and wonders', he now finds himself relativized as just one of many fundamentalists operating in that revivalist tradition.

7. Wimber's distinctive power-centred emphasis will lose its lustre. The agenda of 'signs and wonders', the role of powerful prophets and the function of dynamic praise in Wimber's thinking are intended to produce two major occurrences. First, the believer feels closer to God, and experiences God's power as of old. Second, the Church grows numerically as a result of witnessing such occurrences. There will come a point, however, when some believers no longer have faith in these programmes. Anything from dissatisfaction with results to weariness with immanence may produce this crisis of confidence. At that point, some may begin to question whether God really does meet us in and through power, or whether he has temporarily abdicated omnipotence, and only meets us in his love, this alone being the means of our empowerment.

Renewal, Revival and Healing

This book has attempted to deal with the significance of words and wonders for fundamentalists. It is really beyond the scope of this investigation to ask, 'What actually happens at healing and revival meetings?' Are people really healed? Does God intervene as the result of prayers, and, through people, perform miracle cures? Are 'miracle-workers' like Morris Cerullo genuinely gifted, or simply charlatans? Are occurrences like the recent 'Toronto Blessing' a movement of the Holy Spirit, or a sophisticated example of auto-suggestion and mass hysteria?[5] It should be stated immediately that there are no simple 'answers'. Indeed, attempting to unravel the spaghetti of issues in this field is virtually impossible. Some years ago, a journalist, commenting on a complex political situation, remarked, 'Anyone who thinks that they know what is

going on here does not really understand the situation.' The
delicacy of material and testimony requires careful handling. Yet
it is the task of theology to inquire into the mystery of God, and
of the life and faith posited in humanity. So I want to suggest
some ways of interpreting renewal and revival-related phenomena
in a way that will open discussion rather than closing it.

Wherever Morris Cerullo conducts his missions, questions about
reality and authenticity accompany him. Cerullo's supporters
clearly believe that miracles do happen at his rallies; God does
heal, and people who can bear testimony to this can usually be
produced.[6] Cerullo's detractors, on the other hand, assert that the
cause of the healing is more to do with Cerullo's style of ministry;
powerful rhetoric, heightened expectations and congregational
dynamics are as much responsible for people feeling 'blessed' as
anything else. The chasm between a literal and naive reading of
Cerullo and a more critical approach seems unbridgeable; the
assessment of results depends on the grounded assumptions of the
inquirers. How can theology facilitate the testing of spirits that is
needed here, in order that the key problems can begin to be
addressed?

One way forward is to recognize the complex and relational
field of power at work in revivalism. Whenever power is exercised,
there are always some predictable results. For example, if a 'word
of knowledge' is offered at, say, a youth rally, concerning areas
of sexual guilt such as masturbation or premarital sex, it is obvious
that a number of people present will at least feel a sense of
conviction. This does not mean the 'word of knowledge' is not
genuine; it might be. But if it isn't, the factors at work such as
the hushed, reverential tone in which the 'word' is imparted,
and the congregational expectations, mean that the 'word of
knowledge' will still convict. The same is true for 'words' about
many medical conditions; cancer, backache or childlessness being
typical examples. In fact, all those 'conditions' just mentioned are
simply metaphors for a range of complaints; for example, 'cancer'
describes dozens of medical conditions, some of which are easily
treatable and recognizable, whilst others are not. To say 'I have
been healed of cancer' sounds like a dramatic, conclusive statement.
But it is very far from that. To 'prove' healing from cancer takes
years of scans, tests and good health. Add to this the ambiguity
of cancer and its causes (why do some tumours or lumps simply
disappear, even before an operation and biopsy can be performed?),
and the grounds for definitively claiming a divine healing start to

look rather shaky. Interestingly, few charismatic leaders claim to be of much use in hospital accident and emergency departments. Would a team of devoted healers really be able to do something about a broken leg or a severed artery? Of course not: charismatic healing primarily deals with the internal, unseen world of the body. It is important at this point not to get too sceptical; we are dealing with grey areas here, the very borders between religion and science, body, mind and spirit. In such a field, the key to gaining some understanding is to keep questioning.

Christopher French, a senior lecturer at Goldsmiths College, London University, attributes the 'results' of revival meetings to endorphins, chemicals that are released in the body that enhance its function.[7] He claims that high levels of excitement and expectation produce endorphins, which in turn produce good feelings. The psychological process of feeling, and, maybe, of actually being healed, arises out of the individual 'mapping' their experience on to the religious language and dogma. Attitudes to pain change, and some psychosomatic conditions (including hysterically induced blindness and paralysis) can then be altered through prayer, praise or a sense of divine intervention. What then seems like a miracle to one, is, to another, a complex psychosomatic response to external and internal factors that are somewhat intangible.

This is an important observation in the context of power, since it must be acknowledged that revivalism also produces results and consequences that can 'surprise' participants. Someone may go to a meeting hoping for something particular, but instead find that their 'divine encounter' turns out to be entirely different from their original expectations. This may seem like a miracle, but again, social and psychological factors may need to be acknowledged more readily. A revival meeting permits participants to engage in a massive release of their own energy, to relax, and then to apparently engage with a higher power. That hysterical behaviour, deeply repressed experiences or hitherto taboo desires should surface under the extraordinary conditions of revivalism cannot be surprising. The rhetoric of power, immediacy and love provides a safe linguistic canopy under which hidden tensions can now emerge. Indeed, some psychologists acknowledge that revivalism may do more to help some people in the short-term than can medicine or therapy: an encounter with revivalist phenomena can provide temporary and immediate release from hysterically-related symptoms that could take a psychiatrist months to unlock.[8]

At the same it should be stressed that it is usually *temporary* release. The healing methods employed at revivalist meetings are primarily geared to individuals; yet many problems, including medical ones, arise out of complex social problems such as stress, poverty or family circumstances. The individual can seek healing, and a prayer may well make them feel better. But the prayer will not usually alter the social context in which the individual operates. For example, if a person is suffering from chest pains, a charismatic healer may very well correctly uncover the fact that the person is overweight and a smoker; the smoking and the poor diet arise out of the stress the individual feels – living on a run-down housing estate, unemployed, and a large family to support. The underlying stress is the feeling of weakness, helplessness and illness. A prayer may be offered, and the individual feel better for having their problem acknowledged; they may even feel 'healed'. But if the social or relational conditions remain, the chances are that the individual will once again slip back into illness.

Further complications can occur here. Guilt may arise as a result of people not 'claiming' or realizing their healing. They may feel that it is their own fault that they are ill; perhaps they have sinned, and are being punished by God. Charismatic healers are usually very good at providing long lists of tenuous reasons as to why people are not healed. But what they all universally fail to acknowledge is that the causes of illness are often social, not simply individual. On a global scale, the primary cause of disease and illness is *poverty*; 'signs and wonders' fails to address this in its method. Human beings are socially interactive creatures; healing them depends as much on altering their contexts and the social causes of illness as anything else.

It must also be remembered that revivalism, although originally a reaction to the 'mixed offerings of modernity', is now definitively a post-modern movement. It flourishes under the conditions of post-modernity, freely competing in the spiritual free market, playfully engaging with tradition and experience, whilst remaining broadly true to its foundational dogmas. (The present syncretism between Shamanism and Pentecostalism in some Korean churches provides an excellent example of this.[9]) In a world where Christendom has given way to secularization and post-modernism, most religions struggle to find a definitive identity that offers a bulwark of stability against a constantly shifting social and moral cosmos. Revivalist religion can, on occasions, legitimately be seen as 'what we do with our madness',[10] a form of escapism from the world to a realm where the values of the world are accepted and rejected, adapted and abused, but in a way that delivers clarity, not confusion. For example, the secular culture of the 'quick fix' of instant results and immediacy so often derided by fundamentalists, is mimicked spiritually by movements of healing, revival and church growth.[11]

In a rational, plural and relative world that often confuses and alienates individuals in a 'fog' of competing convictions, revivalism and fundamentalism offer a haven of tradition and certainty with new, competing values that promise clearer horizons. In Michael Foucault's first major work, *Madness and Civilisation*, he develops a theory of human behaviour in which certain traits are designated as 'mad' whilst others are 'sane'.[12] Selectivity is the key. For example, to revivalists some deficiencies are acceptable, others are not. It is all right for Wimber to wear glasses for short-sightedness; no one thinks this is a handicap. But slight deafness is to be prayed for: why is this so?

In Chapter Four, we noted how worship carried the believer into a selective 'other-worldly' realm in which doubt was negated and expectations met. Part of the genius of revivalism and fundamentalism lies in its ability to cast the world as mad and itself as sane. This gives rise to a 'power knowledge', a created discourse that can speak of the world and the experiences of individuals, yet without really being connected to reality. Thus, 'sin', liberalism, demons and malign spirits are blamed for failures and for the insanity of the world, whilst the Spirit accounts for the wisdom of the believers. In this scheme it is not difficult to understand how a 'complete world-view' that expresses so much madness is in fact seen as sanity to those who are 'in the know'; nothing can break this circle, not even reality. In this vision, truth becomes a concretized monologue instead of a dynamic dialogue with the world.

The phenomenon known as the 'Toronto Blessing' illustrates much of this. We have already noted how Wimber depends on new phenomena to help to keep participants within the framework. The old agents of biblical inerrancy and the power of the Spirit are always present to the framework; but new, novel and exciting agents are always needed to keep participants interested and engaged, to perpetuate the myth that this kind of revivalism is fresh and relevant. A good analogy could liken fundamentalism and revivalism to listening to a radio that is very well tuned-in.[13] The post-modern world is full of competing signals, some weak, some strong and some quite foreign; many people find the ensuing confusion of 'reception' both alienating and unsystematic. Fundamentalists and revivalists, however, offer a clear 'signal'; tuning into them necessitates blocking out all other interference. The revivalist tradition within fundamentalism is especially good at holding its 'audience', since excitement and adventure are also part of the experience of being tuned-in, besides the regular diet of certainty.[14]

The 'Toronto Blessing', with its message of fresh revival, revelations and reassurance, represents a novel way of enhancing the power framework and signifying the authenticity of revival faith. But what exactly is the 'Toronto Blessing'? What are we to make of congregations falling over 'in the power of the Spirit', of individuals barking like dogs, and others experiencing God afresh in deeper-than-ever-before ways? Several observations need to be made. First, its occurrence is not surprising given the struggle for particularity that faces all revival movements. Each *needs* its own defining hallmarks, especially in a post-modern era, where relativity is generally assumed and the only way of being noticed by the media-fed public is through novelty, originality and power. Come to that, one hallmark per movement will not do; the public memory is too short. What is required is a number of hallmarks, preferably revealed over a period of time, so that people's attention span is held and constantly kept in a state of expectation for the immediate. Thus, Wimber moves from power evangelism to healing, then to worship, then to prophecy, then to the 'Toronto Blessing'; each 'trend' appearing approximately two to three years apart.

Second, and linked to the first point, the 'Toronto Blessing' is not produced by Wimber himself. His churches now have the capacity to create their own dynamics of power; all that a new movement in the Vineyard needs to succeed is Wimber's imprimatur. Sociologically speaking, the 'Toronto Blessing' represents his movement coming of age; it is able to demonstrate new and appropriate forms of power in ways which attract and astonish, without specific reference to its founding 'father'.

Third, because one congregation in the Vineyard network has shown power like this, many if not all in the network will want to replicate the phenomenon; a failure to do this would place them 'out of communion'. Thus, there is a real sense in which congregations that aspire to Wimber's ecclesial and spiritual vision must experience the 'Blessing' for themselves to remain part of the revival community; 'missing out' could imply anything from disobedience to the will of God to lagging behind in the latest revival phenomenon. This is not meant to imply that the 'Toronto Blessing' is somehow false. Yet it should be remembered that some communities will subconsciously fake, copy or mimic revivalist phenomena for fear of the new 'wave' passing them by.

Fourth, the 'Toronto Blessing' appears to lack any real depth or obvious point. Some British Evangelical leaders have implied that, spectacular though the phenomenon may be, it is by its fruit that it will be known.[15] Those in favour of the movement point to people's deeper awareness of God, but it is hard to see why God might have to make people bark like dogs to induce this. The lack of depth is a serious problem for champions of the 'Toronto Blessing'; the particularity of its novelty and playfulness in a post-modern setting seems to be its main distinguishing feature, if not the point. The laughter and accompanying barking may be psychosomatic responses to deeply embedded traumas about the failure of revivalism to move from being a particular belief to a universal one; in other words, a mild hysterical response that is experienced by individuals in group contexts.

Fifth and last, we should mention that the lack of any serious message in the 'Toronto Blessing' allows interpreters to set their own gloss on the phenomenon. To many it is a sign of revival, a fresh 'wave' of the Holy Spirit.[16] To others still, the 'Toronto Blessing' is a moral sign: Mary Pytches equates the roaring noises associated with the revival meetings with 'restoring [male] authority and leadership to his church'.[17] Some see the movement as an evangelistic opportunity, but few conversions appear to have resulted from it. Others regard the movement as a sign of Christ's imminent return; the increasing number of 'waves' points to this. Yet this is a tricky argument, that begs testing against biblical texts. Perhaps the 'Toronto Blessing' is more a sign of 'Pre-Millenial Tension' (PMT), the well-documented history of religious paranoia and hysteria that accompanies the end of each millennium.[18]

In saying all this, it would be wise neither to affirm nor deny that the 'Toronto Blessing' is a movement from God. It is certainly a complex phenomenon. To those within the power framework, it seems like another moment of divine intervention in a bewildering world that is starved of direction: God's way of saying, 'I'm still here'. To those outside the movement, however, the phenomenon presents itself as a rather peripheral puzzle; it seems to have little to say to that same world, and its specious particularity feels escapist and self-indulgent. The discernment of this spirit will certainly take time.

Overall, my view is that movements like the 'Toronto Blessing', along with the popularity of healers such as Morris Cerullo, represent a retreat into the past. It is well known that under stress, individuals and groups revert to the forms characteristic of earlier phases, especially those learnt in childhood or the genesis of a group. This is most easily seen in prayer, where 'concrete needs and wants' surface, and the inductive theological strategy is invoked to counter the threat of the world.[19] At this point, fundamentalist and revivalist belief provides a safe haven of certainty for individuals and groups, a place in which to be a child again, immunized from the complexities of adult social interaction. A world in which 'daddy' intervenes to make dreams come true, rewards the faithful, punishes the bad, sorts out problems and wipes away all tears. As such, it *does* perform a useful task within the whole context of the body of Christ, reassuring individuals (especially damaged individuals) of the immanence and care of a parenting God. However, it ultimately lacks maturity, sophistication, space for growth and sufficient grounding for serious engagement with the world as it is; as such, it may properly be described as an immature, intermediate stage of faith.[20] Phenomena like the 'Toronto Blessing' and healers like Cerullo only really appeal to the world in which they operate; their effectiveness and ministry is very particular and shows little sign of becoming universal. For all the claims made on their behalf, it should be remembered that most people are drawn to God and the Church through close, lasting relationships, not by miracles or awesome rhetoric.[21]

It would be wrong to end this section without some reference to the larger theological and political dimensions at stake here. Theologically, there are serious questions to ask about the claimed particularity of God's action. The 'signs and wonders' movement seems to be primarily confined to the white middle classes, appealing to mainly thirty-somethings. The vision of God is largely local and domestic, even primitive or tribal – a Holy Spirit of the Home Counties. Why does God heal someone from a painful knee in one town, whilst millions all over the world live under poverty, famine, suffering and injustice? Is it really possible to believe in a God who does a few nice, handy miracles for the chosen few, but nothing in response to the prayers of millions for the needs of billions? The cause-and-effect theology of prayer has been explored at length by many theologians, and in every case the philosophy of fundamentalism and revivalism at this point is found wanting.

Prayer has become wish-fulfilment, a child's fantasy of a 'fix-it' God who can do anything.[22]

Politically speaking, I am not alone in regarding certain types of revivalism and fundamentalism as being predisposed to right-wing, individualistic and anti-corporate political philosophy. Healers and fundamentalist preachers, in calling congregations to look to God alone for salvation, tend to discount social dynamics that need challenging and changing. The social causes of disease, such as poverty, are not usually addressed. Their Victorian forebears did the same – pray and behave, and God will bless you; depend on God alone, not on others. Salvation, judgement and healing are turned into individualistic notions; the idea of corporate sin or redemption is lost. As a result, 'society' fragments, and simply becomes the sum of its individuals. Fundamentalism and revivalism partly creates, and certainly capitalizes, on this; a spiritual 'free market' allows competition for power, whereas an established liberal religion, whilst trying to serve everyone, can lack sharpness and power.[23] The creative way forward in solving the dilemma of identity is to ensure that all churches properly attend to their borders and margins. All too often churches live as though they are central to salvation, making Christ peripheral; the agent displaces the source at the centre of itself – this is common to both established and 'free' churches. But focusing on the margins of belief, of membership, of experience and tradition, draws a church out of itself into creative dialogue with neighbours. Borderlands are always places of exchange, dialogue, ambiguity and reconciliation; they can also be dangerous – you can be shot at from both sides. Yet this is the calling that faces all churches, including those in the fundamentalist and revivalist tradition. We are to be socially engaged, yet transcendent; the truth, yet life. We are not to be places of concentrated power, but to be open, incarnate communities that risk weakness, and even death.

Towards a Conclusion

In the volume *Fundamentalisms Observed* (1992), the editors note that 'the task of understanding fundamentalisms is urgent at a time when these movements are so frequently catalysts in an unsettled world'.[24] The plural form of the key word in the book's title reminds us that fundamentalism is a diverse and dynamic phenomenon that is not easily reducible to a single set of guiding principles.

I have argued that fundamentalism offers adherents a 'complete world-view', so that the context in which it operates is one of competing powers. Fundamentalists resist modernity (an attitude where tradition and/or its authority is challenged), which threatens the basis of their power. Equally, they must fight for supremacy amidst an obvious plurality of beliefs, struggling to reassert their particular view of the power of God, in the face of competing convictions.[25]

I have also drawn attention to the difficulty of differentiating between divine and human power, and divine and human agency. Kathleen Boone, in *The Bible Tells Them So* (1990), points out that in fundamentalist groups, the Bible is ideally regarded as a divine agent ('God-given'), and is therefore inerrant; the interpreter is, however, a human agent, subject to the divine. She then goes on to show how these two agents are actually confused in such groups, so that it is the interpreter who becomes pre-eminent.

One of the main benefits arising from an inductive strategy is certainty for the believers. Yet there is an ambiguous relationship between authority and certainty. Certainty does, in fact, have an authority of its own: it demands allegiance, and issues control to those who propagate it.[26] Some caution needs to be exercised here; though fundamentalism cannot simply be reduced to control, control is at the *centre* of its power framework. To communicate, distribute and mediate power requires control, especially in a network as dispersed as the Vineyards: centralist or core stories and ideologies are essential, if the expanding network is to speak the same language and hold together. The control needed in social relations for fundamentalists is mirrored in their doctrine of God. Omnipotence is a controlling power that competes with freedom, and can manipulate: the love of God is ultimately an agent of that power in this view. But orthodoxy suggests a different picture, that creation becomes fully what it is intended to be through loving co-operation with God rather than a naked assertion of power and control that denies freedom.

The suggestions above can be illustrated more simply if one looks at how truth is sometimes held by groups. For example, in the debate over the priesting of women in the Church of England, an alliance developed between some Anglo-Catholics and some Conservative Evangelicals. Generally, they have little in common. However, on the issue of women priests or women in authority, they can unite. This is because they can agree about the *controlling nature* of revealed truth (although not about its *substance*). Both groups see the *nature* of truth as something unalterable, which is passed down from one generation to the next, or, if you prefer, like a baton in a relay race, passed from one man to the next. (And it would usually have to be a man.) The issue of control – keep women away from power – can be agreed upon in principle, although the two groups arrive at their conclusions from (and for) quite different reasons and presuppositions. The point of dealing with truth in this way is that fundamentalists like their truth to have the same amount of control and power as (it is said) it originally had.[27]

Given these remarks, however, we must ask, what happens when power fails for fundamentalists, control is lost, and the forces of modernity and liberalism seem to have the upper hand? The more usual response under such circumstances is that power is appealed to again, reasserted afresh, and the controlling network reorganized to hold that power. This is illustrated by some of the ultra-Catholic groups who protested against the Church of England General Synod's decision to ordain women to the priesthood. The ultra-conservative Catholic group 'Ecclesia' resorted to rhetoric punctuated by violent 'Holy War' metaphors and images; talk of love, understanding and reconciliation was completely absent.[28] Or, we can listen to the rhetoric of fundamentalist-charismatic Benny Hinn, following some (scholarly) undermining of his understanding of the Spirit:

> Now I'm pointing my finger with the mighty power of God on me . . . You hear this. There are men and women attacking me. I will tell you something under the anointing now, you'll reap it in your children. You'll never win. . .And your children will suffer. . . you'll pay, and your children will. Hear this from the lips of God's servant. You are in danger. Repent, or God Almighty will move his hand . . .[29]

These two examples show that a violent reassertion of power is often threatened by fundamentalist groups, and specifically against those who might have caused the 'power failure'. The power of God is appealed to, instead of his love. Love, by definition (1 Cor. 13), gives freedom to respond, and does not seek to control. But if fundamentalists perceive that their control has been damaged, it is a reassertion of power rather than a commitment to love that will manifest itself. Ultimately, fundamentalists are guilty of loving the power of controlling truths more than the people they are supposed to serve.[30] Their commitment to a God of power always precedes that of a commitment to a God of love, and its consequent implications for society, Church, and theology.

So, in the light of the theme of power, fundamentalism can be understood as a *concentration* of power, both in ecclesiology and theology. This is often read as sectarianism by sociologists, or as wilful religious naivete or bigotry by theologians. In fact, when one considers one of the main tasks of fundamentalism – defending omnipotence in the face of modernity – the phenomenon is better read as 'power concentrated for a particular task'. Quite often, this task can be defined as 'fighting', which requires the concentration of energy, resources, strategy and a degree of singlemindedness. Fundamentalists fight back (against modernity), fight for (a traditional world-view), fight with (doctrines or 'fundaments'), fight against ('the agents of assault on what they hold dear'), and fight under (God, or their 'sign of transcendent reference').[31]

'Concentration of power' is a key phrase here. It implies that fundamentalism is not so much about the beliefs themselves as it is about the manner in which they are held. A good example of how fundamentalism is a concentration of power can be seen when one observes certain Protestant 'Bible-believers'. Although a minority within Christianity, they gain their identity by concentrating on a very small number of essentials, which empower their community. The group of true believers, however, diminishes in proportion to the levels of concentration and certainty which are claimed for beliefs. To many this is unsurprising, since the more you insist on concentration, the more room there is for dissipation and distraction.

It has been argued here that fundamentalism is an *inductive* theological strategy, designed to recover an empowering experience from the past in the present. There is a sense in which contemporary fundamentalism is a relatively new movement that emerged in reaction to modernity. In nearly all its forms, it claims to go back to Scripture for guidance in the present. It tends to disregard the authority of tradition or scholarship, relying instead on some charismatic leader who claims and exemplifies direct insight into the original meaning and power of the text. In the opinion and experience of fundamentalists, tradition and authority have often failed to protect belief from the vagaries of modernity. Consequently, fundamentalists frequently submit themselves wholly to some individual's interpretation, and even appeal to it to criticize tradition.

Last, fundamentalism is *assertive* or counter-assertive in the modern age. It is the true power resisting all others:

> Fundamentalist movements are final desperate attempts to assert the primacy of one cultural tradition...They [fundamentalists] see the basic modern religious conflict as one between an ancient and irreformable truth, embodied in one cultural framework, and destructive forces of secularism and materialism, which must be resisted by a return to the old absolute values.[32]

The use of the word 'assertive' implies that there are claims to be made in fundamentalism. Certainly, this is the case. But those claims are only made in order to receive power, to defend it, and ultimately, to reimpose it, on a society that is deemed to have 'sold out' to other powers which are corrupt. In its assertiveness, fundamentalism is appealing not just to a set of abstract claims, but rather to the empowering possibilities of those claims, which will realign the believer's life via an experience of the ultimate power: God.

Charisma, scriptures, experiences and prophets can all be agents of empowerment, and that empowerment is focused on reasserting the omnipotence of God in the modern situation. This is all very well for Wimber, who 'fits' the methodology chosen. But how might the theme of power enrich the study of other types of fundamentalism?

(i) POWER: THE THEME

In many theories of power, power is treated as a force, which could be directed to certain ends.[33] One consequence of choosing to interpret a particular type of fundamentalism using the theme of power has been to show that the operation of power is very diverse, just as fundamentalism is itself. Neither can be reduced to a simple, brute equation. What has been proposed is more sophisticated, and does justice to the rich complexity of fundamentalist belief and behaviour, namely, that power has an interrelational quality about it, and can only be understood properly by referring to the operating agents that receive, transfer, transform and communicate it. Fundamentalism is a belief system that can be interpreted, whose encompassing framework is fixed by power in a particular way, namely, inductively.[34]

This broad thesis can illuminate the study of other types of fundamentalism, that at first sight appear to be very remote from

Wimber. For example, those organizations engaged in campaigning *against* the ordination of women to the priesthood in the Church of England can, in some respects, be better understood if the theme of power is used as an interpretative scheme. In a very ordinary sense, power is already deemed to be present in an all-male priesthood, and opening priesthood to women would dilute or destroy that power, which is variously labelled: 'apostolic succession', 'headship', 'revealed', 'tradition', and so on. God's omnipresence is limited: true priestly power may only come through male agents. The pattern for this is arrived at via an inductive strategy: Jesus, a male, and now High Priest, was and is a demonstration of God's power in a particular form. If the Church wishes to hold on to or recover its original empowering, the all-male priestly agency must be upheld.

Now, clearly there are many more sophisticated arguments used to endorse this line of thinking, and we must not make light of them. However, the trenchant defence of an all-male priesthood is clearly a power issue that has implications for who God is, what he/she/it can do, and what the Church should do as a consequence. The ideological agents also reveal much: 'ideal' women are mothers and servants, 'ideal' men, priests/presidents and 'fatherly', a metaphor that conflates the identity of the priest with God's. To try to interpret such organizations in the light of their stance on, say, tradition, would be to miss the point. The controlling issue is power, and the 'power framework' that has been constructed – 'tradition', 'Scripture' and 'relations with Rome' – is a tool, or rather agent, of the power that is constantly being sought inductively. So, what is at issue in this type of fundamentalism is the essential agency of maleness as a means of making concrete a particular aspect of divine power. God's self-revelation in the male Christ is invested with particular significance (but not his Jewishness) which in turn demands and protects an all-male priesthood. In the eyes of those who believe this, women priests represent a threat to the very power of God: they might pollute it or dilute it. Ultimately, only withdrawal will guarantee the purity of their power. This is highly ironic: those claiming to be 'catholic' actually start to become sectarian in nature, withdrawing from society in order to protect the omnipotence of God. Yet we should not be surprised at this. The theme of power, in this case, shows that the professed 'catholicity' is in fact bogus; it is an agent of power for the present. If that agent fails to function, it will be cut out of the framework, or, be reinterpreted in a different light.[35]

(ii) DIVINE POWER

One of the allegations in this book is that fundamentalism is an attempt to hold on to omnipotence in the modern age, in a particular style and form. That power is central to both religious experience and to human ideas about God is undeniable. Gerhardus van der Leeuw, amongst others, confirms this, arguing that religion in its essence and manifestation consists in 'being touched by power', 'being effected by power', 'conducting oneself in relation to power', and 'participating in power'.[36]

Fundamentalists are particularly interested in omnipotence, since omnipotence guarantees control. Of course, that control ultimately lies in the mystery of God. Yet fundamentalists are firmly convinced of the existence of 'fixed points of passage' (Clegg), through which this control, order and power ultimately passes. For many fundamentalists, this is an inerrant text, teacher or tradition, which with each subscribing believer must be *experienced*, if divine power is to be shown in their lives. God's omnipotence becomes a framework that is ultimately to be imposed on society, which will have to submit to the new powers. If the fixed points of passage for omnipotence are interfered with in any way, this naturally poses a threat to God, the group's agenda, and all the operating control mechanisms.

What is particularly at issue here is the *nature* of God's power. I have argued that the fundamentalist defence of omnipotence gives rise to a distorted theology and view of the Church, tending to focus on how God distributes power, and how it might be controlled and enacted. Even the most sophisticated attempts to define God's power in relation to Christology and 'divine self-limitation' still tend to place God in total control, reinforcing notions of almightiness in weakness, and so on.[37] Yet, contrary to what many fundamentalists assert, the primary *being* of God is love, not power: all powers are subordinate to his nature, which is love. God approaches creation in love, risking compromise, rejection and defeat.

For fundamentalists, two 'hallmarks' arise directly out of their distorted identity. The first is a fear of 'embodiment' that can take a number of forms. For some fundamentalists, the idea of Jesus as incarnate is notionally satisfactory, since it is partly by this means that they themselves can be empowered. Yet many

fundamentalists who claim to affirm the incarnation will not
countenance Jesus ever being ill, having sexual desires, being
confused at times, or even making a mistake. For other
fundamentalists, their own embodiment presents a problem. In
order to demonstrate God's power as *purely* as possible, an
assortment of channels that God's power might come through are
ruled out. For example, some Roman Catholics, Christian Scientists
and Jehovah's Witnesses share a common belief that it is wrong
to interfere with the 'natural function' of the body. The use of
contraceptives, aspirin and blood transfusions are deemed to be
contrary to God's will, since this might prevent the power of God
being properly embodied in that person. The power of God
therefore becomes something that can 'flow' through natural
functions, but is distorted, and perhaps not even present, in
'artificial' ones.

A second hallmark is a hierarchy in divine power.
Fundamentalists believe that divine power does and can control.
So, they are always seeking a controlling person or doctrine, both
in the life of God and in social relations. In some respects, the
controlling 'mechanism' that characterizes the power framework
can be almost anything: the maleness of God, the inerrant word,
being 'born again'. Any one of these concepts can be used as an
agent of power and control. Yet it is in the life of God that we
must especially note that fundamentalists construct a hierarchy. In
Oneness Pentecostalism it is Jesus who is the principal controlling
person. In certain types of charismatic renewal, it is the Spirit and
the Father. In some forms of conservative evangelicalism, it is God
revealing himself in the Word (i.e., Bible), that is principal, with
the Spirit's role reduced to that of a biblical interpreter. Any notion
of the persons of God in an open, mutual relationship is absent.

(iii) HUMAN POWER

In fundamentalism power is what forms the basis for individual
and communal relations, not love. That is not to say that love
has no place in fundamentalist communities: it does. But the
primary preoccupation of fundamentalists is with protecting the
power of God against other powers. If this is the case, we cannot
be surprised that fundamentalists are often accused of being
'sectarian'. Total protection requires vigilance, security, and
isolation of the object from any potential threats. The necessity
of protecting the source of power for a given group is an important
point. Often, the source of power is a 'still point' for a community,

around which other things may change, yet the power itself remaining undiminished. In terms of human institutions, this tends to place power over love. Although love is valued, power is valued more highly, since it is constant: love can compromise, change, and does not always insist on its own way. However, power, as a basis for community, runs no such risks.

Traces of this trend within fundamentalist groups occur with alarming frequency. Differences of opinion are rarely countenanced; doctrine is often placed above unity (in spite of what some in the 'anti-women priests' movements seem to be saying); hierarchies, schisms and egalitarian claims are common. To the outsider, such problems might appear to be trivial. Yet they are far from that. Each occurrence is a direct consequence of the 'base' upon which fundamentalist communities are built. In choosing the apparent 'rock' of power and certainty, it is not usually recognized that certainties have a habit of developing a 'sand-like' quality, especially in the context of modernity and plurality.[38]

In considering the operation of human power within fundamentalist groups, certainty is a key concept. The stating of fundamentals and their efficacy depends on their certainty. This can be theoretical, practical, pragmatic, or even 'mystical' certainty. But what does certainty look like? There is no one answer to this; but, for fundamentalists, certainty is either something that is done to truth, or a quality that is discerned within it. Fundamentalists, in all their diverse dynamism, tend to 'pin down' truth – even a new truth – and then hold it in such a way that it becomes still and fixed: from this position, fixed passage points for divine power are established. Believers can then be held to those fixed points. The truth is not free to move, change or develop: it is fixed, and, ultimately, actually controllable to some extent. In reflecting on this, one cannot help noting that Jesus met his death this way, because of some people's attitude to truth and certainty. There is a case for saying that Christ – dynamic, free truth, embodied in a human being, who left few rules and wrote only in the sand – is literally pinned down on some planks of wood. In fact, there is no certainty, and nor can there be. For it is a familiar fact of experience that the only things of which we can be certain are those which do not affect the human heart at all. Fundamentalism, in its power-centredness, often attempts to bypass this ambiguity, and establish its certainty and power *independent* of humanity. This is part of the appeal of fundamentalism, as well as its intrinsic weakness: to those who possess the truth, it is all; to those who do not, it is a distant puzzle.[39]

Of course, certainty as a fixed point for demonstrating power does not exist for its own sake. It is present for many different reasons. However, the primary, and perhaps most obvious, reason is that certainty results from the desire to see order, especially in the face of the turbulence generated by the modern situation. As we have noted before, fundamentalist communities are seldom static; there is always a delicate balance between the desire for stability and the desire for change. In Wimber's case, we noted that 'signs and wonders' fulfil this obligation, providing both a dynamic programme as well as an agreed theological core that is essentially unchanging. Other fundamentalist groups behave similarly, offering a form or type of order that is essentially fixed, which affords a secure basis of empowerment for subscribing believers. Certitude is the absence of doubt, and, as such, is an ideal channel for power, since dissipation is rarely if ever risked.

That certainty and power are intimately linked in fundamentalist communities cannot be denied. Even a cursory glance at a fundamentalist group or trend illustrates this. For example, a belief in a faultless Bible is ultimately untenable. But the *function* of an 'inerrant scripture' is to provide a power-base in a community that in this case comes through a particular and certain fixed point. An inerrant text, teacher or tradition is a means of asserting power where there is a perceived vacuum; here, certitude replaces faith. Indeed, we may say that certainty is as different from faith as power from love. Faith as an act implies a continuous journey of aspiration;[40] it is concerned with a vision of the truth which has constantly to be reviewed, renewed and striven towards and held on to; it is never beyond doubt, yet neither is it firmly in one's grasp.[41] Certainty and power, however, are concerned with attainment. Doubt, a necessary part of faith, has no place in assertive certitude. As such, certitude 'overshoots faith, craving for sureness': instead of a flexible vision, there is a blueprint or programme.[42]

Summary

Chapter Two hinted at one of the more fundamental questions that faces Christianity in the modern world, namely, how does God exercise his power, and what kind of power is it that is revealed? Wimber's answer to this question, which is generic for other fundamentalists, is that God's power is almighty, God is omnipotent (in a particular kind of way), and that there are established divine and human agencies that can show this to be the case. Certainly, in Wimber's case, miracles, signs and wonders are said to be irresistible evidence of God's being. In this theology, a miracle is thought of as, so to speak, a 'localized and controlled explosion' of controlling power.[43] The miracle becomes the principal indicator of God's existence, and of the kind of power exercised – one that is irresistible and irrefutable. The sociological manifestations that arise out of this theology are, at least in part, what gives fundamentalism its control and power over believers.

But this view of power seems corrupted. Christianity does not centre itself on a 'God of knock-down power', but on a 'creative servant God of invincible love'.[44] Because of the fear of the ambiguity of freedom and love, fundamentalism feeds on the mentality that wants a God of all-controlling power. So, religions are constructed that do exactly what Freud, Marx and Durkheim say they do – meet our psychological needs, support vested interests, and provide patterns of bonding and control that can operate in society. Wimber's basic error is to see signs and wonders as evidence of God's assertive control and power, whereas miracles are in fact evidence of love committed to the world, and to bringing that world into a sharing of God's creativity and love. To put it another way:

> Miracles are part of encountering the openness and presence of God within the textures, structures and activities of the created world. They are produced and experienced by means of the space which is kept open or made open, in that world by the intercourse of God with free and searching persons. . .An authentic and genuinely revelatory miracle is always a mysterious combination of active faith along with a sense of, and conviction about, a gift which goes beyond the ordinary. There is always a way of interpreting or explaining a 'miracle' which does not oblige anyone to attribute it to God . . . God does not force himself on people. He offers himself to us for our response, obedience and collaboration.[45]

Miracles, of course, can and do evoke faith, even deep faith, but they do not compel faith. They are *gifts*, and therefore not intended as objective agents that will pressurize people into faith. They are not so because faith is not like that, and neither is God. Miracles are not proof of power, to be replicated today. They are gifts of love to be received by faith, as part of that same love that is poured out in Jesus Christ.[46]

The overvaluing of power at the expense of love is a major problem in fundamentalism, and leads to a distorted theology and view of the Church. Ultimately, it leads to a quest for agents that will deliver certainty and control of that power. We have noted how the experience of knowledge often fulfils that function of power, guaranteeing to the body of believers a degree of security that no longer requires further searching. Yet we must agree with the author of the fourteenth century *Cloud of Unknowing*, who states that 'by love God may be gotten and holden, but by thought and understanding never'.[47] Fundamentalists ultimately seek concrete faith through propositions, which are validated inductively. This is in contrast to a God who reveals himself relationally, not only in Jesus (the Word, or proposition, made flesh), but also in the dynamic particularity of the economic Trinity. It is in the Trinity that one must locate the ground and being of God, divine agency, action, and his relation to the world. Such a view does not lead to certainty about God and his relation to the world. But it does invite a free and loving response, and the beginnings of faith.

Ultimately the quest for authority, control and certainty within fundamentalist groups must be understood in its proper context. It is a search for a way of receiving, holding and demonstrating divine power, against any other prevailing powers that pose a threat. Yet there are at least three problems with the inductive theological strategy that is deployed by fundamentalists, and I conclude with them.

First, the problem of 'false' religious experience is not new to fundamentalists. An exclusive claim on God requires the denial of other groups who might claim the same, yet be different. Equally, groups that are very similar yet 'not of the fold' sometimes require an even stronger rebuttal. For example, it is interesting to note that the most vilified religious group for Wimber's churches is the 'New Age' movement. This could be because the *experiences* and practice of Wimber's followers are so similar in many instances, that a very sharp distinction has to be drawn.[48] (Fundamentalists with a more scriptural orientation tend to vilify their nearest neighbours too. Jehovah's Witnesses, Mormons and others, are taken to task over their *interpretation* of texts and the experiences this should lead to.) Clearly, if the inductive strategy is seeking *the* original, empowering experience or text, those who have travelled a different route need treating with caution, or eventually falsifying.

Second, there is the problem of the chosen historical basis for the essential beliefs. Inevitably, a degree of relativity is implied in selecting some texts as important over others, some traditions as more valuable than most. Of course, practitioners of the inductive model justify their selectivity on the basis that they are pursuing the *essence* of Christianity. So, 'signs and wonders' as a means to church growth and more besides, can be said by subscribers to be pre-eminent. However, the strategy is always open to counter-claims. It is at the mercy of other groups who suggest different essentials, or seek to show God's power in different ways.

Third, every inductive model has to confront the problem of certainty. Particularly in the case of fundamentalists, certitude is so often bound up with the charisma of the chief exponent. During their life, they are a primary source of information for followers; after their death, they become a subject for interpretation. At this point, certainty can often become a rather shaky commodity. The rich irony for fundamentalists is that the inductive strategy, used to 'prove' the power of God, is in fact highly susceptible to the relativity of post-modern times.[49] This problem will ensure that fundamentalism continues to be a dynamic, restless force in the future, as it struggles for the pure, empowering essence of early Christianity, a greater experience of divine power, and a certainty of the power that will convince the world.

So, I think that the final word belongs not to a theologian, nor to a sociologist, but to a poet. Donald Davie, in his poem 'Ordinary God', invites us to cast off the vision of the all-powerful God so beloved by fundamentalists and revivalism, and embrace a God that respects humanity and encourages maturity:

> 'Do you believe in a God
> who can change the course of events
> on earth?'
> 'No, just
> the ordinary one.'
>
> A laugh,
> but not so stupid: events
> He does not, it seems, determine
> for the most part. Whether He could
> is not the point: it is not

stupid to believe in
a God who mostly abjures.

The ordinary kind
of God is what one believes in
so implicitly that
it is only with blushes or
bravado one can declare,
'I believe', caught as one is
in the ambush of personal history, so
harried, so distraught.

The ordinary kind
of undeceived believer
expects no prompt reward
from an ultimately faithful
but meanwhile preoccupied landlord.[50]

Notes

CHAPTER ONE

1. K. C. Boone, *The Bible Tells Them So: The Discourse of Protestant Fundamentalism*, London, SCM, 1990, p. 10.
2. This is a standard definition. See for example *The Oxford English Dictionary*.
3. Martin Marty, 'Fundamentalism Reborn', in *Religion and Republic*, Boston, Beacon Press, 1987, pp. 299–300.
4. Marty, 'Fundamentalism Reborn', p. 3.
5. See N. C. Sellers, *Biblical Conclusions Concerning Tongues*, Miami, n.p., 1972, p. 26; J. Falwell (ed.), *The Fundamentalist Phenomenon: The Resurgence of Conservative Christianity*, Garden City, Galilee-Doubleday, 1981, p. 71.
6. See Falwell, *The Fundamentalist Phenomenon*, pp. 128–131, for a thorough overview of fundamentalist antagonism towards Billy Graham.
7. Carl Henry, *God, Revelation and Authority*, vol. 4, Waco, Texas, Word Books, 1979, pp. 100, 122.
8. See David Ford, 'Faith in the Cities', in C. Gunton and D. Hardy (eds.), *On Being the Church*, Edinburgh, T. & T. Clark, 1989, p. 243.
9. The British Evangelical Alliance incorporates a broad cross-section of denominations and movements. Members include 'house churches', organizations (British Youth for Christ, Proclamation Trust, etc.) and representatives from denominations, ranging from Anglicans to 'The Jesus Army'. The EA represents evangelical, fundamentalist, conservative and charismatic viewpoints. It organizes annual public marches involving around one million people across the UK ('March for Jesus'), annual conventions ('Spring Harvest', attracting over 100,000 people a year), as well as organizing political and media-based campaigns. At present, the EA is not a member of the ecumenical instrument in England, 'Churches Together in England' (CTE). The reasons for this are unclear, but probably centre on its desire to keep its goals sharp and distinctive, a fear of colluding with 'liberals', and of being identified with a broad/pluralist expression of Christianity.
10. G. Lindbeck, *The Nature of Doctrine*, Philadelphia, Westminster Press, 1984, pp. 33ff.
11. Lindbeck, *The Nature of Doctrine*, p. 34.
12. An example of this would be the Universities and Colleges Christian

Fellowhip's (UCCF, linked to IVP, Inter-Varsity Press) insistence on 'penal substitution' as the only way of understanding the atonement. Members are required to sign a 'statement of faith' in which other possible interpretations are denied. For a fuller analysis, see Steve Bruce's *Firm in the Faith*, Oxford, Gower Publishing, 1984.

13. See Stephen Sykes on 'Power', in *The Identity of Christianity*, London, SPCK, 1984, p. 11; see also Stephen Pickard, *The Purpose of Stating the Faith*, PhD thesis, University of Durham, 1990.

14. David Watson (1943–84) was a prominent leader in the British evangelical-charismatic movement, who first met Wimber in 1981. For a fuller discussion of David Watson's prominence in British church life, see P. Hocken, *Streams of Renewal*, Exeter, Paternoster Press, 1986, and Edward England (ed.), *David Watson: A Portrait by his Friends*, Crowborough, Highland Books, 1985.

15. Roger Foster's Ichthus Fellowship and Terry Virgo's New Frontiers churches would be included in this, as would individual Anglican, Baptist, and Methodist churches, along with other non-aligned fellowships and churches.

16. J. Wimber, *The Dynamics of Spiritual Growth*, London, Hodder & Stoughton, 1990, pp. 29ff: 'I realized that the Bible was written in such a manner that to reject one part was to reject it all. This was a power point, a discovery that put me on the narrow path to salvation'.

17. Wimber: 'In order to see God's church multiply as it is doing in the rest of the world, the western church must become involved in power evangelism. We must allow the Holy Spirit to empower us ... when we encounter the lost we must have the power – the ability to see into men's hearts and know their sin and their need, the ability to heal those who are ill, the ability to free those who are bound by Satan'. ('Signs and Wonders in the Growth of the Church', C. P. Wagner (ed.), *Church Growth: State of the Art*, Wheaton, Illinois, Tyndale Press, 1989, p. 224).

18. *Equipping the Saints*, Special UK edition, Fall 1990, p. 28.

19. Actually, Wimber has not *authored* these books so much as *authorized* them. His associate Kevin Springer compiles the books from Wimber's tapes and notes, with Wimber doing the final editing.

20. See, for example, T. Payne and P. Jensen, *John Wimber: Friend or Foe?*, Sydney, St Matthias Press, 1990. This is a bitter, unsystematic attack from some conservative evangelicals. Four more decent and recent books of related interest are J. F. MacArthur, *Charismatic Chaos*, Grand Rapids, Michigan, Zondervan, 1992; R. M. Enroth, *Churches that Abuse*, Grand Rapids, Zondervan, 1992; this describes Wimber's churches as 'potentially abusive', but includes too many extreme case-studies and insufficient in-depth analysis; M. S. Huton (ed.), *Power Religion: The Selling Out of the Evangelical Church*, Los Angeles, Moody Press, 1992; and J. R. Coggins and P. G. Hiebert (eds.), *Wonders and the Word*, Winnipeg, Manitoba, Kindred Press, 1989.

21. Wimber's view of church history is not very different from that of

British Restorationists, who believe the Holy Spirit was 'lost from' or neglected by the Church since the time of the apostles. Apart from a few isolated and persecuted minorities, who Restorationists claim were 'in touch' with the Spirit (such as Anabaptists, Montanists, etc.), they assert that the gifts of the Holy Spirit were ignored by the Church, until now, when through small groups and 'house churches', God is *restoring* the fullness of the spiritual blessings that the early apostles knew. For a fuller discussion, see A. Walker, *Restoring the Kingdom*, London, Hodder & Stoughton, 1988 (2nd edn).

22. To borrow a phrase from Harnack. Although Harnack's idea of transpotentiation was that the Church had transferred its power to institutionality, and the power of the gospel for transformation of the inner life was thus lost.

23. Wimber, in Wagner, *Church Growth: State of the Art*, p. 224.

24. Wimber, in Wagner, *Church Growth: State of the Art*, p. 216.

25. See Max Weber, *The Theory of Social and Economic Organisation*, London, Macmillan, 1964.

CHAPTER TWO

1. Cheryl Forbes, *The Religion of Power*, Grand Rapids, Zondervan, 1983, p. 54. See also R. Quebedeaux, *By What Authority?*, San Francisco, Harper & Row, 1982.

2. Forbes, *The Religion of Power*, p. 17.

3. Forbes, *The Religion of Power*, pp. 58-9. Forbes has in mind here so-called 'possibility' or 'positive' thinkers, who, she claims, influence American evangelicalism. An interesting example of this, though obviously not mentioned by Forbes, would be Roland Griswold, *The Winning Church: Church Growth and Evangelism for Today*, Wheaton, Illinois, Scripture Press, 1986.

4. Forbes, *The Religion of Power*, p. 60.

5. Forbes, *The Religion of Power*, p. 86.

6. D. Hardy and D. Ford, *Jubilate: Theology in Praise*, London, Darton, Longman & Todd, 1984, p. 21. However, the phrase 'jazz factor' is not really accurate. Jazz began after Pentecostalism and as a musical sense is more commonly associated with mellowness and liberalism (Berger).

7. Hardy and Ford, *Jubilate*, pp. 79ff.

8. Paul Cain, *Paul Cain at the Vineyard*, Anaheim, Vineyard Publications (6 audio-cassettes: no manual), 1989, tape 2, side 1. Cain specifically mentions that criticism or judgement of himself or Wimber will open the individual 'to a lot of judgement and severity' (from God). This severity might include hardship or sickness; at one point he says 'those who oppose the prophetic will die'. He warns that family and friends may also be affected by the actions of an individual critic. Similarly, Bob Jones, another of the 'Kansas Six', claims that God speaks to him annually on the Jewish Day of Atonement. In Jones's own terminology,

the Lord places him 'under the Shepherd's Rod' and gives him a message for the whole Church for the coming year. Jones's 1989 'Shepherd's Rod Prophecy' gave an interesting account of why so many prophecies go unfulfilled: '[God] said, "If I release the hundred-percent rhema right now, the accountability would be so awesome and you'd have so many Ananias' and Sapphiras' going on that the people couldn't grow; they'd be too scared"'. (Audio-cassette, Kansas City Fellowship, October 1989).

9.   'Slain in the Spirit': a relatively modern expression denoting a religious phenomenon in which an individual falls down and the cause of this is attributed to the Holy Spirit (see note 14, below).

10.   See A. McFadyen, *The Call to Personhood*, Cambridge, Cambridge University Press, 1991, p. 207.

11.   See K. Barth, *Church Dogmatics*, Edinburgh, T. & T. Clark, 1958, IV, ii, chap. 15, p. 648: 'The true growth which is the secret of the upbuilding of the community is not extensive but intensive; its vertical growth in height and depth ... It is not the case that its intensive increase necessarily involves an extensive. We cannot, therefore, strive for vertical renewal merely to produce greater horizontal extension and a wider audience ... If it [the Church and its mission] is used only as a means of extensive renewal, the internal will at once lose its meaning and power. It can be fulfilled only for its own sake, and then – unplanned and unarranged – it will bear its own fruits'.

12.   Stephen Sykes, *The Identity of Christianity*, London, SPCK, 1984, p. 208.

13.   J. Wimber, *Power Evangelism*, London, Hodder & Stoughton, 1985, p. 37.

14.   I would bear this out in the following way, in the table below. The observation of a particular manifestation is listed on the left of the page, and the contrasts denoted 'Eighteenth century revival'; and 'John Wimber's work and works'.

CONTRASTS IN REVIVALS

	Eighteenth-century revival	John Wimber's work and works
(i) Particular aspect of God being focused upon:	the holiness of God, and the need for individuals / the Church to be likewise	the healing power of God, and the need for individuals / the Church to likewise
(ii) Primary needs of respondents to message:	to have sins forgiven	to be physically / emotionally healed and / or empowered
(iii) Falling down at meetings or being 'slain in the Spirit':	individuals usually fall on their faces, as in the Bible (Matt. 7.16; Luke 5.8; Acts 9.4; 1 Cor. 14.25)	individuals usually fall on their backs

(iv) When manifestation occurred:	during preaching	during a 'clinic'
(v) Attitude of preacher:	Wesley did not encourage the phenomenon, often ignoring it	very much encouraged
(vi) Congregational proxemics:	people fell down on their own, sometimes involuntarily, or as a conscious response to a particular conviction	individuals fall down once others have gathered around them and prayed for them during a clinic
(vii) Reaction of preacher to people being 'slain in the Spirit':	Wesley claims he ignored them or had them carried away	fallen person becomes focus of activity, since this is where 'the Spirit is resting'

Of course, this table does not mean Wimber is bogus in his claims to divine power: it simply shows the discrepancies in his hermeneutics. We must also note the extensive work done by sociologists and historians of revivalism in the last twenty years. Many now distinguish between modern revivals (post-Finney), and those before. Finney's *Lectures on Revivals of Religions* (1835) provided Free Churches with a practical handbook on how to organize a revival. See R. Carwardine, *Transatlantic Revivalism*, Westport, Conn., Greenwood Press, 1978: 'By the 1850s in most evangelical churches a more calculated, more obviously "worked up" revivalism had replaced what traditionalists regarded as "waiting for God's good time"'. (p. xiii).

15.   More recently, Wimber has based his analogy on the Korean war of the 1950s.

16.   J. Wimber, *Power Points*, manual with tapes, Anaheim, California, Mercy Publishing, 1985, p. 43.

17.   See for example G. E. Ladd's *The Presence of the Future*, London, SPCK, 1980. (Originally published as *Jesus and the Kingdom*, New York, Harper & Row, 1964). Chapters 1, 6 and 7 seem to be echoed in Wimber's treatment of eschatology, which I discuss in Chapter 6.

18.   E. Troeltsch, *The Absoluteness of Christianity* (1902), London, SCM, 1976, p. 60.

19.   Wimber, *Dynamics of Spiritual Growth*, p. 3. Wimber attributes this comment to C. S. Lewis' discussion of the transformation of humanity found in *Mere Christianity* (London, Collins Fount Editions, 1977, pp. 180–1). However, even a casual reading of Lewis in this instance does not suggest the word 'replica' is appropriate.

20.   Wimber, *Dynamics of Spiritual Growth*, p. 4.

21.   Wimber, *Dynamics of Spiritual Growth*, p. 5.

22.   Wimber lists reasons why people are not healed (*Power Healing*, p. 164), including: not enough faith in God, unconfessed sin, unbelief, incorrect diagnosis of problem or poor prayer method. If any of these symptoms occur in either the healers or the persons desirous of healing, it is held that healing might not take place.

CHAPTER THREE

1.   M. Weber, *The Theory of Social and Economic Organisation*, London, Macmillan, 1964, pp. 152ff. I am most grateful to Janet Bigland-Pritchard for many of the insights expressed here. See her *The Theme of Power in the Theology of Adolf Von Harnack*, University of Durham PhD, unpublished, 1990.

2.   See, for example, Michael Mann, *The Sources of Social Power*, Cambridge, CUP, 1986; Rollo May, *Power and Innocence*, New York, Norton & Co., 1972; Robin Lakoff, *Talking Power*, New York, Basic Books, 1990.

3.   See, for example, Leonardo Boff, *Church, Charism and Power*, London, SCM, 1986. No disrespect to liberation theologians is intended here. An emphasis on the powerlessness and risk necessarily involved in the incarnation is to be welcomed, as is a stress on the unique character of the power of God. But if that is *only* used as a tool to undermine existing power structures, one has to question the gain of such an exercise.

4.   See, for example, the work of Charles Hartshorne, especially his *Omnipotence, and Other Theological Mistakes*, New York, NY State University Press, 1984.

5.   Quite why Matt. 28. 16–20 is deserving of the title 'the Great Commission' is a puzzle. This is not a phrase Matthew employs himself; it seems to have originated in the early nineteenth century, during the peak of European Protestant missionary expansion. Each of the Gospels offers a rival version of 'the Great Commission'. Mark 16. 15–18 is Wimber's usual choice, because of its reference to 'casting out demons'. Luke concludes his Gospel with a Great Commission (Luke 24. 44–9). John has several commissions, of which 18. 34–5 and 19. 21–4 are perhaps most notable. However, we should note that the Gospels are clear about what is the 'Great Commandment' (Mark 12. 28–34, etc.), which Jesus seemed to think should serve as a missiological, ecclesiological and theological foundation for the disciples.

6.   See also Robert Towler, *The Need for Certainty*, London, Routledge, Kegan Paul, 1984.

7.   See E. Miller and R. Bowman, *Report*, from the Christian Research Institute, February 1985, p. 1: 'While Bible teaching is not emphasized enough, the role of experience in the Christian life appears to be somewhat over-emphasized. People in the Vineyard frequently seem to be willing to allow their spiritual experiences to be self-authenticating. They seem too willing to assume that whatever transpires in their midst is from

God. That is not to say that the leaders do not attempt to show that their experiences are scriptural, but that experience far too often is their starting point'.

8.   Stewart Clegg, *Frameworks of Power*, London, Sage, 1989, p. 37.

9.   See, for example, P. Daudi, *Power in the Organisation*, Oxford, Blackwell, 1986.

10. There is no question that these two interests are linked, although I know of no serious work that supports this view. Material from The Church Growth Institute at Fuller Seminary, California, the British Church Growth Association and the Bible Society talks about the 'health' of the Church, 'health' being an umbrella concept that shelters principles of growth, management, evangelism and the implementation of spiritual gifts on the congregational structure, including healing.

11. Clegg, *Frameworks of Power*, 1989, pp. 130ff.

12. Clegg, *Frameworks of Power*, 1989, p. 197.

13. Clegg, *Frameworks of Power*, 1989, p. 198.

14. Clegg, *Frameworks of Power*, 1989, pp. 198–202.

15. P. D. Anthony, *The Ideology of Work*, London, Tavistock, 1977.

16. A. Strauss, *Negotiations: Varieties, Contexts, Processes and Social Order*, London, Jossey Bass, 1978, p. 201.

17. B. Barnes, *The Nature of Power*, Cambridge, Polity Press, 1988, p. 103.

18. R. Adams, *Energy and Structure*, Austin, University of Texas Press, 1975.

19. P. Daudi, *Power in the Organisation*, 1986, p. 266.

20. D. H. Wrong, *Power: Its Forms, Bases and Uses*, New York, Harper & Row, 1979, pp. 2, 6, 21, etc.

21. cf. Tom Smail, *The Power of Love*, audio-cassette, London, C. S. Lewis Centre, 1990, tape 1, side 1. See also P. Hocken, *Streams of Renewal*, Exeter, Paternoster Press, 1987, and A. R. Mather, *The Theology of the Charismatic Movement*, University of Wales PhD, unpublished, 1983.

22. According to Anthony Giddens, Weber's theory of charisma is the most enduring sociological theory of all time.

23. Max Weber, *The Theory of Social and Economic Organization*, New York, Oxford University Press, 1947, pp. 328, 358–9; idem, *On Charisma and Institution Building*, Chicago, University of Chicago Press, 1968, pp. 22, 24.

24. Arthur Schweitzer, 'Theory and Political Charisma', *Comparative Studies in Society and History*, March 1974, pp. 150–86.

25. Thomas E. Dow, 'The Theory of Charisma', *The Sociological Quarterly*, vol. 10, Summer 1969, p. 190.

26. Max Weber, *On Charisma and Institution Building*, Chicago, University of Chicago Press, 1968, p. 24.

27. P. Wagner, *Church Growth: State of the Art*, Illinois, Tyndale House, 1989, p. 125.

28. L. Karon, 'Presence in *The New Rhetoric*', *Philosophy and Rhetoric*, vol. 9, Spring 1976, p. 97.

29. Eric Hoffer, *The True Believer*, New York, Harper & Row, 1965, p. 105.

30. Martin Spencer, 'What is Charisma?', *The British Journal of Sociology*, vol. 24, September 1973, p. 348.

31. I. Schiffer, *Charisma: A Psychoanalytic Look at Mass Society*, University of Toronto Press, 1973, p. 37.

32. Wimber's language about Satan tends towards making him a virtually incarnate being. See especially *Power Healing*, London, Hodder & Stoughton, 1986, pp. 111ff.

33. 'Satan murdered him', was an incidental remark made by Wimber at his Brighton Conference in 1986.

34. J. Wimber, *Power Healing*, London, Hodder & Stoughton, 1986, pp. 159ff. See also 'I am a Wounded Soldier' (1985), by Danny Daniels, in *Songs of the Vineyard*, Eastbourne, Kingsway, 1987.

35. Arthur Schweitzer, 'Theory and Political Charisma', *Comparative Studies in Society and History*, vol. 16, March 1974, p. 153.

36. See J. Wimber, *Power Evangelism*, London, Hodder & Stoughton, 1985, pp. 44ff. There is an abundant supply of such stories circulating in this kind of fundamentalist universe. In particular, I refer the reader to the remarkable profile of Paul Cain in *Equipping the Saints* (A 'Vineyard Publication'), vol. 3, no. 4, 1989.

37. Ann R. Willner, *Charismatic Political Leadership: A Theory*, Princeton, Center of International Studies, Princeton University, 1968, pp. 103–4.

38. Erwin Bettinghaus, *Persuasive Communication*, New York, Holt, Rinehart & Winston, 1980, p. 113.

39. Mark Knapp, *Non-verbal Communication in Human Interaction*, New York, Holt, Rinehart & Winston, 1978, p. 158.

40. L. Rosenfeld and J. Civikly, *With Words Unspoken: The Non-verbal Experience*, New York, Holt, Rinehart & Winston, 1976, p. 71.

41. Sidney Jourard, 'An Exploratory Study of Body-Accessibility', *British Journal of Social and Clinical Psychology*, vol. 5, 1966, pp. 221–31.

42. Not actually touching in healing meetings arose as a result of climatic conditions. It was simply too hot and sweaty to lay hands on people in California, in buildings that were not air-conditioned. Wimber's original meetings were often held in vacant warehouses; the Vineyard practice of almost touching therefore developed, and is now adopted all over the world at Wimber/Vineyard meetings, irrespective of climate.

CHAPTER FOUR

1. Eric Hoffer, *The True Believer*, New York, Harper & Row, 1965, p. 28.

2. L. P. Gerlach and V. H. Hines, *People, Power, Change: Movements of Social Transformation*, New York, Bobbs-Merrill, 1970, p. 160. Gerlach and Hines assert that beliefs are at their most 'closed' – i.e., optimum

ideological height – during worship. This is because worship is usually an area in which doubt and debate are negated, where the needs of believers and those outside the community of worship can be addressed through the picture of God offered in the praise and supplication.

3. Lionel Adey, *Hymns and the Christian 'Myth'*, Vancouver, University of British Columbia Press, 1986, p. 153.

4. See the work of Claude Levi-Strauss and Jurgen Habermas, who asks, 'Who benefits from these ideologies?': J. Habermas, *Knowledge and Human Interests*, Boston, Beacon Press, 1971. Also see Clifford Geertz's 'Religion as a Cultural System', in *A Reader in Comparative Religion: An Anthropological Approach*, ed. William Lessa and Evon Vogt, New York, Harper & Row, 1972. See also C. Geertz, *The Interpretation of Cultures*, New York, Basic Books, 1973, and 'Deep Play', in *Myth, Symbol, and Culture*, ed. C. Geertz, New York, W. W. Norton & Co., 1971.

5. We are indebted to Sandra Sizer for this phrase, which she coins in describing the eighteenth century fundamentalist-revivalist hymn writers of the age. See S. Sizer, *Gospel Hymns and Social Religion*, Philadelphia, Temple University Press, 1978, chapter 3. We should note too that the view being expressed here is very Durkheimian. See his *Elementary Forms of Religious Life* (1912), trans. J. Swain, New York, The Free Press, 1965, pp. 31ff. For a discussion on Durkheim and power, especially 'power interests' in society as indicators of pathological (i.e., unhealthy) conditions within, the reader is referred to S. Fenton, R. Reiner and I. Hamnet, *Durkheim and Modern Sociology*, Cambridge, Cambridge University Press, 1984.

6. Wesley expressly noted the plan of order in his Preface to the 1877 *Collected Hymns*: 'The hymns are not carelessly jumbled together, but carefully arranged under proper heads, according to the experience of real Christians' (pp. iv–v). For a discussion of the history of the use of hymns, see L. F. Benson, *The English Hymn: Its Development and Use in Worship*, London, Hodder & Stoughton, 1915, and H. Davies, *Worship and Theology in England*, Princeton, Princeton University Press, 1975 (vol. 5).

7. cf. for a fuller explanation, J. Wimber, G. Kendrick and T. Virgo, *Worship Conference*, London, Vineyard Ministries International, 1989. This is a collection of 8 audio-tapes and a written syllabus, recorded at the Brighton Conference Centre, 1989.

8. The 'blessing gesture': arms are fully extended in front of the worshipper, slightly raised, the palms of the hands facing outwards, directed towards the stage area, or overhead. Often the hands move in an 'encompassing motion', almost as though something tangible was being held or framed by the worshipper.

9. *Songs of the Vineyard*, No. 37. Copyright © 1982 Mercy Vineyard Music/Kingway's Thankyou Music.

10. Songs of love: 22, 25, 33, 34, 36; Songs of power: 1, 18, 20, 37; Songs of holiness: 11, 12, 13; Songs about praise: 9, 43, 44. Jeremy Begbie, in

'The Spirituality of Renewal Music: A Preliminary Exploration', *Anvil*, vol. 8, no. 3, 1991, pp. 227–39, offers six different categories of song: exuberant praise to God; jubilant testimony and exhortation; intimacy; majesty; hushed reverence; battle.

11. See, for example, *Songs of the Vineyard*, No. 20. Copyright © 1982 Mercy Vineyard Music/Kingway's Thankyou Music.

12. For further discussion, see also J. Begbie, 'Renewal Music', *Anvil*, vol. 8, no. 3, p. 230.

13. *Songs of the Vineyard*, No. 1. Copyright © 1985 Mercy Vineyard Music/Kingway's Thankyou Music. (Variations in the verses sometimes include replacing 'tears' for 'fears', and 'the' with 'my').

14. Songs addressed to 'You' account for almost 50% of Vineyard worship; songs to God as 'Lord', about 30%.

15. *Songs of the Vineyard*, No. 10. Copyright © 1982 Mercy Vineyard Music/Kingway's Thankyou Music.

16. *Songs of the Vineyard*, No. 18. Copyright © 1982 Mercy Vineyard Music/Kingway's Thankyou Music.

17. Hardly any of Wimber's early songs are 'battle songs', although a good proportion of the material in *Songs of the Vineyard (Vol 2)* does fit this description (e.g., 152, 164).

18. See W. G. McLoughlin, *Modern Revivalism*, New York, Ronald Press, 1959; B. A. Weisberger, *They Gathered at the River*, Chicago, Quadrangle Books, 1958; W. R. Cross, *The Burned Over District: The Social and Intellectual History of Enthusiastic Religion in Western New York, 1800–1850*, New York, Harper & Row, 1961. This last book, although now over thirty years old, remains an unsurpassed history.

19. S. Sizer, *Gospel Hymns and Social Religion*, p. 52. Although Sizer coins the term 'community of feeling', I mean something different in employing the term. For Sizer, the 'community of feeling' is located in the intense emotionalism of revivalism, which eventually becomes domesticated in late nineteenth century rhetoric. My application of the term refers more explicitly to a transcendent community that identifies itself by organizing and directing its feelings in worship, *without* reference to social or historical situations.

20. *Songs of the Vineyard*, No. 5. Copyright © 1982 Mercy Vineyard Music/Kingway's Thankyou Music.

21. *Songs of the Vineyard*, No. 49. Copyright © 1985 Mercy Vineyard Music/Kingway's Thankyou Music.

22. *Songs of the Vineyard*, No. 36. Copyright © 1982 Mercy Vineyard Music/Kingway's Thankyou Music.

23. For example, Wesley's hymn, 'Jesu, Lover of My Soul': 'While the nearer waters roll/ While the tempest still is high/ Hide me, O my Saviour, hide/ Till the storm of life is past/ Safe into the haven guide/ O, receive my soul at last'.

24. *Songs of the Vineyard*, No. 18. Copyright © 1982 Mercy Vineyard

Music/Kingway's Thankyou Music. cf. the discussion of ambiguity in ideology in Gerlach and Hines, *People, Power, Change*, pp. 169–74.

25. In worship songs, the simplistic mantra-like formulations, when repeated sufficiently, reduce the capacity for thinking. See Emille Durkheim's *Elementary Forms of Religious Life* (1912), trans. J. Swain, New York, Free Press, 1965, pp. 411ff, 484ff. See also J. Begbie, 'Renewal Music', *Anvil*, vol. 8, no. 3.

26. See Wayne Booth's *Modern Dogma and the Rhetoric of Assent*, Chicago, University of Chicago Press, 1974, p. 17. See also D. Snow and R. Machalek, 'On the Presumed Fragility of Unconventional Beliefs', *Journal of the Scientific Study of Religion*, March 1992, vol. 21, no. 1, pp. 15–26; and S. M. McFarland and J. C. Warren, in 'Religious Orientations and Selective Exposure Amongst Fundamentalists', *Journal of the Scientific Study of Religion*, June 1992, vol. 21, no. 2. MacFarland and Warren argue that fundamentalists 'suspend' belief above reality, in order to address the complexity of the modern world with faith.

27. An exception would be G. Cray, 'Justice, Rock and the Renewal of Worship', in R. Sheldon (ed.), *In Spirit and in Truth*, London, Hodder & Stoughton, 1988, p. 3.

28. Walter Hollenweger, 'Music in the Service of Reconciliation', *Theology*, vol. XCII, 1989, pp. 276ff.

29. B. Castle, 'Hymns – More than Songs of Praise', *Theology*, vol. XCIV, 1991, pp. 101–6.

30. Wimber: 'Some songs you just can't get out of your head, others you can't get out of your heart; worship is the essential foundation for every activity ... our hope is that you will experience worship that is vital and intimate'. (From the preface to *Touching the Father's Heart*, 1989). For a perspective from Restorationist circles, see C. Bowater, *Creative Worship: A Guide to Spirit-filled Worship*, Basingstoke, Marshall-Pickering, 1986.

31. A. P. Merriman, *The Anthropology of Music*, Evanston, Northwestern University Press, 1964, p. xi.

32. *Songs of the Vineyard*, No. 9. Copyright © 1978 Scripture in Song.

33. From the song 'More Love, More Power'. *Songs of the Vineyard*, p. 110. Copyright © 1987 Mercy Vineyard Music/Kingway's Thankyou Music.

34. N. Luhmann, *Trust and Power*, London, John Wiley & Sons Ltd., 1979 (combined edition). (Originally published in Stuttgart, Germany, 1973 and 1975 respectively.) Part of the basis for this theorizing can be found in G. Lakoff and M. Johnson, *Metaphors We Live By*, Chicago, University of Chicago Press, 1981.

35. *Songs of the Vineyard*, No. 37. Copyright © 1982 Mercy Vineyard Music/Kingway's Thankyou Music.

36. *Songs of the Vineyard*, No. 50. Copyright © 1982 Mercy Vineyard Music/Kingway's Thankyou Music.

37. *Songs of the Vineyard*, No. 18. Copyright © 1982 Mercy Vineyard Music/Kingway's Thankyou Music.

38. *Songs of the Vineyard*, No. 32. Copyright © 1982 Mercy Vineyard Music/Kingway's Thankyou Music.

39. *Songs of the Vineyard*, No. 34. Copyright © 1985 Mercy Vineyard Music/Kingway's Thankyou Music.

40. A phrase borrowed from Berger's *Social Construction of Reality*, and echoed in *The Heretical Imperative*.

41. For a fuller discussion on the links between Christian Science and charismatic theology, see D. R. McConnell, *A Different Gospel*, Peabody, Mass., Hendrickson, 1988, and J. MacArthur, *Charismatic Chaos*, Grand Rapids, Zondervan, 1992, pp. 228ff.

42. This is Wimber's notion of 'conformity to Christ', discussed in Chapter 3.

43. Personal correspondence with the Professor of Music Criticism at Bristol University, 9 February 1991.

44. cf. W. Edgar, *Taking Note of Music*, London, SPCK, 1986.

45. 'Major modes' employ a particular series of scales that convey 'cheerful' or 'joyous' moods; in contrast, 'minor modes' employ a series of notes that possess a 'sadder' quality. Controversy rages over whether this is intrinsic to the physical nature of the music or simple convention.

46. Once again, this is a very Durkheimian idea. Society, in the form of the celebrating community, *is* power. See the Doctrine Commission's *We Believe in the Holy Spirit*, London, Church House Publishing, 1991, p. 21, and also J. Hopewell, *Congregation*, London, SCM, 1987, for this discussion of 'adventure' as the dominant motif in charismatic fundamentalist texts.

47. A. Walker, *Restoring the Kingdom*, London, Hodder & Stoughton, 1987, 2nd edn, Chapter 13.

48. *Songs of the Vineyard 2*, 54, 56, 70 and 80. Note especially Song 70, in which the worshippers sing as though God were addressing them: 'I will change your name. You shall no longer be called wounded, outcast, lonely or afraid . . . [you] shall be confidence, joyfulness, overcoming one, friend of God . . .' (Mercy Publishing, 1987).

49. Even in this song, however, the words bear out our case (emphasis mine):
'I am the wounded soldier
and I will not leave the fight,
because the Great Physician is healing me'.
However, we should note that Wimber has changed some of his views on healing, following his throat cancer in 1993.

CHAPTER FIVE

1. John Wimber, *The Cross*, Anaheim, California, Mercy Publishing, 1986, manual, p. 5, tape no. 1.

2. The language of experience contains perhaps as many problems as

the language of power. The most serious one is the danger of imprecision, but, like power-language, experience-language can still be of service provided it is carefully deployed. For example, instead of 'the experience of divine power', one could speak of the existential encounter or receptivity, or of the individual being enabled by the divine. One needs to overcome the rather static quality of the word 'experience' in English. What is meant by 'an experience of divine power' by Wimber is not just a sense of the numinous, nor even just 'a heart strangely warmed'. By 'experience' Wimber means an empowering encounter resulting in an ontological change.

3. See C. P. Wagner, *Church Growth: State of the Art*, Wheaton, Illinois, Tyndale House, 1989, p. 37. The term 'Third Wave' was coined by Wagner: 'The first wave was the Pentecostal movement, the second the charismatic movement, and now the third wave is joining them' (C. P. Wagner, *The Third Wave of the Holy Spirit*, Ann Arbor, Vine, 1988, p. 13). Wagner sees the Third Wave as a movement of the Holy Spirit among evangelicals beginning in the 1980s; it is described as being 'distinct from [but] very similar to the first and second waves'. Wagner himself dislikes being labelled as a 'charismatic', and does not necessarily share the views propounded by other Third Wave leaders. Nevertheless, we may agree with J. F. MacArthur when he describes Third Wave belief as 'an obsession with sensational experiences and a preoccupation with apostolic charismata: tongues, healings, prophetic revelation, words of knowledge and visions' (*Charismatic Chaos*, Grand Rapids, Michigan, Zondervan, 1992, p. 130).

4. See C. P. Wagner, 'A Third Wave?', *Pastoral Renewal*, July–August 1983, pp. 1–5; 'The Third Wave', *Christian Life*, September 1984, pp. 90ff.

5. See C. P. Wagner, 'Church Growth', in *A Dictionary of Pentecostal and Charismatic Movements*, (ed. S. M. Burgess, G. B. McGee and P. H. Alexander), Grand Rapids, Zondervan, pp. 184ff.

6. J. Wimber, *The Kingdom of God*, Anaheim, California, Mercy Publishing, 1985, p. 43.

7. Wimber, *Signs, Wonders and Church Growth I*, manual Mercy Publishing, 1984, p. 8, sec. 5.

8. *Signs, Wonders and Church Growth I*, manual, p. 8, sec. 5.

9. Subordinationism as a term is intended to convey the notion that Jesus is subordinate to the will of the Father and the power of the Spirit. Wimber's brand of subordinationism does not correspond to any mainstream heresies that go by the same name in the first four centuries. Wimber's 'hierarchy of being' most closely resembles Origen's pre-Nicene Christology, in which the Father is the ultimate one, and the Logos-Spirit is a mediating link between ultimate and created essences. The place of Jesus in this non-economic Trinity is as an example.

10. A strong emphasis on the *name* of Jesus undoubtedly originates from the influential Oneness Pentecostal Movement of the early twentieth

century. Oneness Pentecostalism first emerged in 1914, when some Assemblies of God ministers, influenced by nineteenth century revivalism and holiness movements, challenged Trinitarian theology. In particular, baptism according to a Trinitarian formula was rejected, and believers re-baptized only in the name of the Lord Jesus Christ (following Acts 2.38). By the late 1920s, a distinctive emphasis on devotion to the name of Jesus had become apparent in hymnody, piety and teaching, as a source of spiritual power. The use of the name of Jesus as an almost 'magic' word or formula, that can mechanically transform situations and people, is present in many fundamentalist groups today, including some who would claim to be orthodox Trinitarian.

11.   See for example *The Dynamics of Spiritual Growth*, pp. 64ff. Although Wimber mentions the Trinity here, his ultimate power theology contradicts it. Whilst it is true that Wimber would be unhappy about being identified as non-Trinitarian, his theology of power is so deeply hierarchical that it is impossible to see anything that could be construed as an economic Trinity. In fact, we may go further here, and suggest that the dissolution of the Trinity is inevitable in fundamentalist groups. The Oneness Pentecostals eventually became Unitarian in outlook, because they placed the 'name' of Jesus as the ultimate source of their spiritual power. From the other end of the spectrum, some people within modern conservative evangelical movements like the British-based Proclamation Trust find the Trinity problematic, as it does not appear to be sufficiently grounded in Scripture.

12.   *Songs of the Vineyard I*, no. 4, or *Songs of the Vineyard II*, no. 44, would be excellent examples.

13.   Naming and invoking the Spirit with the words 'Come, Holy Spirit' is a cue for the Spirit to operate with some force at Wimber's clinics. At the behest of the leader, the invoking of the Spirit is said to produce dramatic and beneficial effects on the congregation. Only leaders already open to the Spirit can invoke it effectively. Wimber is fond of pointing to the failure of Simon Magus and the Jewish exorcists, recounted in the early chapters of Acts. For accounts of what happens when 'Come, Holy Spirit' is uttered, see *Power Evangelism*, pp. 39ff and pp. 147ff, and *Signs, Wonders and Church Growth I*.

14.   Although I have only heard associates of Wimber use this metaphor, Wimber himself often speaks of the Holy Spirit 'blowing people away', or, occasionally, minds being 'blown'. Both phrases imply force that has violent potentiality. Modern revivalists such as Benny Hinn use the mechanistic metaphors of gun and shooting much more readily. See B. Hinn, *Good Morning Holy Spirit*, Milton Keynes, Word, 1991.

15.   *Signs, Wonders and Church Growth I*, sec. 5, p. 1.

16.   *Signs, Wonders and Church Growth I*, sec. 5, pp. 1, 3.

17.   Speaking in tongues tends to be played down by those who are advocates of the 'Third Wave' in connection with church growth. This is, in my view, for three purely practical reasons: 1. some people who

'minister in the power of the Spirit' do not speak in tongues; 2. emphasis on tongues tends to produce division and strife in congregations and denominations; 3. an emphasis on tongues does not appear to produce church growth, whereas, it is held, 'signs and wonders' do.

18. *Power Healing*, p. 164.

19. An excellent example of this can be viewed in Kevin Springer (ed.), *Power Encounters*, San Francisco, Harper & Row, 1988. In a chapter entitled 'Come Holy Spirit', Mike Flynn describes an encounter with a woman who needed 'inner healing' (pp. 140–8). See P. Selby, *Liberating God*, London, SPCK, 1990, for a useful critique of internalized, fulfilment-centred approaches to healing.

20. Wimber frequently describes exorcisms, both in literature and at rallies. See *Power Healing*, pp. 111ff. His demonology is inventively dualist, giving rise to some novel analogies. For example, in an unpublished 'Healing Seminar' (3 tapes, 1981, tape 1), he states: 'There are many demons that don't have a body. Having a body [for a demon] is like having a car. They want to have a car so they can get around. If they don't have a body, they're a second-class demon. They're not first-class. I'm not kidding you. That's the way it works. And so [to them] having a body is a big deal. That's why they won't want to give it up'.

21. Confirming this information is difficult, as those sources providing the information wish to remain confidential.

22. See Conference notes, *Teach Us to Pray*, 1986.

23. C. P. Wagner, *Territorial Spirits: Insights into Strategic Level Spiritual Warfare from Nineteen Christian Leaders*, Chichester, Sovereign World Publishing, 1991.

24. Wagner, *Territorial Spirits*, p. 39.

25. But one can also actually touch God. See *Touching the Father's Heart*, Worship series, manual plus tapes, 1990.

26. Wimber contradicts himself on what power Satan actually has. In *Power Healing*, for example, readers are told that they have nothing to fear from Satan: he is not like God, since he is created by him and therefore subordinate to him. Satan's 'opposite' enemy of the same strength is the Archangel Michael (p. 117). Yet these assertions need to be contrasted with the power and capacities ascribed to Satan in *Power Points*, *The Kingdom of God*, and parts of *Signs, Wonders and Church Growth II*.

27. I am indebted to Rollo May for this phrase. See *Power and Innocence*, New York, Norton, 1972.

28. See, for example, P. Jensen and T. Payne, *Wimber: Friend or Foe?*, London, St Matthias Press, 1990.

29. Wimber, *The Cross*, manual, p. 68.

30. Wimber does not use the phrase 'born again' often. He prefers the less oblique 'becoming a new person' or 'regeneration', both of which imply power and transformation.

31. Wimber barely focuses on the resurrection of Christ in his works.

His interest tends to lie much more in Jesus' raising of others from the dead.

32.   Wagner, *Church Growth: State of the Art*, pp. 215ff.

33.   Blane Cook, 'Seminar Notes on Physical Healing', Wembley Conference, 1985.

34.   For an account of their power and impact, see Mike Flynn, 'Come, Holy Spirit' (note 19, above).

35.   For example, in talking to some members of the British-based Proclamation Trust, one or two have insisted that a disagreement over the interpretation of a text with its leader, the Rev. Dick Lucas, would be unlikely, since he would ultimately be correct in his exposition. Some of his followers regard his hermeneutical skills so highly that they can no longer distinguish between the actual text of Scripture, and the Rev. Lucas' reading of it. For a fuller account of the dilemma in distinguishing between divine and human agency, see Christoph Schwobel, *God: Action and Revelation*, Kampen, Pharos Books, 1992, pp. 23ff.

CHAPTER SIX

1.   David Pytches and his colleagues at St Andrew's, Chorleywood, have 'planted' Vineyard-style churches at various locations in England. Describing them as Independent Anglican Fellowships (or 'Anglican-friendly'), they remain linked to St Andrew's, rather than being under the control of the Diocesan Bishop or affiliated to the existing parish structures in which they operate. A 'plant' in Watford, Hertfordshire, currently meets in the parish of Christ Church, but works and worships in relation to St Andrew's. For a fuller explanation of how Pytches believes this might work in the future, see D. Pytches and B. Skinner, *New Wineskins*, Guildford, Eagle Press, 1991.

2.   For example, the list of supporters in Britain who affirmed Wimber and the 'Kansas Six' included David Pytches, Terry Virgo, Roger Forster, Graham Cray (presently Principal of Ridley Hall, Cambridge), Sandy Millar and David MacInnes. See the *Church of England Newspaper*, 27 July 1990.

3.   David Pytches, former Bishop of Chile and now vicar of St Andrew's, Chorleywood, was (it is suggested) invited by Wimber to leave the Anglican Church and head up the UK Vineyard network. (In a recent interview, Wimber claimed this 'rumour' was absurd, but then added that an offer might have been made in jest: David Gibb, Interview, unpublished, 10 September 1992.) Whatever the truth was, Pytches has made no move, but continues to remain an important focus for UK Vineyard activity. Wimber's problem in controlling his USA Vineyards began, ironically, after he was seriously ill with an angina attack. Wimber was advised that he should not continue as Pastor of the Vineyard. So he (allegedly) handed over the Pastorship to Sam and Gloria Thompson. However, Wimber recovered quickly, and then demanded his former

position back. Further splits amongst Vineyard pastors followed, specifically over the status of Wimber's authority, and also over the issue of planting Vineyards in the UK. Some pastors opposed this, whilst others supported the move. In 1988, the Revd Chris Lane, curate at St Andrew's, Chorleywood, left the Anglican Church to begin a Vineyard in St Albans.

4. *Signs, Wonders and Church Growth I*, manual, sec. 1, p. 10.

5. This echoes the type of claim made by 'Jesus People' in the 1960s, namely that 'Jesus is the greatest "high"'. In *Signs, Wonders and Church Growth I*, manual, sec. 1, pp. 11ff, for example, we are told that the experience of drugs, alcohol or sex does not compare with the 'kick' one gets from the Spirit.

6. See *Worship Conference*, 1989, with Graham Kendrick and Terry Virgo.

7. John Wimber, *The Church in the 90s*, Anaheim, Mercy Publishing, 1990, essay by Paul Cain, pp. 19ff.

8. Commenting on the growth of the early Church as described in Acts, C. P. Wagner states that: 'While Christianity was being presented to unbelievers in both word and deed, it was the deed that far exceeded the word in evangelistic effectiveness' (*The Third Wave of the Holy Spirit*, Ann Arbor, Vine, 1988, p. 79). Wimber makes the same point in *Power Evangelism*, p. 45.

9. A. Harnack, *What is Christianity?* (1900), Augsburg, Fortress Press, 1986 edn, p. 28.

10. See J. Hopewell, *Congregation*, London, SCM, 1987, p. 24.

11. Hopewell is surely right here when he describes this kind of mechanistic fundamentalism as 'consecrated pragmatism'. Wimber is constantly looking for methods or forms that will reify power and demonstrate efficiency. Anything that does not appear to do this seems to receive scant attention from the Vineyard and other church growth schools.

12. For a slightly different perspective, see the discussion on 'power complex' in James Cobble, *The Church and the Powers*, Peabody, Mass., Hendrickson, 1988.

13. Rhetoric concerning such instances is fairly common at Vineyard conferences, although substantiation remains a problem. A number of works sympathetic to Wimber have appeared in recent years that purport to be thorough investigations into Wimber's claims. However, they are much less than that. Two books to be mentioned in this category are: Rex Gardner, *Healing Miracles*, London, Darton, Longman & Todd, 1986, and David Lewis, *Healing: Fiction, Fantasy or Fact?*, London, Hodder & Stoughton, 1989. The first book is by a retired general practitioner. The second, despite being written by someone who claims to be a doctor and to know something about medical conditions, is by a social anthropologist. We should note that some evangelicals remain sceptical about testimonies concerning digit, limb and eye replacement, supernatural dentistry and raising the dead. See J. F. MacArthur, *Charismatic Chaos*, Grand Rapids, Michigan, Zondervan, 1992, p. 132.

14. Peter May, a practising medical doctor from Southampton and prominent evangelical, has argued this through the columns of the *Church of England Newspaper* (cf. 15 June 1990, etc.). In his articles, he attempts to establish that 'Christ-like' healings (i.e., ones similar to those recorded in the Gospels), very rarely happen in the twentieth century. Further still, he claims that the healing miracles cited by Wimber are never substantiated medically. He has publicly challenged David Pytches to offer 'proof' of any one miracle: so far, the challenge has not been met. Although Peter May appears to have a vested interest in curbing the more eccentric claims of charismatic fundamentalists, his work has led to some revisionism by some supporters of Wimber, most notably Rex Gardner: 'I do agree with Peter May that far too many miraculous cures are being claimed on palpably inadequate evidence' (*Church of England Newspaper*, 6 July 1990, p. 13). Another investigation by some Sydney medical doctors into Wimber's healings also states that 'at this stage [we] are unaware of any organic healings which could be proven' (*The Briefing*, 24 April 1990, p. 19).

15. Wimber, addressing a conference in Sydney on 'Spiritual Warfare' (1990) states that, 'In the next decade the world will turn to Jesus as never before . . . neutrality towards the gospel will be a thing of the past. How will this happen? Through a revitalised Church which by its unity, faith and godliness will recover the lost apostolic powers and with them will cure AIDS . . . and impress the gospel upon hundreds of millions'. See also John Wimber, *The Kingdom of God in the Last Days*, Anaheim, Mercy Publishing, 1988, p. 186. Kevin Springer: 'We have not witnessed any miraculous healing [of AIDS]. By that I mean the total removal of any trace of the AIDS virus. However, we have seen many conditions improve dramatically. [Homosexuals] . . . need to be prepared for difficult questions. God uses AIDS so that homosexuals, in many instances for the first time, begin to address the issue of sexual brokeness'.

16. See L. Caplan (ed.), *Studies in Fundamentalism*, London, Macmillan, 1987, and L. P. Gerlach and V. H. Hines, *People, Power and Change: Movements of Social Transformation*, New York, Bobbs-Merrill, 1970, pp. 34ff.

17. Many sceptical evangelicals have levelled the change that Cain is connected to William Branham. See Ernie Gruen, *The Kansas City 'Prophets'*, Kansas, Full Faith Church of Love Publications, 1990, and articles by Clifford Hill in *Prophecy Today*, vol. 6, nos. 4, 5 and 6. Hill wrote his criticisms after meeting Cain. The publishers Hodder & Stoughton had invited Hill to write a favourable Introduction to a book by David Pytches (*Some Said it Thundered*, London, Hodder & Stoughton, 1990), which introduced the ministry of the prophets to the UK 'market'. Hill refused to write the Introduction after meeting Cain, claiming that he [i.e., Cain] was similar to 'a host of other occult performers who use various demonic sources to channel their messages'. These accusations

did not prevent Wimber and Pytches from bringing Cain and some others of the 'Kansas Six' to London.

William Branham (1909–65) was a charismatic fundamentalist in the revival tradition, prominent after the Second World War. His powers of discernment (prophecy, words of knowledge, etc.) remain legendary even today. However, Branham attracted notoriety for some of his views and practices. He believed that Eve had had sex with the serpent, which accounted for fallen human nature. (There are overtones of this in Cain's 'elected seed' theology, and in his fondness for total sexual purity.) Branham also claimed to be the Angel (of Revelation 3.17), and prophesied that by 1977 all denominations would be consumed by the World Council of Churches; this event would be followed by the Second Coming of Christ. Branham died in 1965, yet many of his followers expected him to be resurrected. Like Cain, Branham and some of his followers believed that he was probably the product of a divinely orchestrated conception.

18. See *Equipping the Saints*, Special UK edition, Fall 1990, pp. 5, 27.

19. *Equipping the Saints*, Fall 1990, pp. 11–12, and *Christianity Today*, 14 January 1991, p. 21. Cain claims that an angel appeared to him on his first date with a girl, and told him that God was jealous. Thereafter, Cain claims to have been 'free from all sexual desires'. Interestingly, his language about Christ contains many sexual overtones. One of his more remarkable statements at the Vineyard was that 'Jesus is turned on by our desire for him'.

20. See *Church of England Newspaper*, 27 July 1990, p. 1.

21. *Equipping the Saints*, vol. 5, no. 1, Winter 1991.

22. John Wimber and Paul Cain, *Paul Cain at the Vineyard*, Anaheim, Mercy Publishing, 1990, tape 2, side 1.

23. See *Church of England Newspaper*, 10 April 1992, p. 1.

24. R. L. Peabody, *The International Encyclopedia of Social Sciences*, vol. 1, Basingstoke, Macmillan, 1968, p. 473.

25. Besides Clegg, see Douglas Webster, *Pentecostalism and Speaking in Tongues*, London, Highway Press, 1964, and Gerlach and Hines, *People, Power and Change*, pp. 55ff.

26. The 'church growth' school of thinking differentiates between 'cell', 'congregation' and 'celebration', which describe the size and type of worship participating believers may expect.

27. Sam and Gloria Thompson, Blane Cook and Paul Cain have all left the leadership of the Vineyard in recent years, all for reasons that are connected with the maintenance of unity. In 1992, Jack Deere, a prominent Vineyard leader, also left. Later that same year, Ken Gulliksen also departed.

28. Gerlach and Hines, *People, Power and Change*, p. 57.

29. From Terry Virgo's 'New Frontiers' to David Pytches' parish church of St Andrew's, Chorleywood.

30. The expression 'Wimberized' or 'Wimbered' has been in common usage amongst charismatic evangelicals since the early 1980s.

CHAPTER SEVEN

1. On this, see P. Berger, *The Heretical Imperative*, London, Collins, 1980, pp. 153ff., and Robert Towler, *The Need for Certainty*, London, Routledge & Kegan Paul, 1984.

2. The wrath of God is something Wimber hardly mentions at all in his writings, yet his evangelical background makes it unthinkable that he has not, at some stage, been exposed to this notion. Some evidence of exposure is traceable in his renderings of the doctrine of penal substitution (or substitutionary atonement), which compete with his more dynamic theory of the cross, in which Satan loses his power over creation at the very point when he thinks he has gained it.

3. See Nigel Wright, *Themelios*, vol. 17, no. 1, October/November 1991, p. 20: another major concern is '. . . the nature of religious experience and specifically the interface between the spiritual and the psychic. This is yet an inadequately explored area, but is profoundly suggested by the entire Wimber phenomenon'. See also Morton T. Kelsey, *The Christian and the Supernatural*, London, Search Press, 1977, and N. Wright, *The Fair Face of Evil*, London, Marshall Pickering, 1989, pp. 115–23.

4. For example, Origen's much-quoted maxim that 'You cannot pray for the cool of the winter in the heat of summer' fails to impress some believers. I recently interviewed a follower of Wimber, who patiently explained to me that if enough people wished for winter conditions in summer, then those conditions would be available and present. In his view, the only thing that prevented this happening was the desire of the majority to have a warm summer. God would change the ordering of seasons if enough prayerful people demanded it.

5. Many of Wimber's followers read the text 'You shall do greater things than I' (John 14.12) literally. For some, this is an indication that newer and more spectacular occurrences may be expected in the Vineyard and beyond.

6. The emphasis on the Old Testament is most interesting, and mirrors a trend that can be located in Restorationism. The desire to return the Church to the experience of the first century has a number of consequences: (i) the Old Testament itself takes a higher profile in forming the life of the community, (ii) the 'tribalism' of some parts of the OT is considered attractive, providing a rationale for being separate from society and occasionally waging war against elements of it, and (iii) believers attempt to copy what they perceive to be OT patterns of worship, including using Jewish rhythms for songs. (In fact, those rhythms almost certainly do not predate 1800.) For a fuller account, see *The Use of the Old Testament in House Churches*, Bramcote, Nottingham, Grove, Booklet no. 48.

7. J. Moltmann, *The Church in the Power of the Spirit*, London, SCM, 1977, p. 20.

8. J. Begbie, 'The Spirituality of Renewal Music', *Anvil*, vol. 8, no. 3, 1991, pp. 227ff.

9.   See G. von Kittel (ed.), *Theological Dictionary of the New Testament*, Grand Rapids, Eerdmans, 1967, vol. 1, pp. 491–2.

10.   See D. Hardy and D. Ford, *Jubilate: Theology in Praise*, London, Darton, Longman & Todd, 1984, p. 80.

11.   T. Smail, 'The Love of Power and the Power of Love', *Anvil*, vol. 6, no. 3, 1989, pp. 223ff.

12.   e.g., John 12.31.

13.   For example, some of Wimber's followers and 'colleagues' (e.g., Colin Urquhart) assert that Jesus 'never had a day of sickness in his life: if he didn't, neither should you!' Whilst it is true that the Gospels do not record Jesus ever having a bout of 'flu, there are problems with this view. For example, he did suffer and die. Further still, if Jesus' humanity was *real*, how would he have made antibodies to combat the common sicknesses of his day without ever having been ill?

14.   Smail, 'The Love of Power', p. 227.

15.   'The Love of Power', p. 228.

16.   *Signs, Wonders and Church Growth I*, sec. 5, p. 12.

17.   Moltmann, *The Church in the Power of the Spirit*, p. 300.

18.   Hardy and Ford, *Jubilate*, p. 148.

19.   Moltmann, *The Church in the Power of the Spirit*, p. 27. See also Hans Kung, *The Church*, London, Burns & Oates, 1967, p. 95.

20.   See Wimber, *The Kingdom of God in the Last Days*.

21.   See *The Kingdom of God in the Last Days*.

22.   See Begbie, 'The Spirituality of Renewal Music', p. 236.

23.   Moltmann, *The Church in the Power of the Spirit*, p. 93.

24.   Smail, 'The Love of Power and the Power of Love', p. 229.

25.   For example, communities like L'Arche in France, pioneered by Jean Vanier; Charnwood in Britain; or the work and writings of Henri Nouwen.

26.   Hardy and Ford, *Jubilate*, p. 51.

27.   Begbie, 'The Spirituality of Renewal Music', p. 237.

28.   K. Barth, *Church Dogmatics*, Edinburgh, T. & T. Clark, 1957, II, ip. 587.

29.   T. F. Tracy, *God, Action, and Embodiment*, Grand Rapids, Eerdmans, 1984, pp. 143–4.

30.   G. M. Jantzen, *God's World, God's Body*, London, Darton, Longman & Todd, 1984, p. 152.

31.   S. Kierkegaard, *Christian Discourses* (tr. W. Lowrie), Oxford, Oxford University Press, 1959, p. 132.

32.   For further discussion, see M. Wiles, *God's Action in the World*, London, SCM, 1986, pp. 22–5.

CHAPTER EIGHT

1.   Andrew Walker, quoted in *Christianity Today*, 18 May 1992, pp. 27ff. (This is an extensive article on American Restorationism and its pervasiveness.)

2. See J. F. MacArthur, *Charismatic Chaos*, Grand Rapids, Zondervan, 1992.

3. Readers interested in cognitive dissonance, the term used to describe the social, psychological and theological mechanisms that a group or individual use to cope with 'unrealized' prophecies, are referred to the work of Leon Festinger; *When Prophecy Fails: A Social and Psychological Study of Modern Groups that Predicted the Destruction of the World*, New York, Harper & Row, 1956, and *A Theory of Cognitive Dissonance*, Stanford, Stanford University Press, 1957, are both exemplary introductions.

4. B. Wilson, *The Noble Savages: An Essay on Charisma – The Rehabilitation of a Concept*, Berkeley, University of California Press (Quantum Books), 1975, p. 93.

5. See Guy Chevereau, *Catch the Fire*, London, Marshall Pickering, 1994; Dave Roberts, *The Toronto Blessing*, Eastbourne, Kingsway, 1994; Patrick Dixon, *Signs of Revival*, Eastbourne, Kingsway, 1994; and Dean Jeffery in the preface to the official *Church of England Yearbook*, 1995.

6. Timothy Pain and Clive Manning, *Miracles are Impossible: You Decide*, Hemel Hempstead, Battle Books, 1993.

7. *All in the Mind*, BBC Radio 4, 21 April 1994.

8. This was the view expressed by Dr Simon Wessley, King's College, London, in 1993.

9. See H. Cox, *Fire From Heaven: Pentecostalism, Spirituality, and the Reshaping of Religion in the Twenty-first Century*, Addison-Wesley, 1994.

10. See R. Holloway and B. Avery, *Churches and How to Survive Them*, London, Collins, 1994, pp. 108ff.

11. For a good discussion of this, readers are especially referred to Wilf McGreal's *Guilt and Healing*, London, Geoffrey Chapman, 1994, pp. 60ff.

12. A good discussion of Foucault and his fundamental ideas is to be found in Didier Eribon's *Michael Foucault*, London, Faber, 1992.

13. Holloway and Avery, *Churches and How to Survive Them*, p. 108.

14. James Hopewell, *Congregation*, London, SCM, 1987, p. 70.

15. *Church Times*, 8 August 1994.

16. The use of the metaphor 'wave' is unfortunate here: waves do not last very long, although there is always another one close behind. More importantly, it is theologically contentious to say that God moves in 'waves'. Others speak of the revival or 'rain from heaven'. This is also unfortunate: rain does not come from heaven, but from the earth. What makes rain is hot air and complex climatic conditions.

17. *Church Times*, 8 August 1994.

18. 'Pre-Millenial Tension' is a phrase coined, I believe, by Andrew Walker. It is certainly true that there has been an increase in phenomena associated with this; disaster with David Koresh's Davidian Cult in Waco, the Solar Temple in Switzerland and Canada, and the mass-suicide of the church of Jim Jones all point to a worrying equation of PMT, charisma and fundamentalism.

19. F. Watts and M. Williams, *The Psychology of Religious Knowing*, London, Geoffrey Chapman, 1988, p. 111. The authors point out that the type of prayer we are discussing is common to children in the 7+ age group.

20. See Vaughan Roberts, 'Reframing the UCCF Doctrinal Basis', *Theology*, Nov–Dec 1992. Roberts uses the work of James Fowler [*Stages of Faith*, 1981] to describe UCCF belief as characteristically 'literal' or 'synthetic', the child-to-adolescent stage of development.

21. Both Marc Europe and research done by Gavin Reid bear this out.

22. So what can God not do? If raising the dead is possible, what kind of dead person? Presumably not someone who has been cremated, or perhaps decapitated like John the Baptist. I do not mean to be churlish here, but it seems to me that a discussion of things that God cannot do needs to happen before a wide selection of vague miraculous claims are made.

23. A 'classic' example of an exposition of this agenda is D. Pytches and B. Skinner, *New Wineskins*, Guildford, Eagle, 1991. The authors argue for the dissolving of Anglican parochial boundaries and structures so that the 'strong' or fashionable churches can increase in number, without having the financial burdens of supporting those churches that are alleged to be weak or 'not doing their job'. In this scheme the corporate social vision of Anglicanism is to be replaced by a form of 'privatization'.

24. Martin Marty and R. Scott Appleby (eds.), *Fundamentalisms Observed*, Chicago, University of Chicago Press, 1992, from the preface.

25. Ironically, the doctrines of biblical inerrancy and Papal infallibility arose, historically speaking, at about the same time. Both must be seen as attempts to reassert perfect divine agents in a world that was beginning to be dominated by some of the conditions of modernity.

26. See R. Towler, *The Need for Certainty*, London, Routledge & Kegan Paul, 1984, for a fuller discussion.

27. For two perspectives on this from different theological traditions, see T. Wright, *The New Testament and the People of God*, London, SPCK, 1992, and H. Walton, 'An Abuse of Power 2: A Polemic Concerning the Priests of God and the Ministers of Religion', in *Modern Churchman*, New Series, vol. 34, no. 2, pp. 21ff.

28. Interview on BBC Radio 4's 'Sunday Programme', 22 November 1992, with Fr Francis Bown, a leader of Ecclesia. Examples of similar rhetoric abound. A vicar from Lincoln diocese called for women priests to be 'burnt as witches' in 1993. The Additional Curates Society, in its magazine editorial, Jan. 1993, wrote: 'It is Truth we should be bothered about, for equality and justice are the key words in our modern pagan society'.

29. Benny Hinn, quoted in *Christianity Today*, 15 October 1992, following an address to an audience at Melodyland Christian Center, Southern California. Hinn's rhetoric is similar to that of Paul Cain, who

promised divine retribution for anyone who opposed the ministry of Wimber or himself.

30. In a slightly different way, S. T. Coleridge was alive to the dangers of putting doctrines of God before the very being of God. In *Aids to Reflection*, London, Taylor & Hessey, 1825, p. 101, he writes: 'He who begins by loving Christianity [by which he meant its tradition or fundaments] better than truth, will proceed by loving his own sect or church better than Christianity and end in loving himself better than all'.

31. Marty and Appleby, *Fundamentalisms Observed*, pp. 1ff.

32. Keith Ward, *A Vision to Pursue*, London, SCM, 1992, p. 206.

33. Stewart Clegg, *Frameworks of Power*, London, Sage, 1989, p. 273.

34. Clegg, *Frameworks of Power*, p. 274.

35. Keeping women in their place (i.e., submissive), and men in their's (i.e., one of headship or authority), is a common though not universal feature of Christian fundamentalism. Wimber has no female prophets, apostles or pastors to my knowledge. Although I have not heard him explicitly teach that women should not be allowed to hold authority or teach, women do seem to be conspicuous by their absence in leadership roles. Of course, women are encouraged to be 'supportive', and there is evidence that some in the Vineyard are now hoping to 'release women into ministry', although I'm unclear as to who or what they are being set free from. See Carol Wimber and Penny Fulton, *Women After God's Heart*, VMI Publishing. A wider perspective on women's experience within fundamentalism can be gained from reading Gita Saghal and Nira Yuval-Davis (eds.), *Refusing Holy Orders: Women and Fundamentalism in Britain*, London, Virago, 1992.

36. Gerhardus van der Leeuw, *Religion in Essence and Manifestation*, vol. 1, Gloucester, Peter Smith Publishers, 1967, p. 191.

37. e.g., K. Barth, *Church Dogmatics*, Edinburgh, T. & T. Clark, 1957, II, i, p. 294.

38. I am indebted to Anthony Thiselton for this insight. Responding to critiques of *We Believe in the Holy Spirit*, London, CIO, 1989, from fundamentalist charismatics, he noted that 'many of the texts appealed to by some groups simply cannot bear the weight that is placed upon them'. In other words, if too much stress is placed on a proof-text or fundament, it tends to crumble. A more developed perspective on this trend is available in Philip S. Lee, *Against the Protestant Gnostics*, Oxford, Oxford University Press, 1989. Lee argues that Christianity, especially in the fundamentalist-revivalist tradition of the twentieth century, has tried to move from faith to *gnosis* (i.e., 'certainty. . .inner knowledge or "fact"') as the basis for faith.

39. Towler, *The Need for Certainty*, p. 100.

40. Towler, *The Need for Certainty*, pp. 100–1.

41. Or, put more eloquently by A. J. Balfour in *The Foundations of Belief*: 'Our highest truths are but half-truths. Think not to settle down for ever in any truth, but make use of it as a tent in which to pass a

summer's night. But build no house of it, or it will be your tomb. When you first have an inkling of its insufficiency and begin to discern a dim counter-truth looming up beyond, then weep not, but give thanks. It is the Lord's voice whispering, "Take up thy bed, and walk"'.

42. Towler, *The Need for Certainty*, p. 107. Another way of tackling this issue would be to ask whether the nature of Christian truth is primarily intended to be *propositional* or *relational*. A. L. McFadyen, in his (unpublished) paper delivered to the Society for the Study of Theology (Cambridge, 1991), argued that Christians believe Christ is the pre-eminent embodied form of Truth. Consequently, like Christ, truth is always with us, yet ahead of us; known, yet not known fully.

43. D. Jenkins, *God, Miracle and the Church of England*, London, SCM, 1987, p. 28.

44. Jenkins, *God, Miracle and the Church of England*, p. 29.

45. *God, Miracle and the Church of England*, p. 30.

46. *God, Miracle and the Church of England*, pp. 31ff.

47. *The Cloud of Unknowing*, from the British Museum MS, with an Introduction by Evelyn Underhill, 5th edn, London, John Watkins Publications, 1950, p. 77.

48. cf. *Equipping the Saints*, vol. 3, no. 3, Summer 1989. Yet we must ask here, what is the difference between what some New Age healers practise, compared to Wimber and Cain's talk of 'feeling electricity', 'auras', 'waves', 'seeing coloured lights over people indicating conditions', and so on? Some recent general theological writing has touched on the relationship between the New Age and charismatic fundamentalism, and exposed the common ground with some sharpness. For example, Keith Ward (*A Vision to Pursue*), describes charismatic fundamentalism as *part* of the New Age. Similarly, John Hick in *An Interpretation of Religion* (Basingstoke, Macmillan, 1989), highlights the structural similarities between certain types of charismatic religion and New Age phenomena.

49. See R. Gill, *Competing Convictions*, London, SCM, 1989, pp. 13ff.

50. Donald Davie, 'Ordinary God' in *To Scorch and to Freeze: Poems About the Sacred*, Manchester, Carcanet Press, 1988, and quoted in Grace Davie, *Religion in Britain Since 1945: Believing Without Belonging*, Oxford, Blackwell, 1994.

Glossary of Terms

Agent: A person or thing that performs an action or produces an effect, in the name of or on behalf of another.

Backward-looking legitimation: The process whereby groups or individuals seek to validate present practice by attempting to show it is consistent with history or tradition.

Circuits of power (model of): The boundaries by which power is contained, as well as the avenues and agents through which power flows.

Cognitive dissonance: The result of knowingly processing lack of agreement in such a way as to make it harmonize.

Conflate: To combine or fuse together different elements in such a way as to make a whole.

Cultural-linguistic: Describes the 'system' of ritual, language and belief in church or community life.

Disposition: The temperament, tendency or inclination of a given individual or group. The power to habitually dispose.

Ecclesiology: The study of the Church as an institution in relation to its belief and behaviour. The doctrine of the Church or a given Christian community.

Episodic: The opposite of dispositional; something incidental, sporadic or momentary.

Epistemology: The study of theories of knowledge.

Fundaments: The core beliefs or articles of faith by which a group chiefly defines itself. The primary doctrinal foundations of a particular community.

Hegemony: A master-principle that controls others. Authority, but usually in the service of dominance. A community in which a hierarchy of persons or beliefs is established by their apparent supremacy.

Ideology: A doctrine or notion that is an idealized, visionary theory. An often abstract system of ideas concerning phenomena, especially social life.

Inductive: A persuasive form of reasoning. It uses particular facts, knowledge, observations or inferences about experience, especially from the past, to draw general conclusions about the present.

Inerrancy: A quality attributed to someone or something that is incapable of error owing to its perfection or inspired nature.

Morphology: The science of structures or forms, especially in organisms and in language.

Nodal points: A still point of convergence within a moving body that often acts as a place for distributing power or controlling it.

Noetic: Describes the powers of perception or of pure intellect.

Over-realized eschatology: The beliefs of individuals or groups who expect phenomena commonly associated with the future Kingdom of God to be present now.

Phenomenology: The division of any science that describes and classifies its phenomena.

Reify: To convert ideas or experiences into something material. To demonstrate power; making something real in order to create belief.

Routinization of charisma: The establishment of institutions, channels or agents through which power and its benefits are deemed to be regularly effective.

Theodicy: A theology that attempts to deal with problems of evil and suffering.

Index

The Society for Promoting Christian Knowledge (SPCK)
has as its purpose three main tasks:

- **Communicating the Christian faith in its rich
  diversity**
- **Helping people to understand the Christian faith
  and to develop their personal faith**
- **Equipping Christians for mission and ministry**

SPCK Worldwide runs a substantial grant programme to
support Christian literature and communication projects
in over 100 countries. Special schemes also provide books
for those training for ministry in many parts of the world.
All gifts to SPCK are spent wholly on these grant
programmes, without deductions.

SPCK Bookshops support the life of the Christian
community by making available a full range of Christian
literature and other resources, and by providing support
to bookstalls and book agents throughout the UK. SPCK
Bookshops' mail order department meets the needs of
overseas customers and those unable to have access to
local bookshops.

SPCK Publishing produces Christian books and
resources, covering a wide range of inspirational,
pastoral, practical and academic subjects. Authors are
drawn from many different Christian traditions, and
publications aim to meet the needs of a wide variety of
readers in the UK and throughout the world.

The Society does not necessarily endorse the individual
views contained in its publications, but hopes they
stimulate readers to think about and further develop
their Christian faith.

For further information about the Society, please write to:
SPCK, Holy Trinity Church, Marylebone Road,
London NW1 4DU, United Kingdom.
Telephone: 0171 387 5282